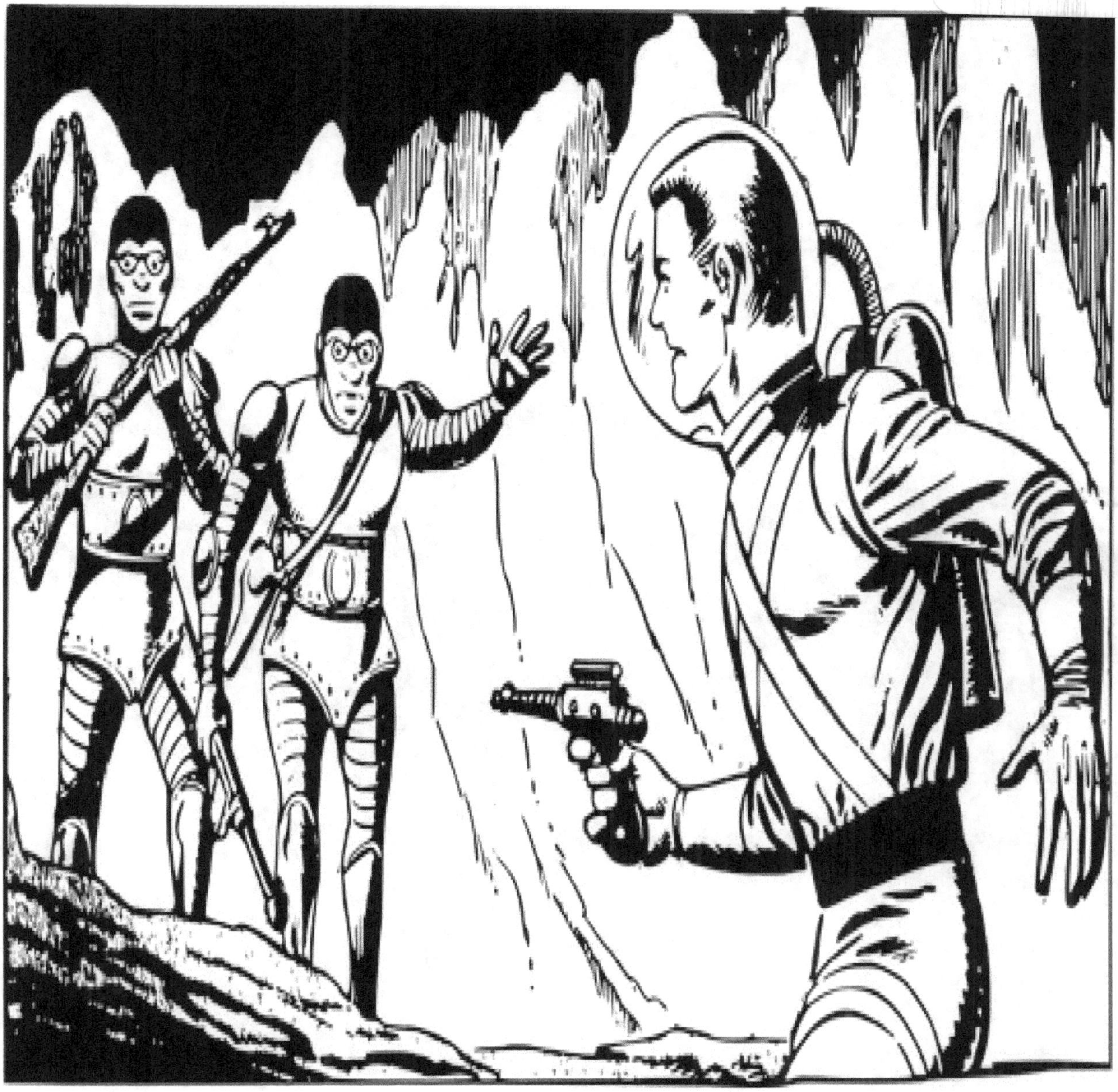

Hurry up _____! We'd better
(your name)

get coloring if we're gonna

survive this trip!

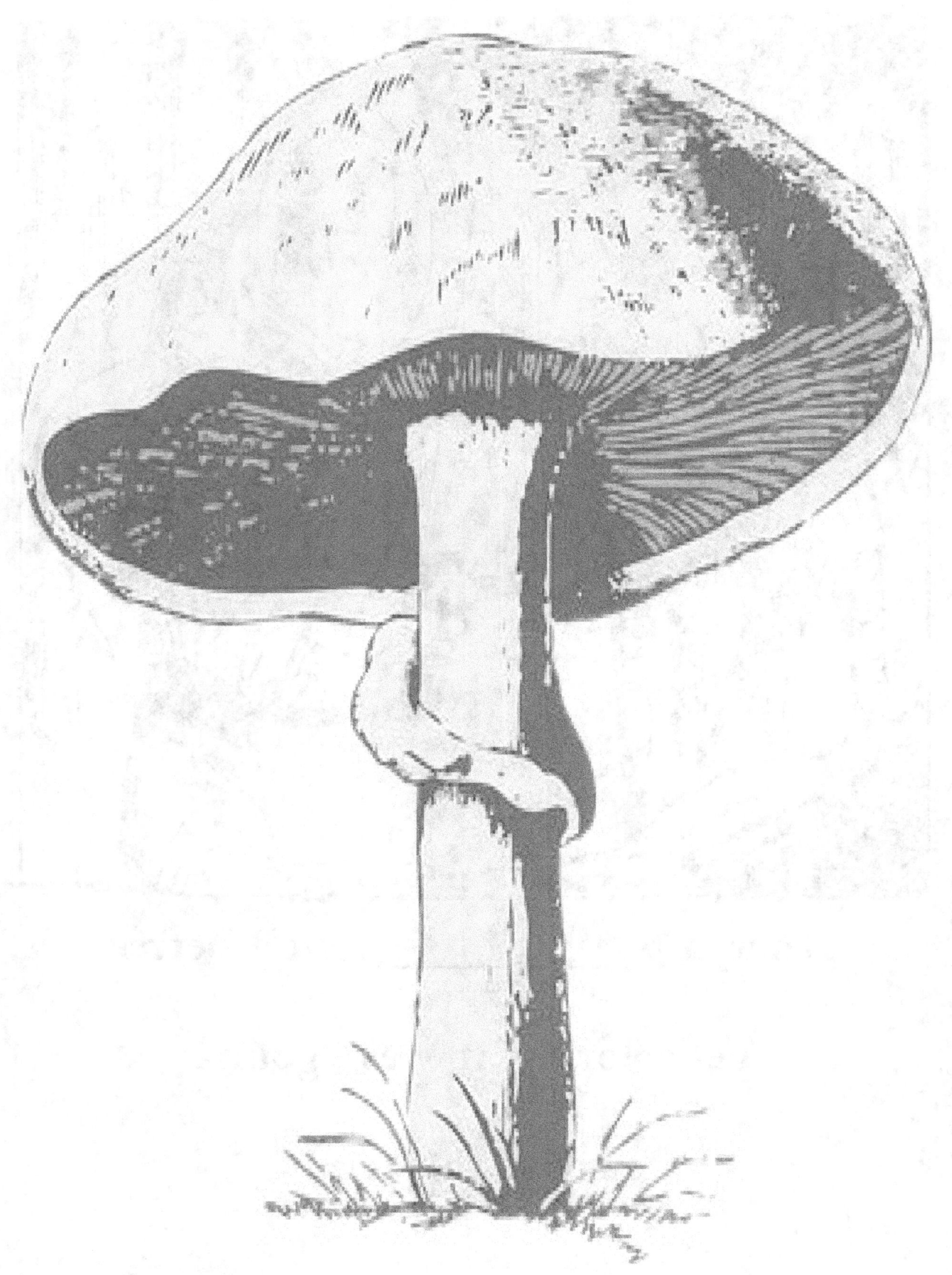

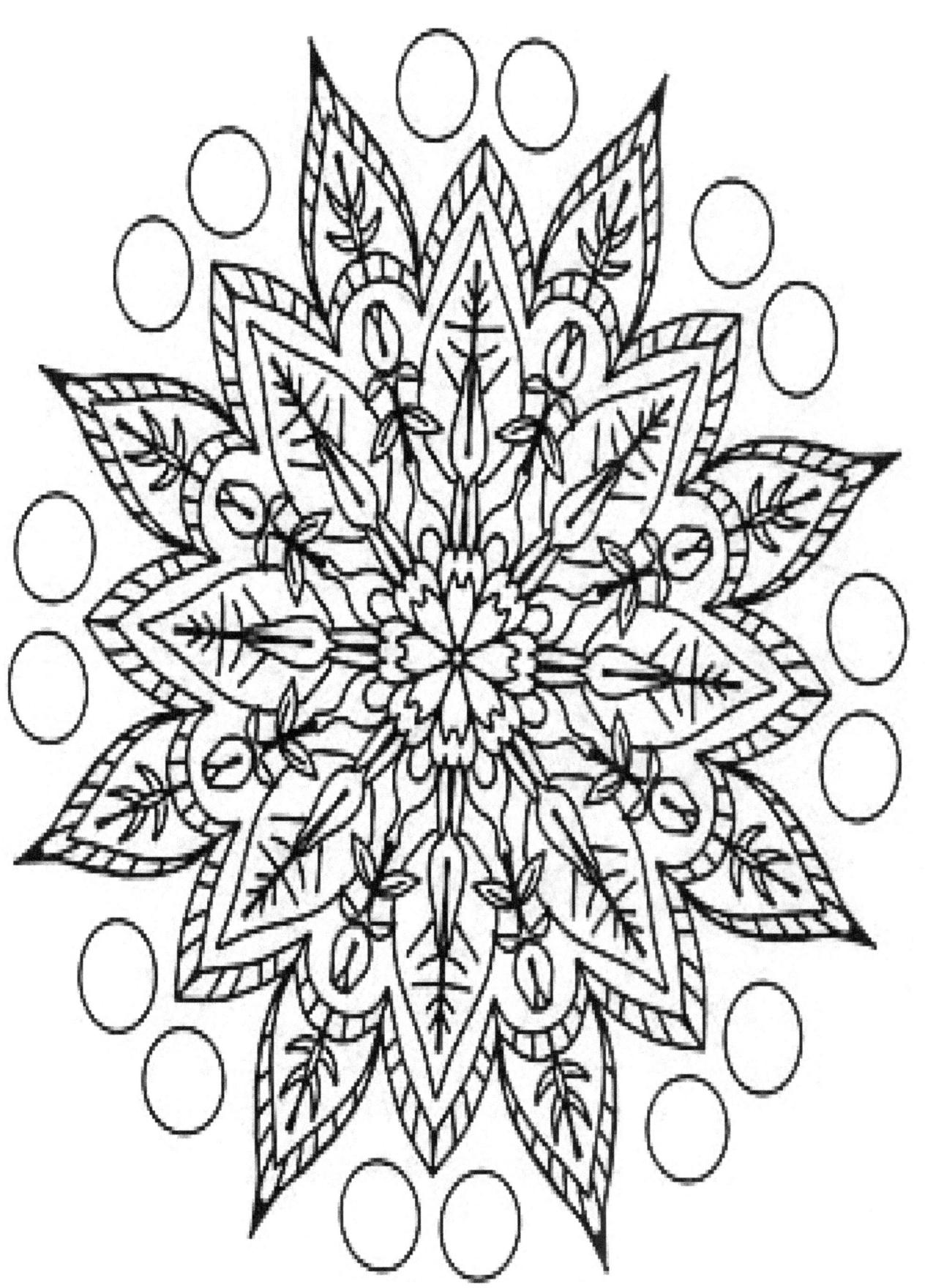

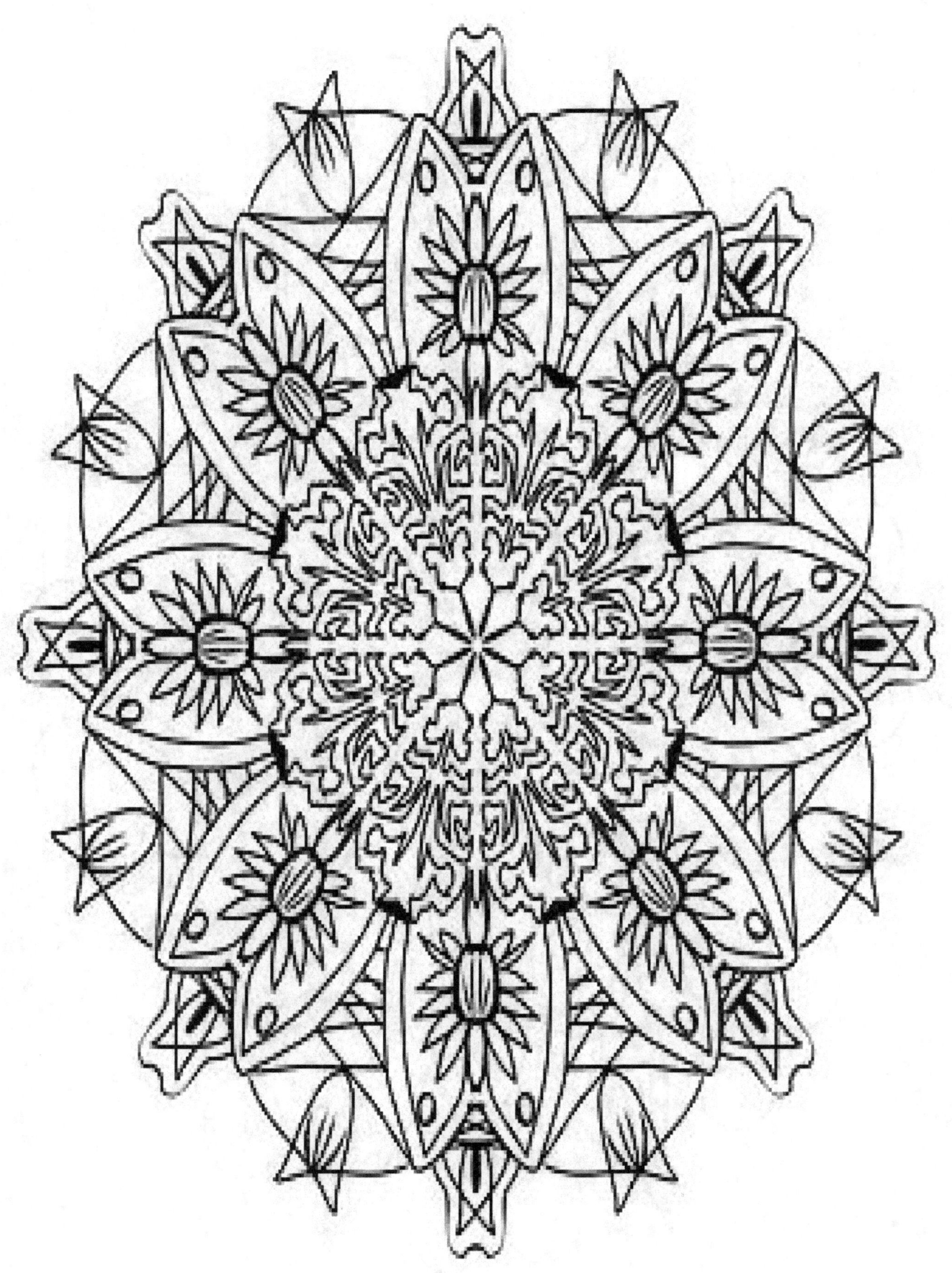

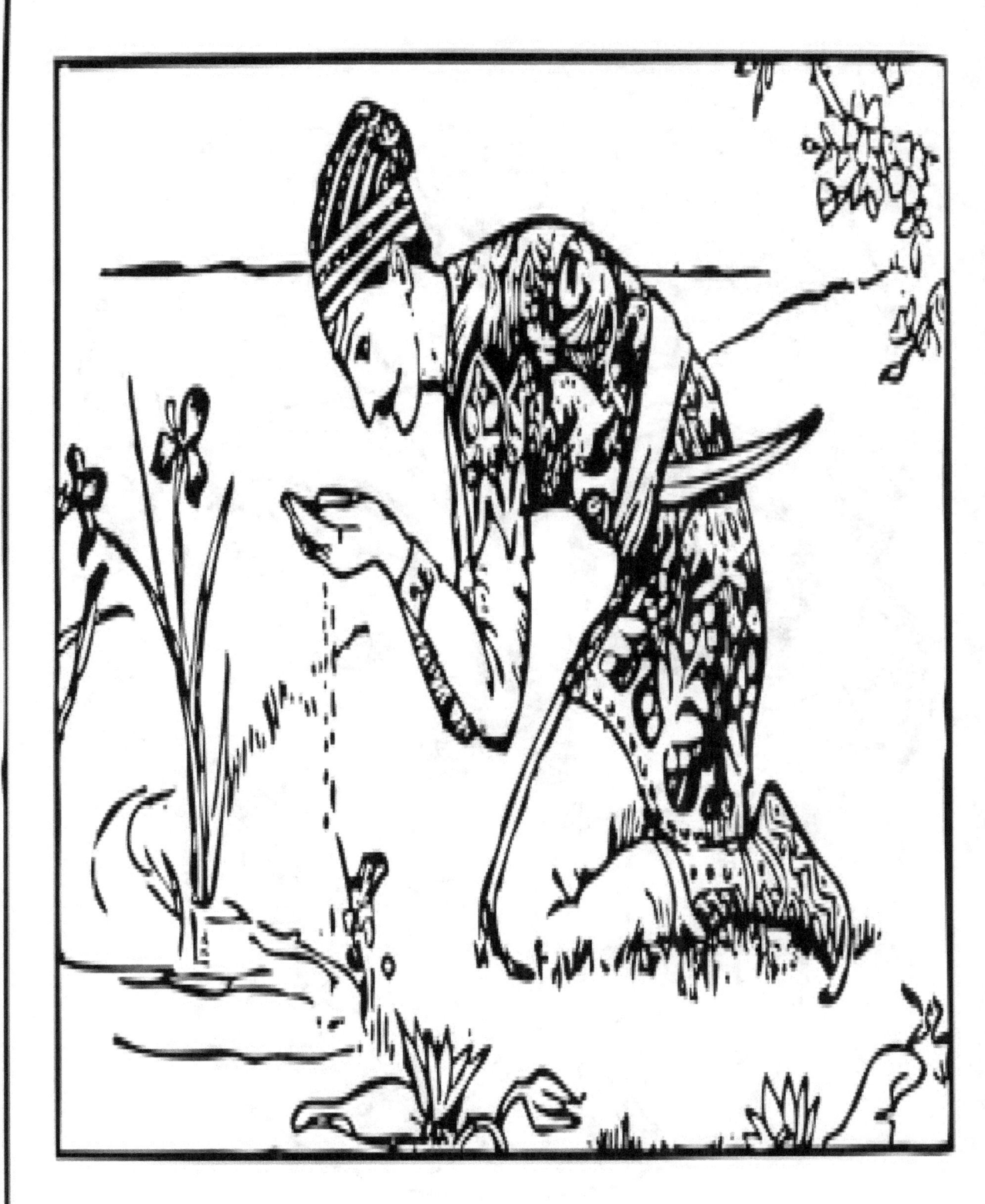

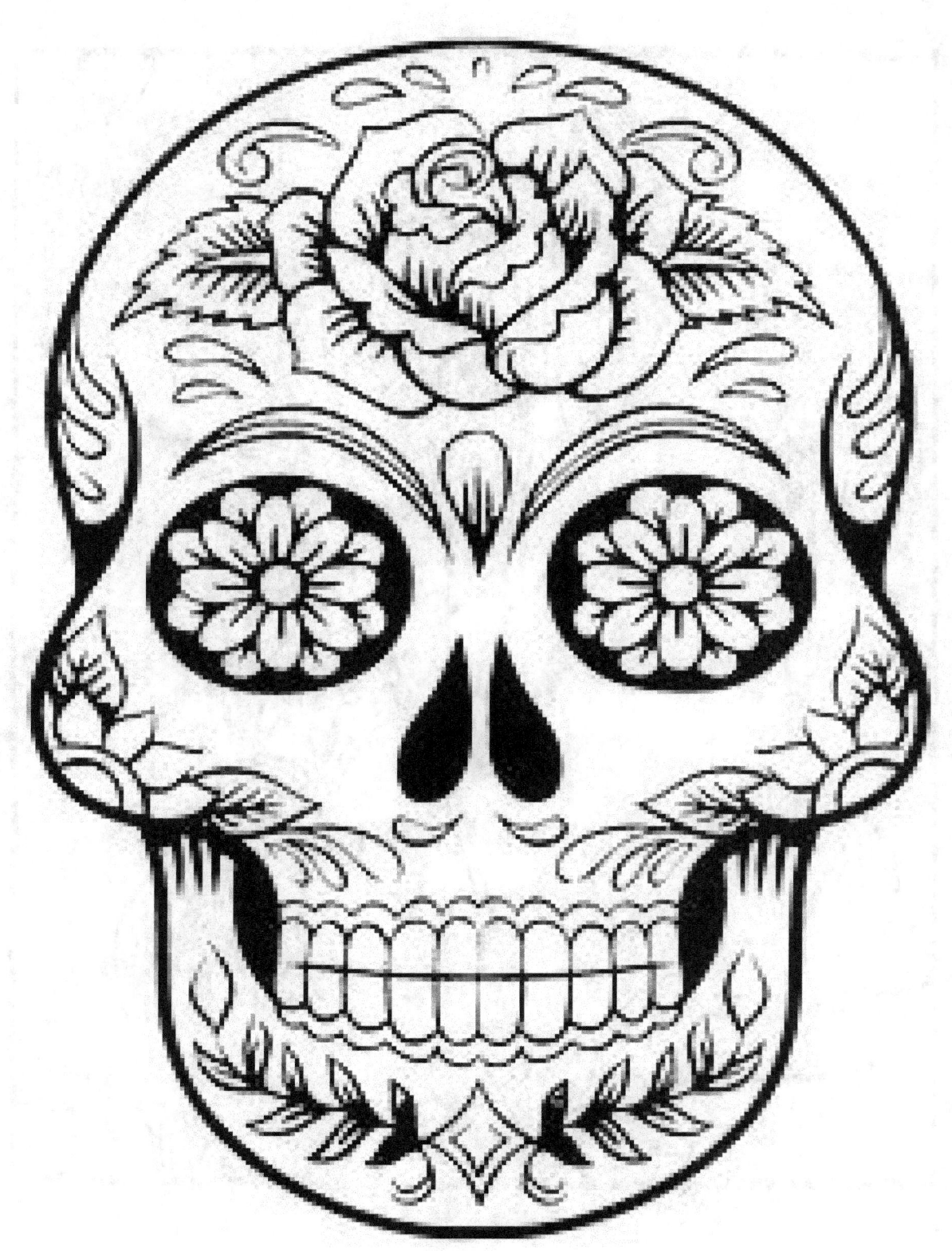

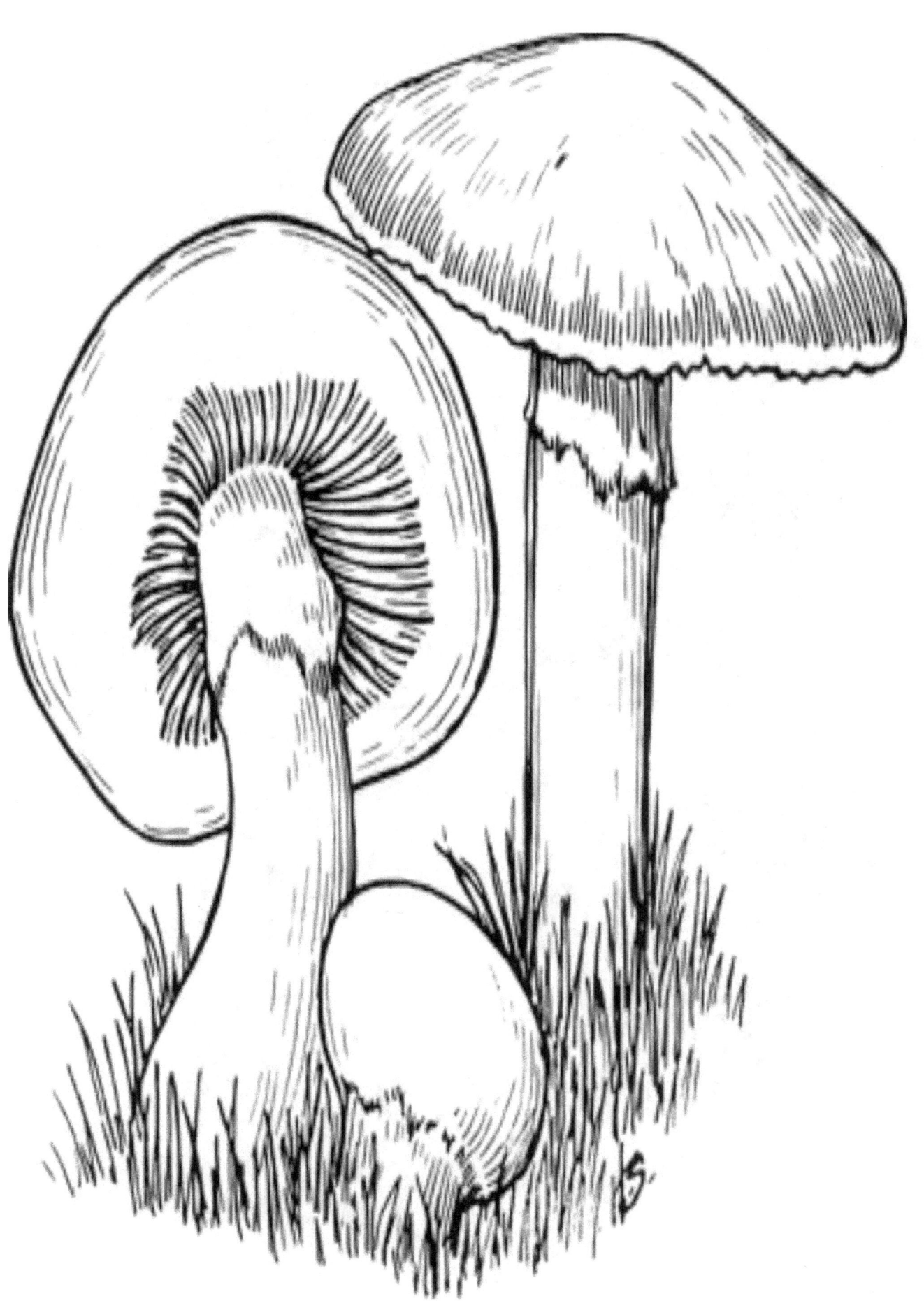

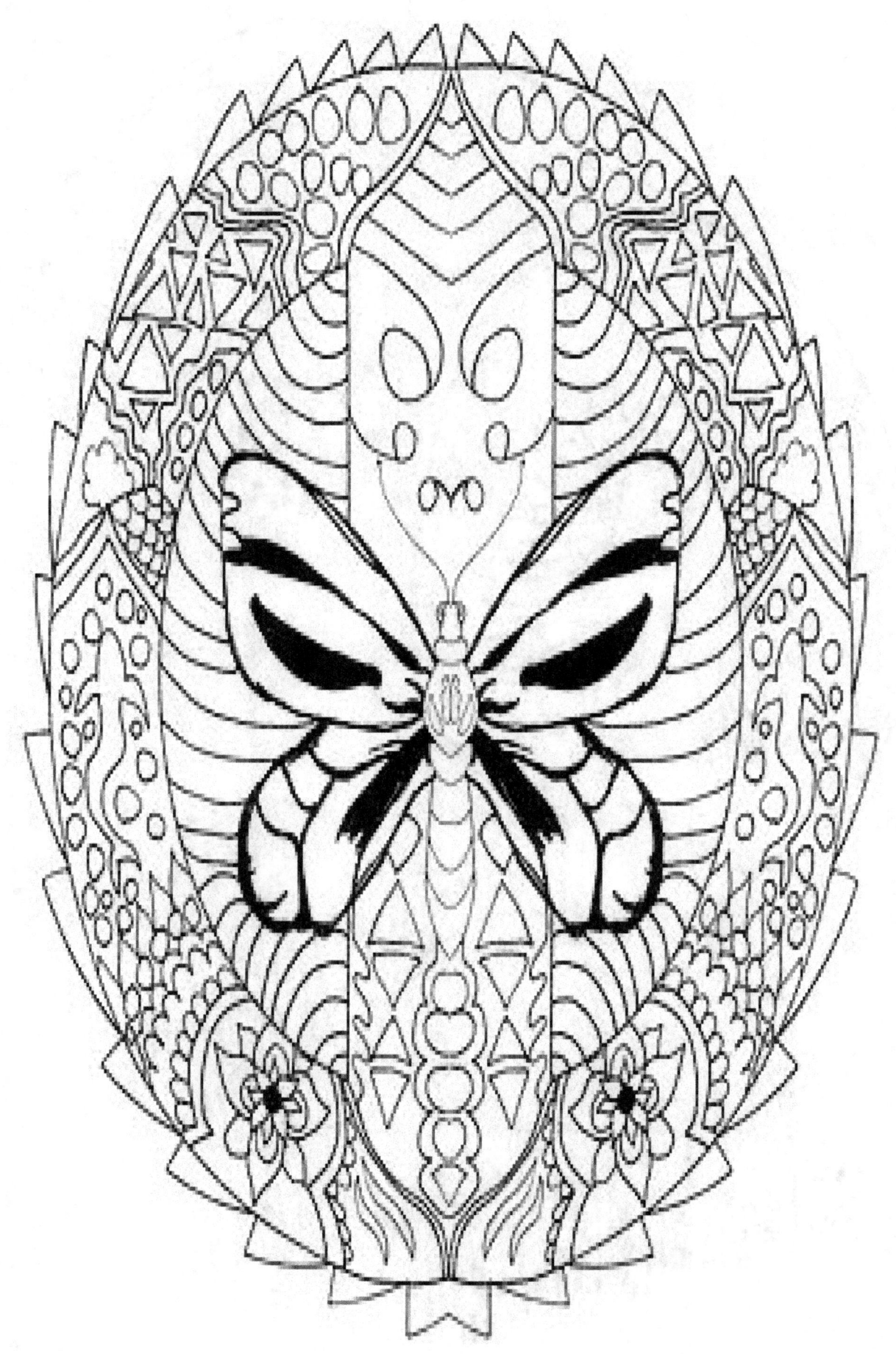

HOME SWEET

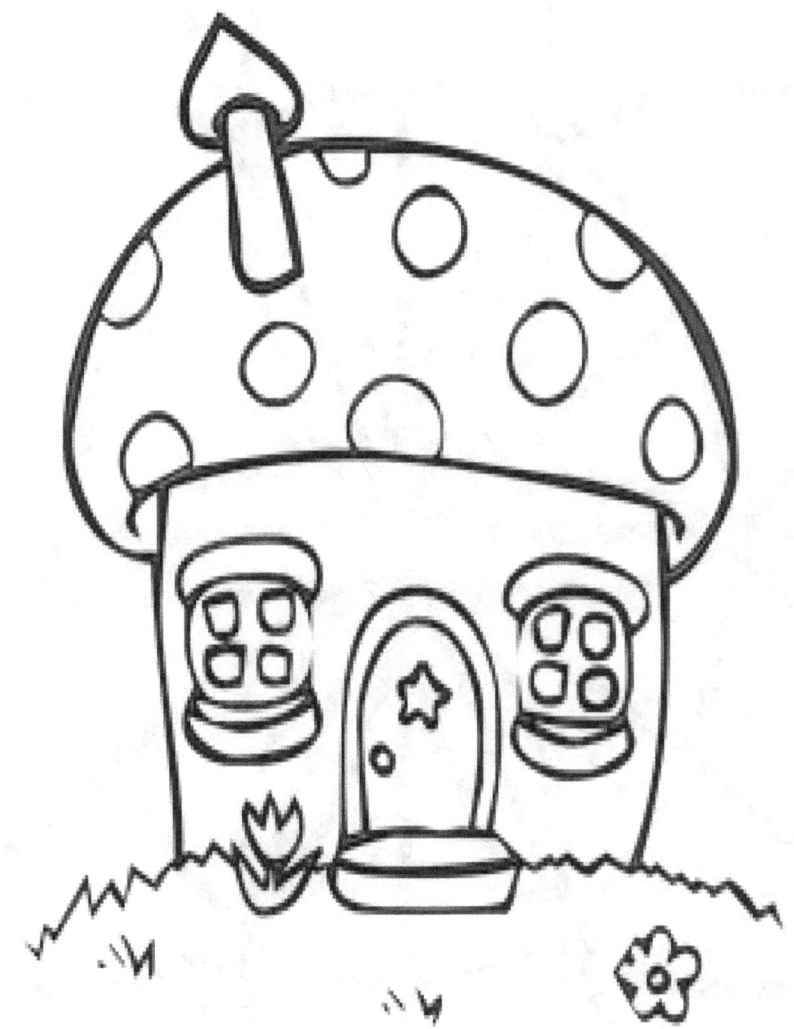

SHROOM

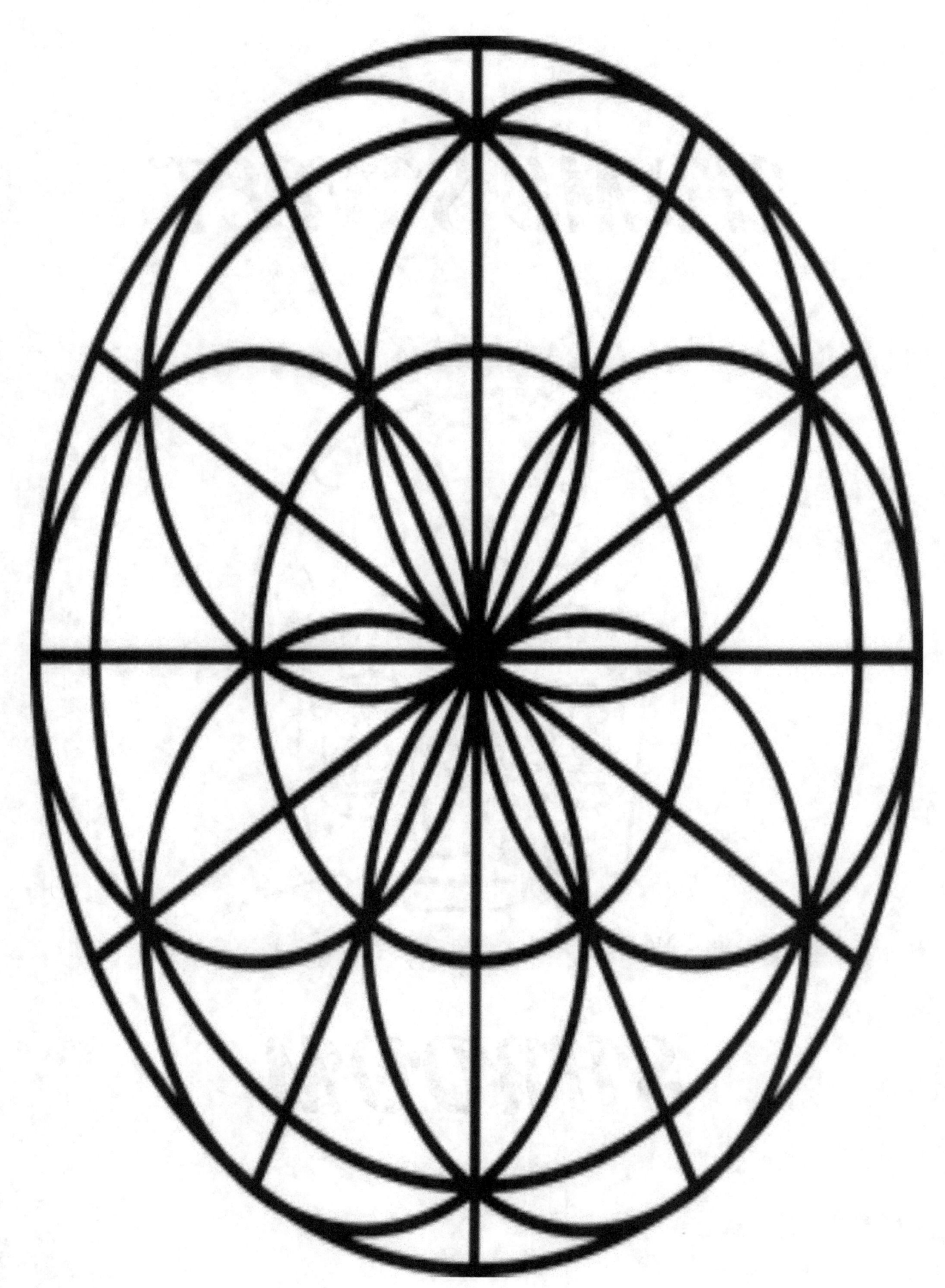

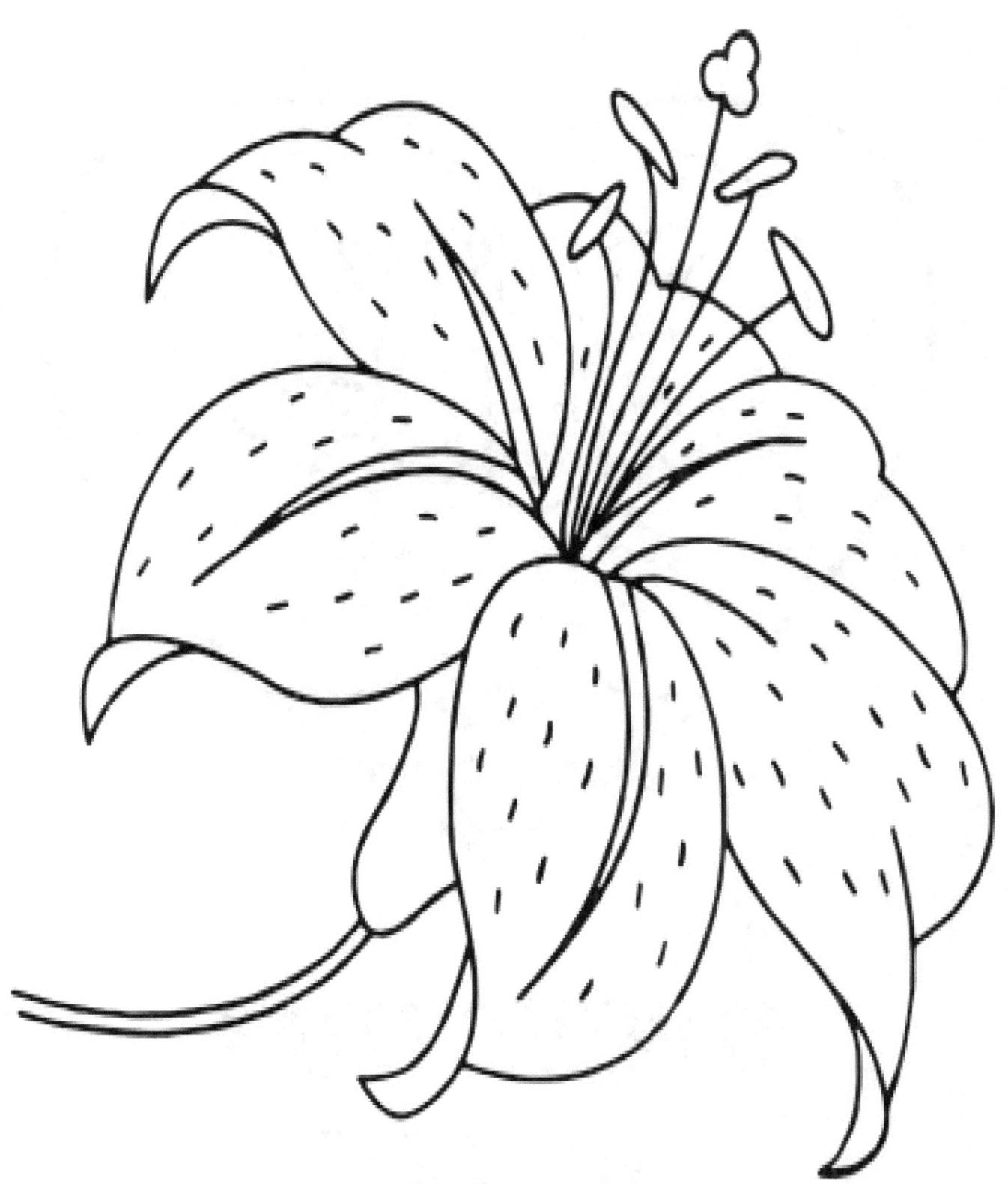

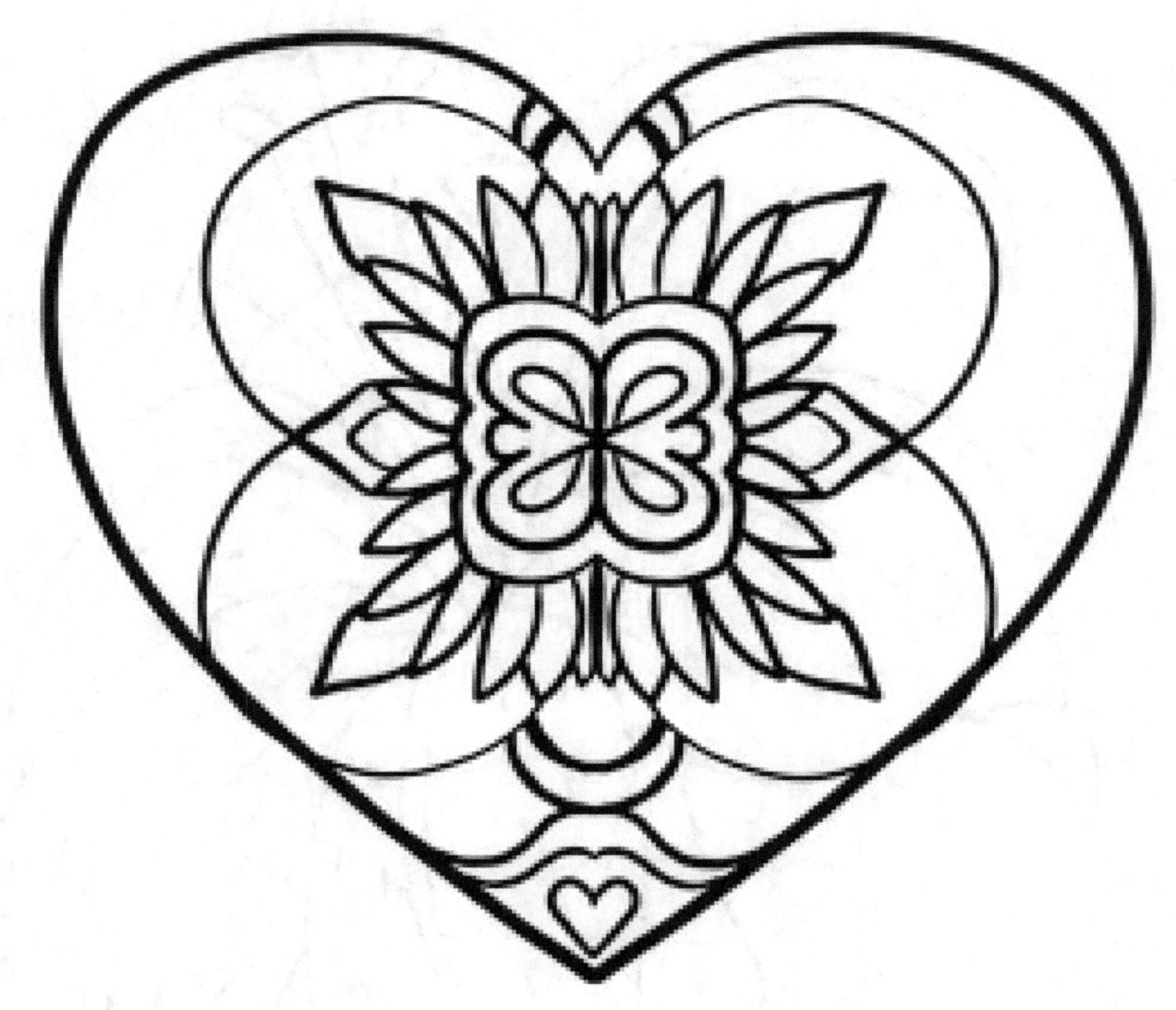

OPEN YOUR
HEART

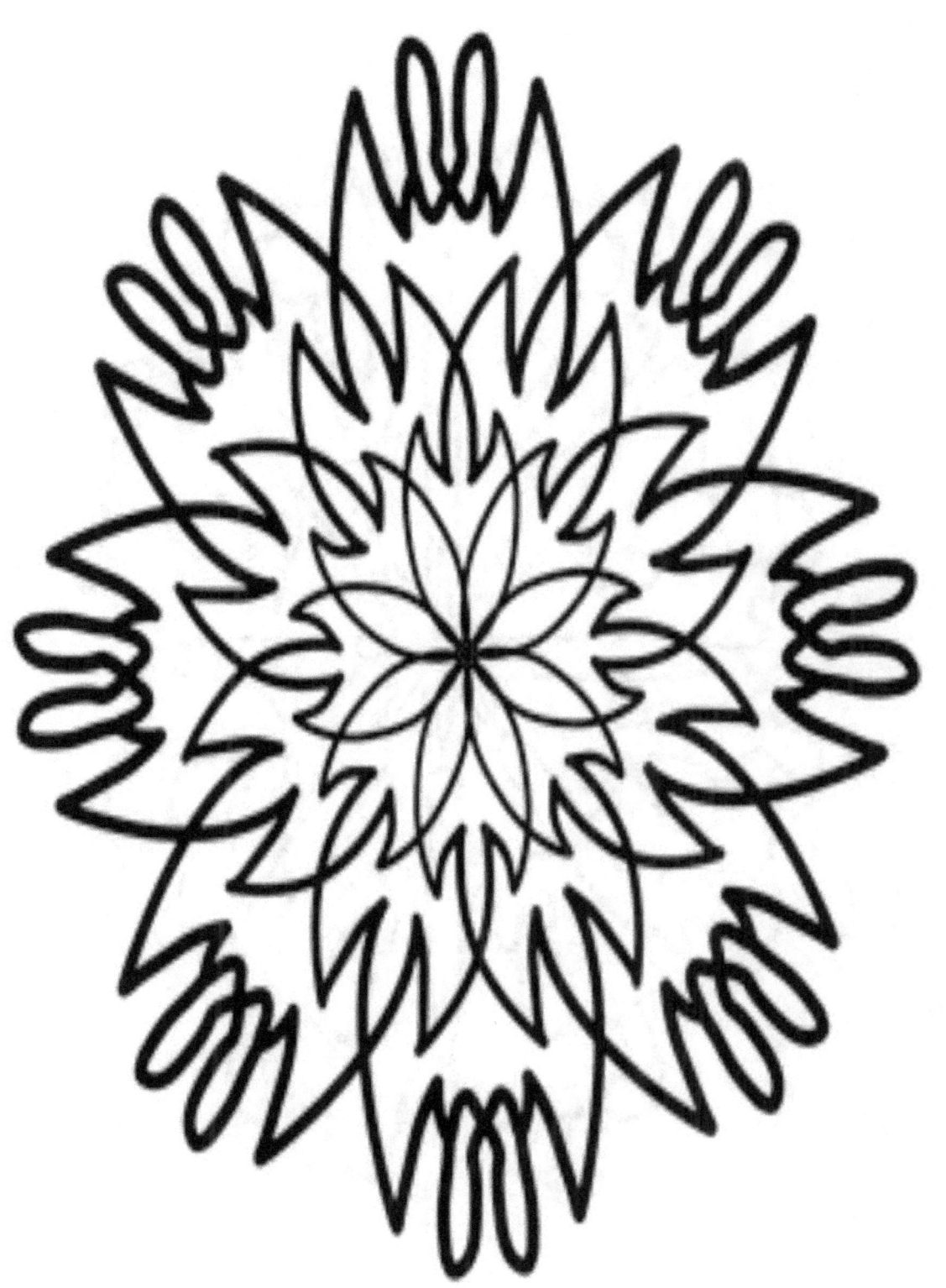

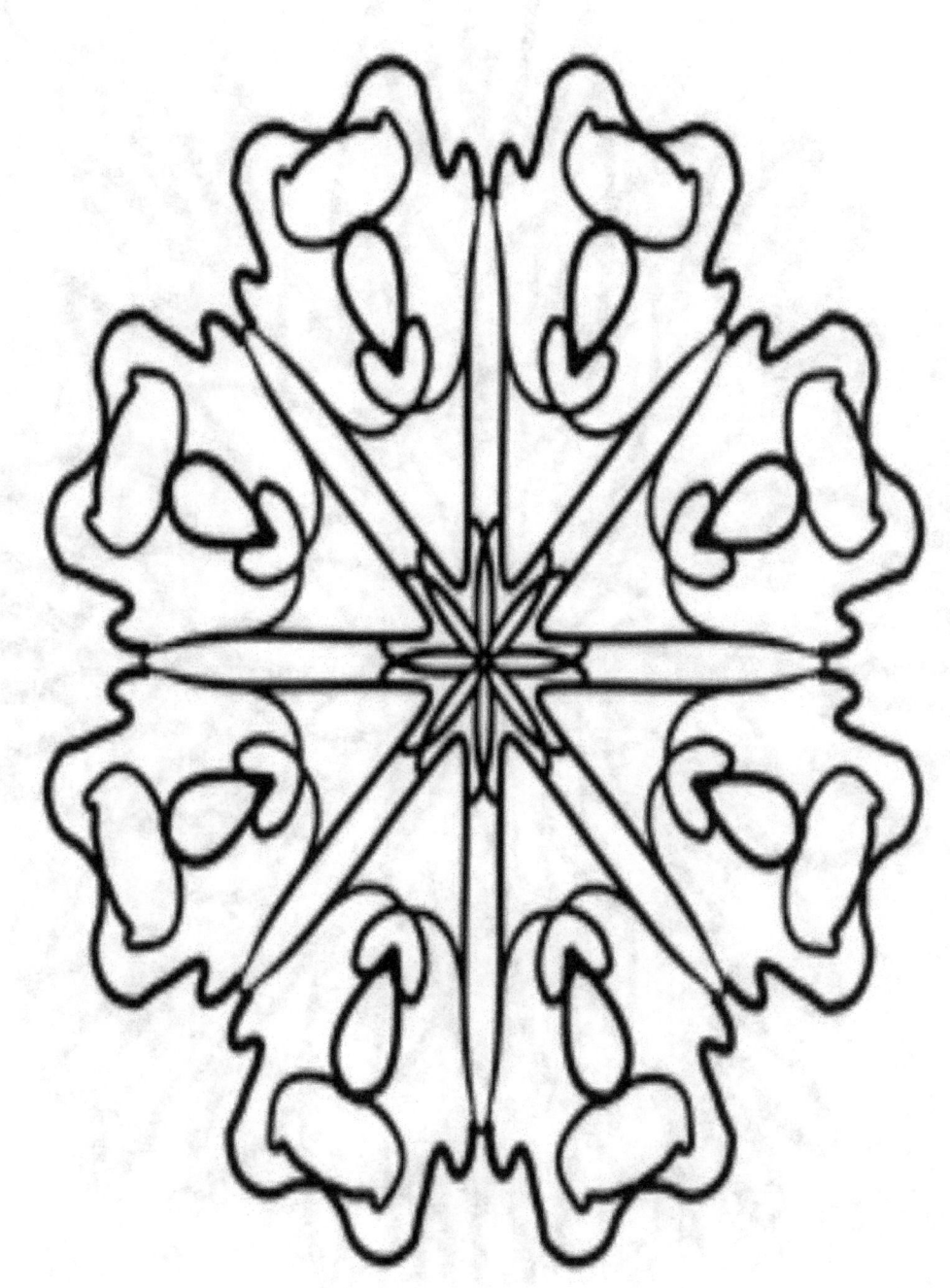

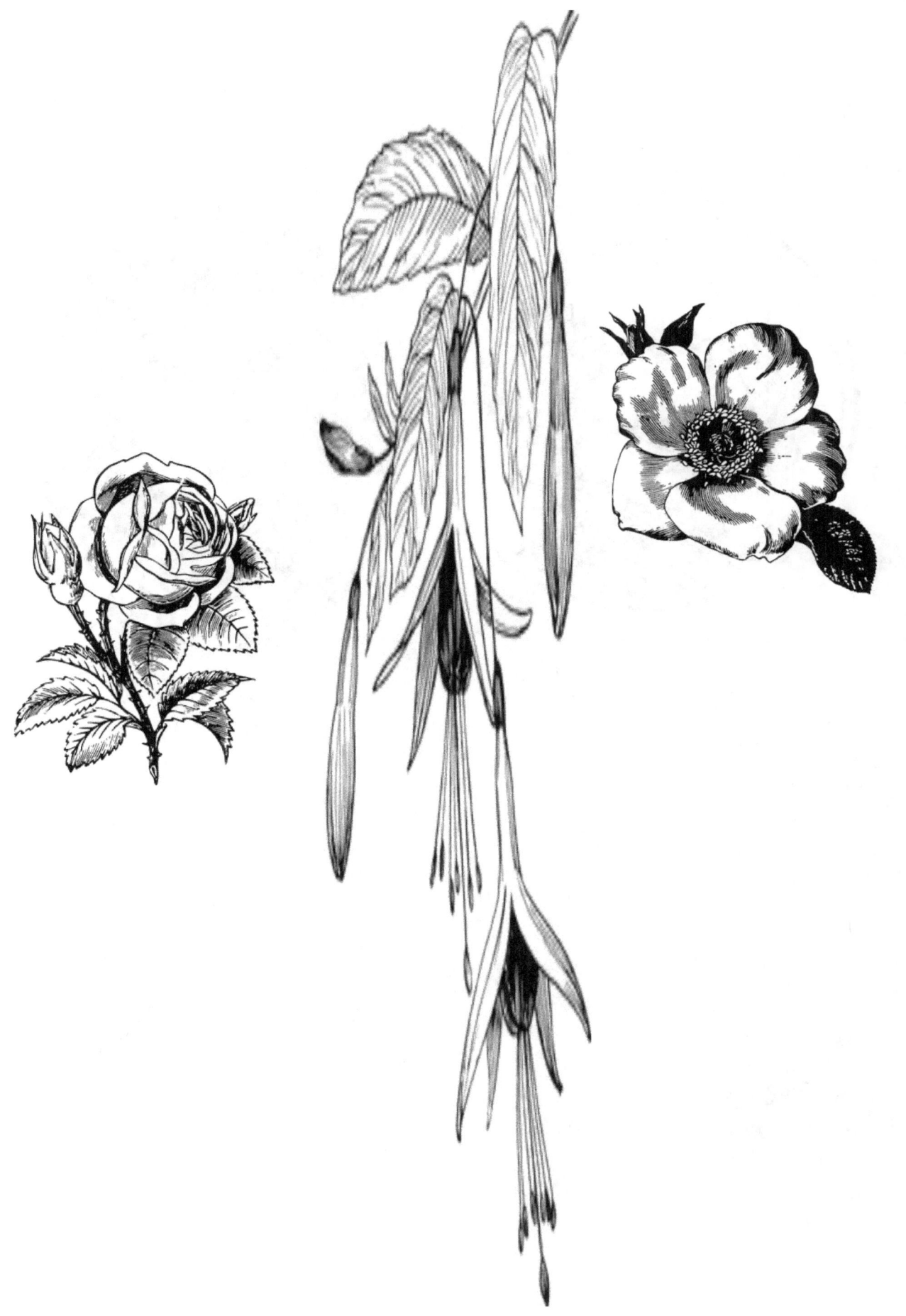

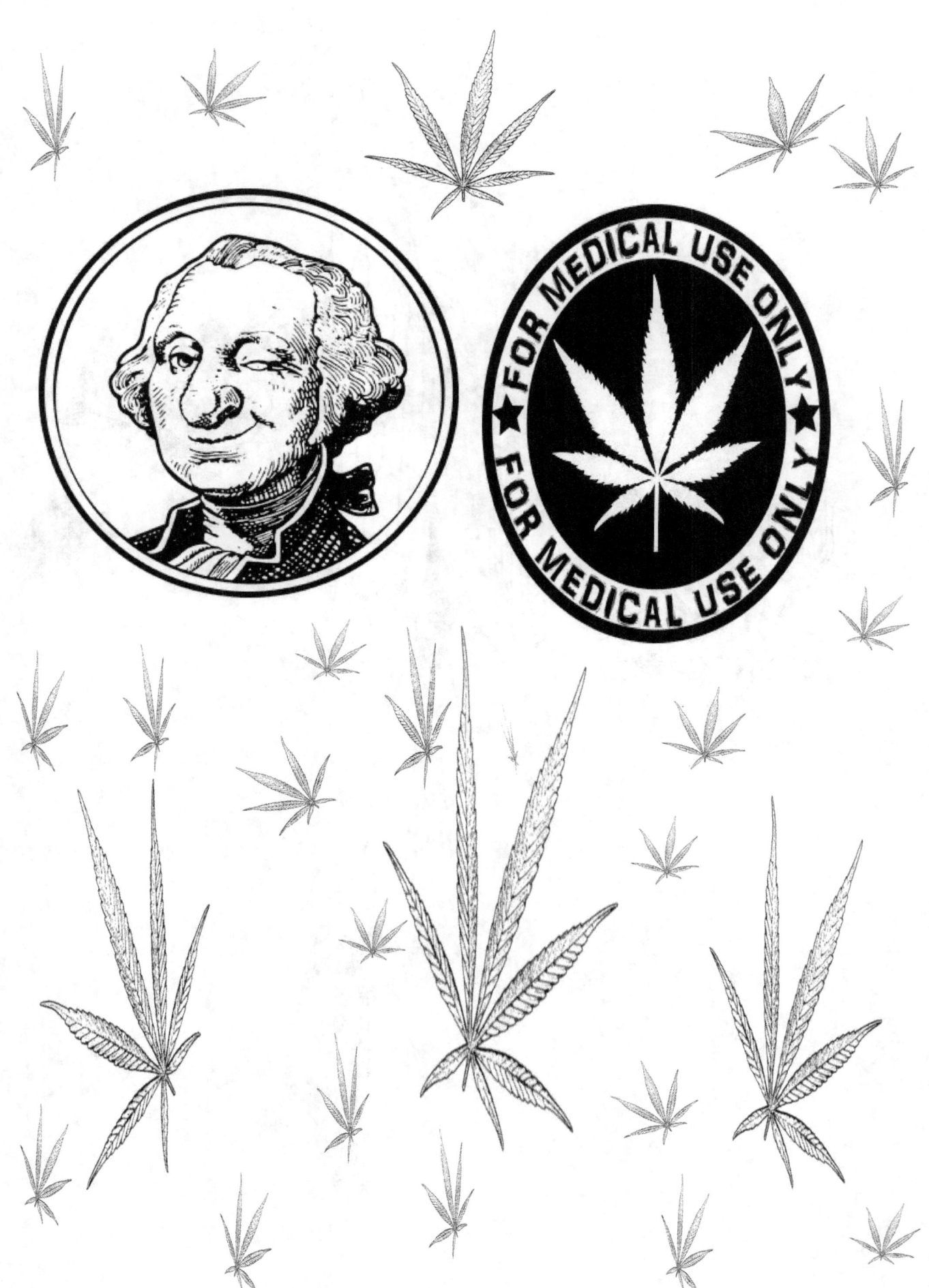

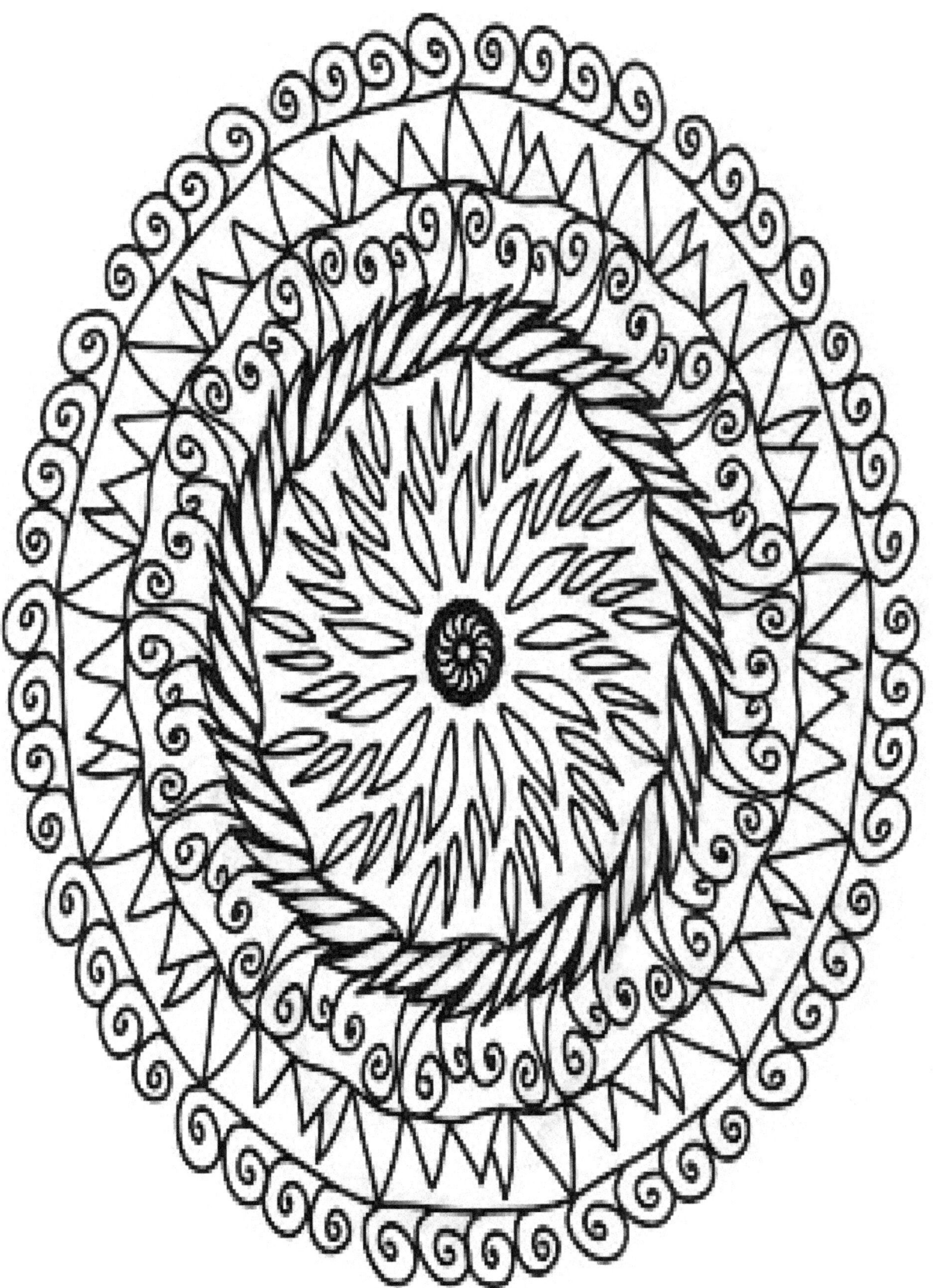

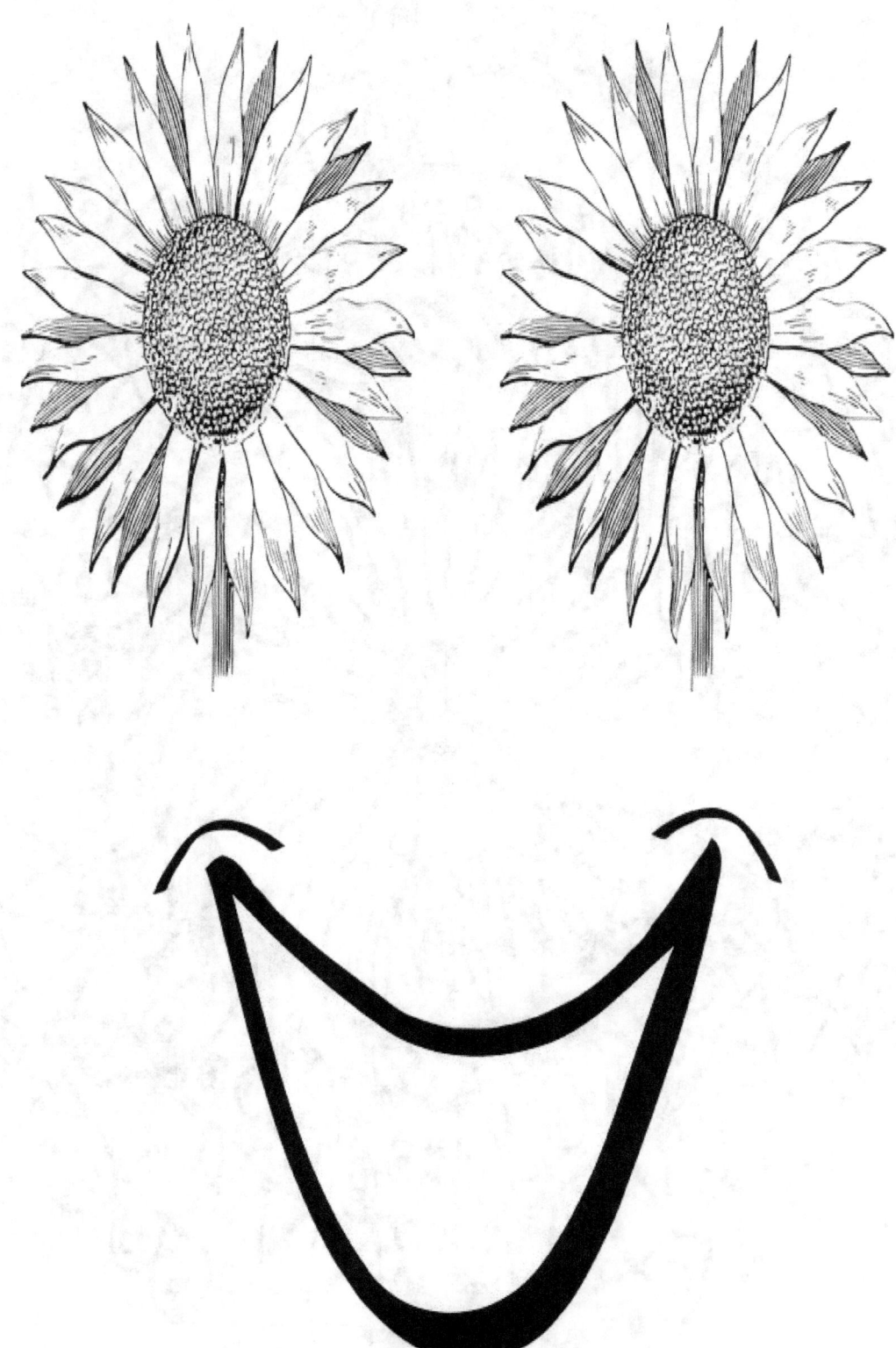

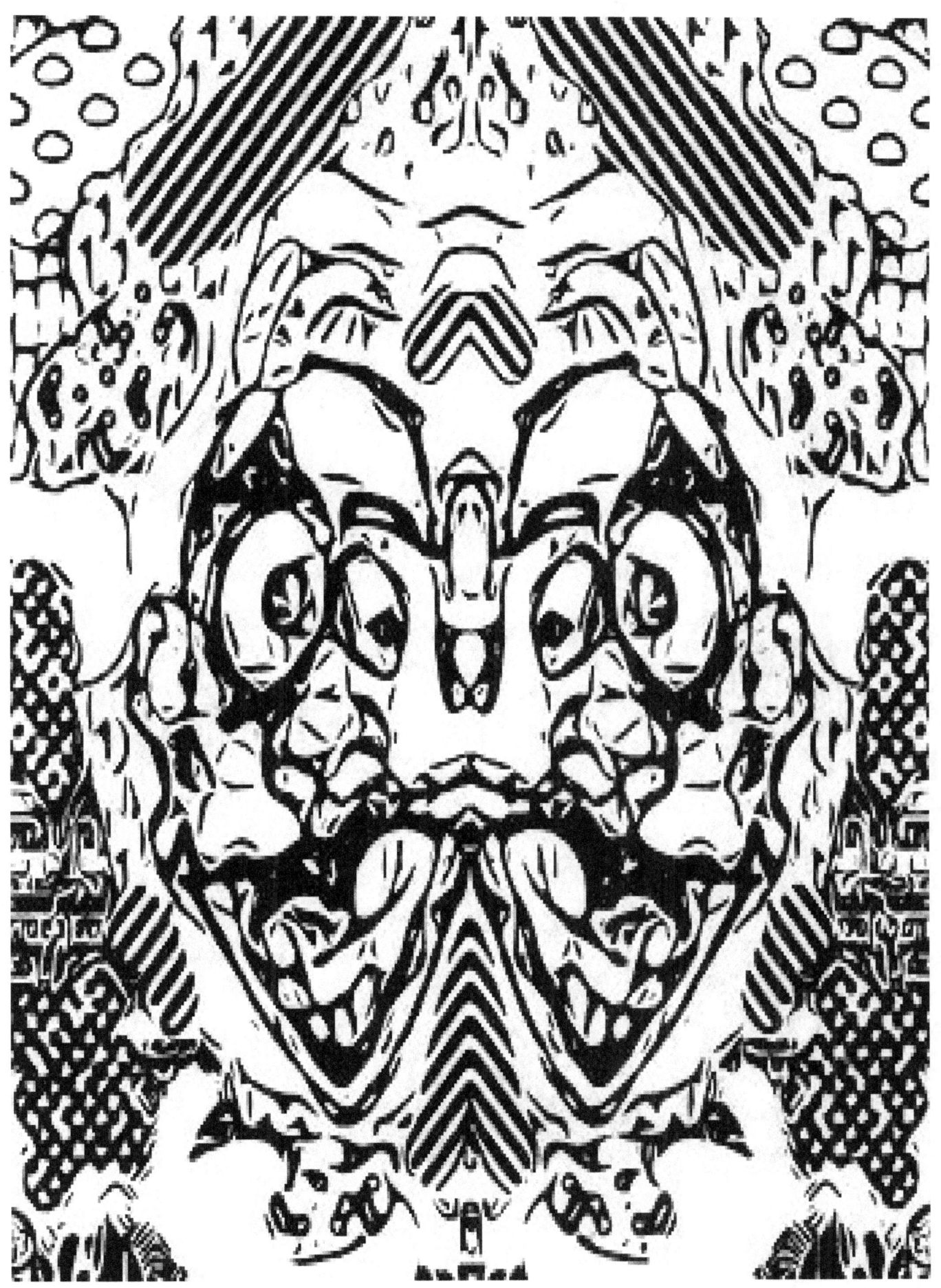

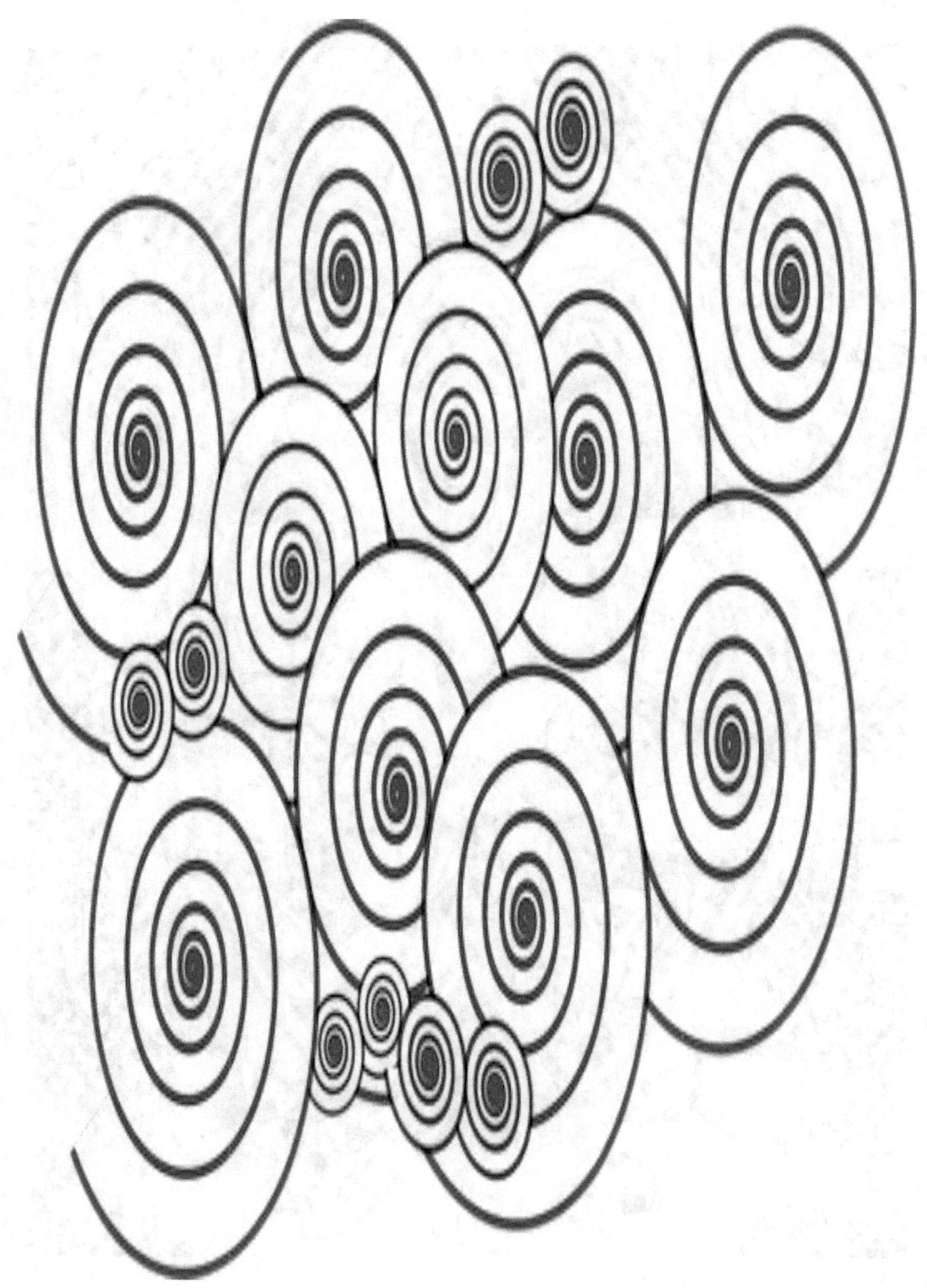

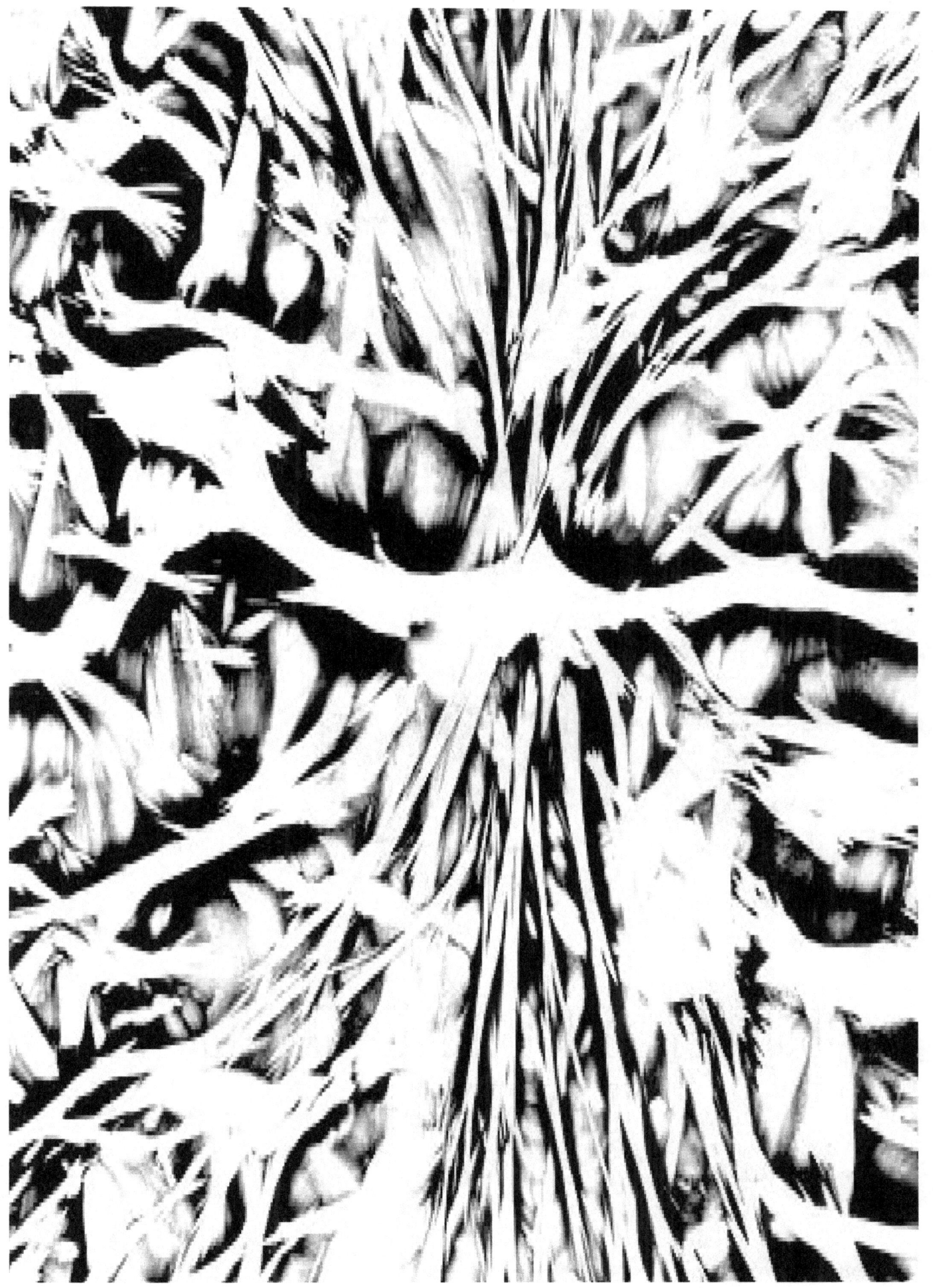

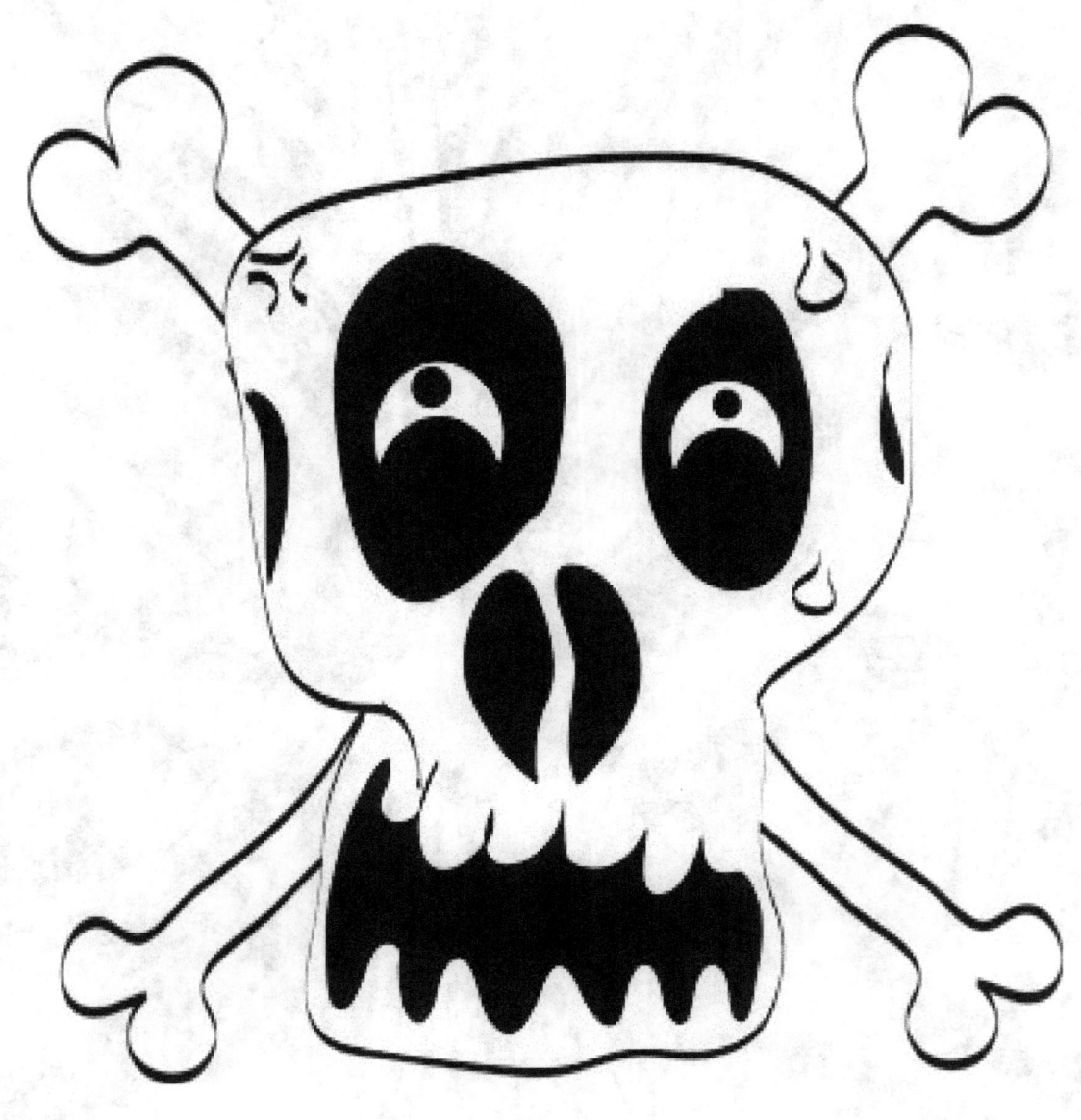

Oh God! I think I'm..
LIVING!

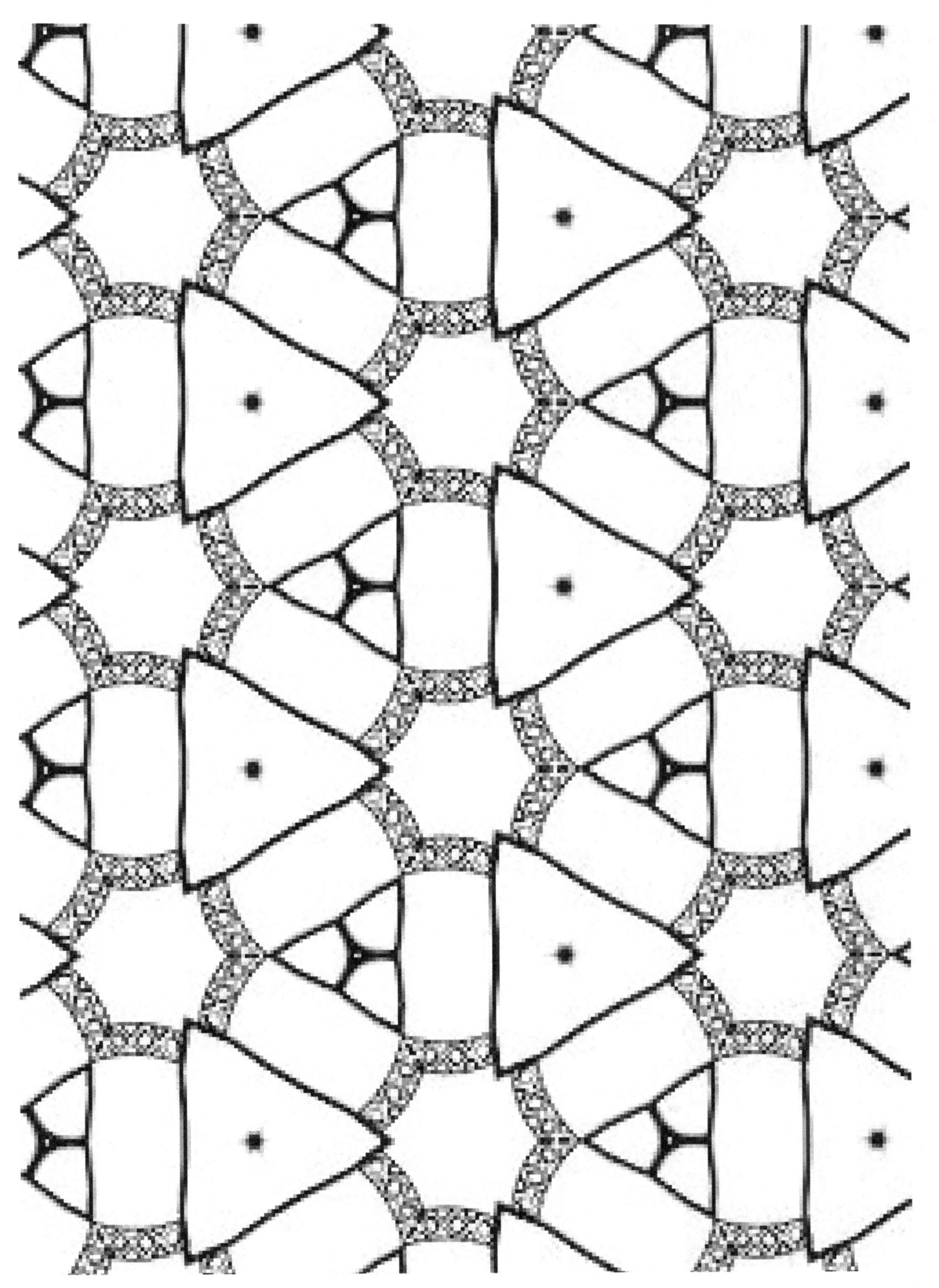

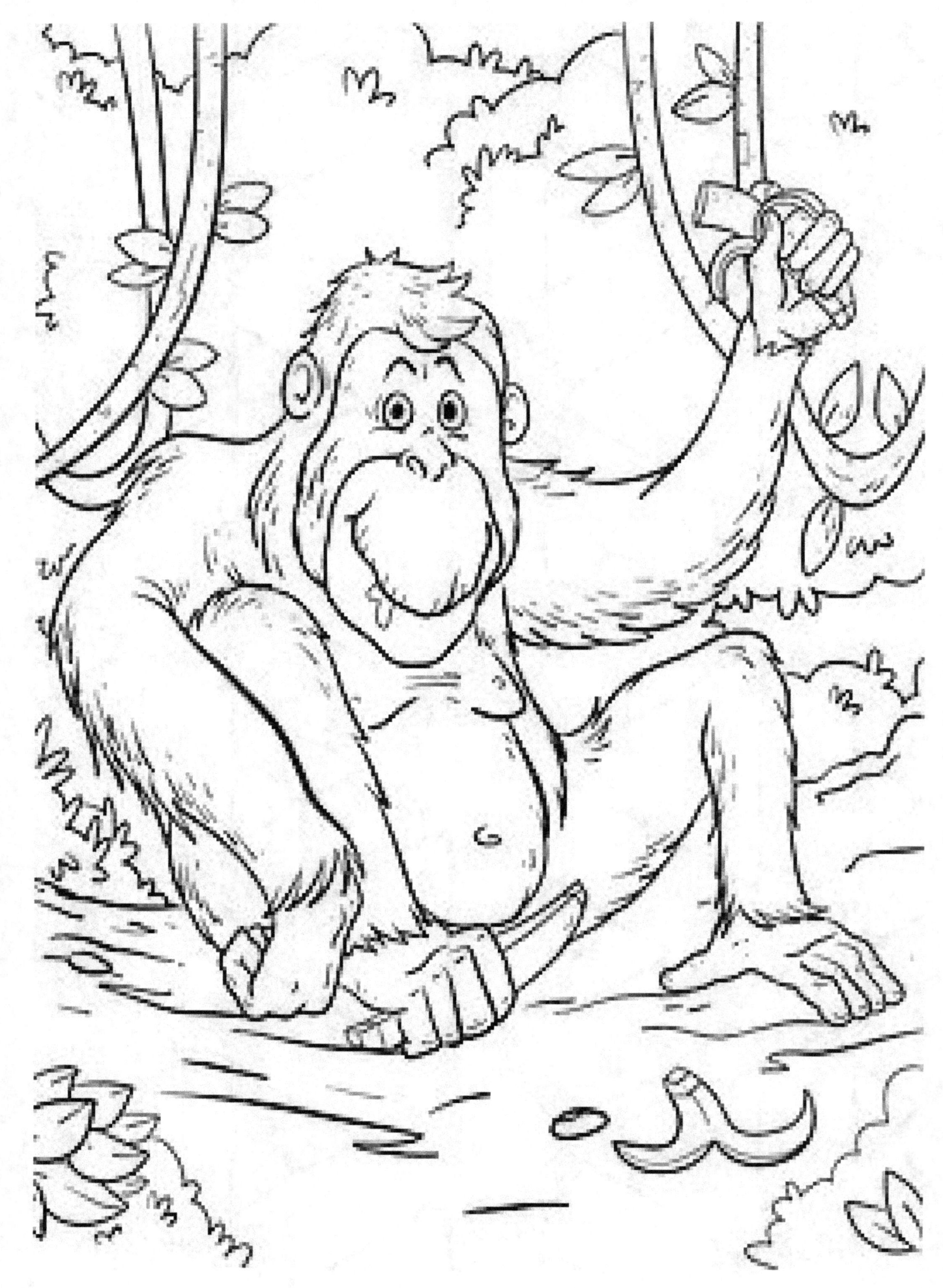

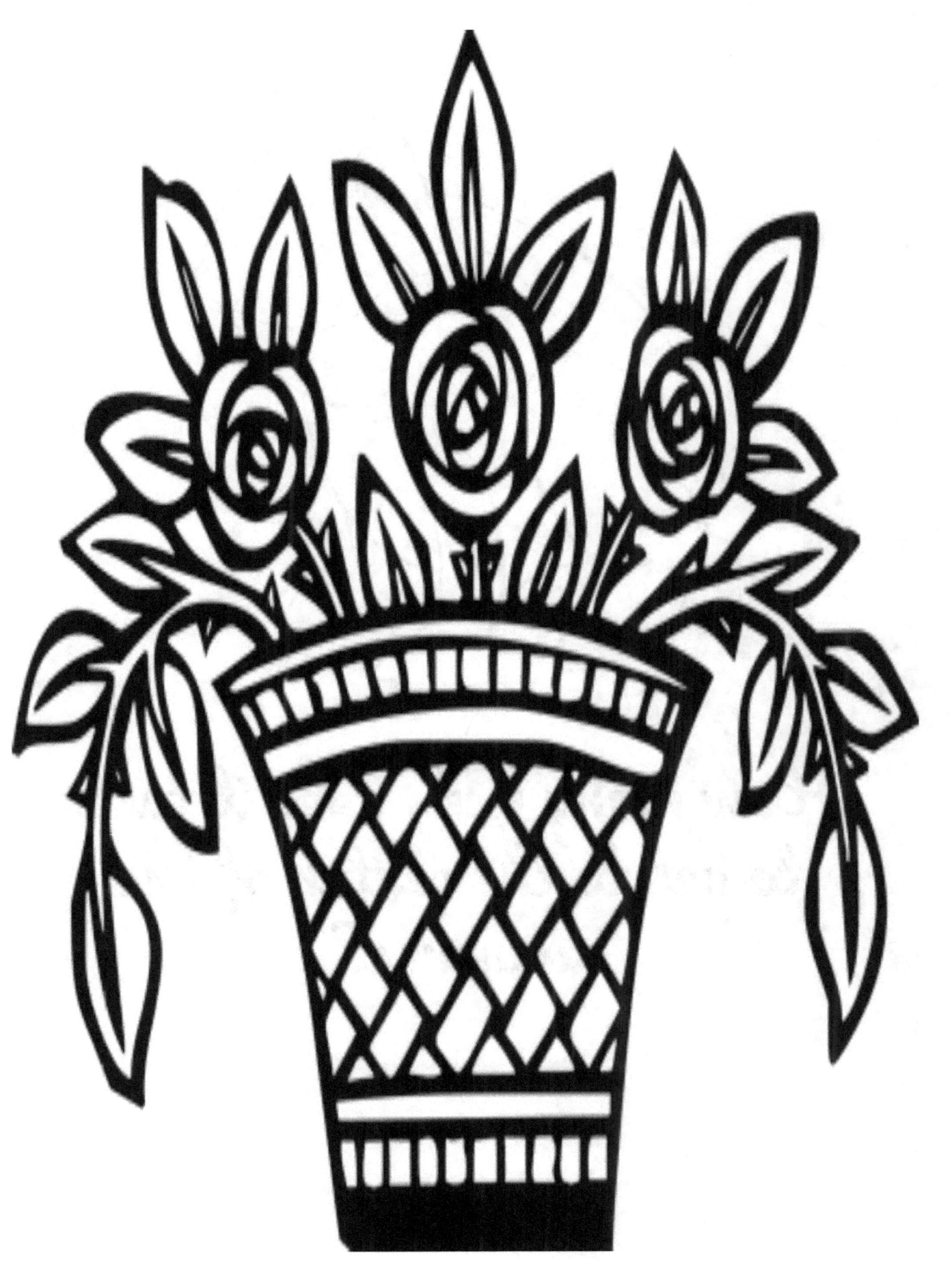

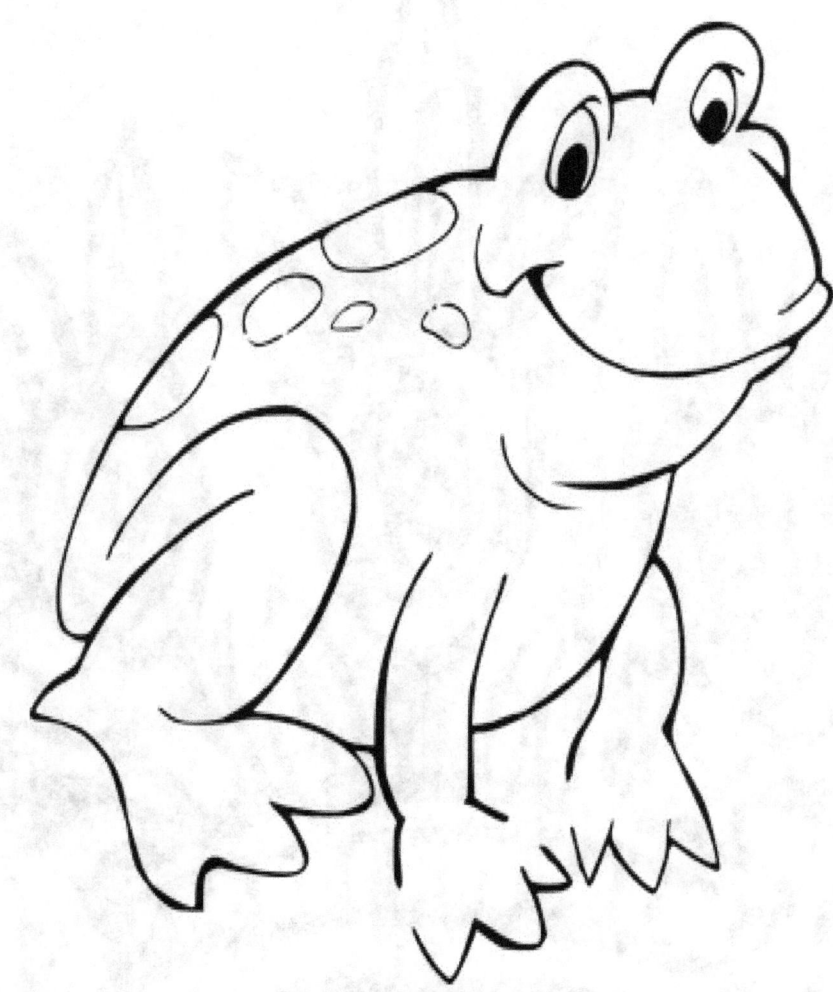

How many licks does it take to get to the center of the universe?

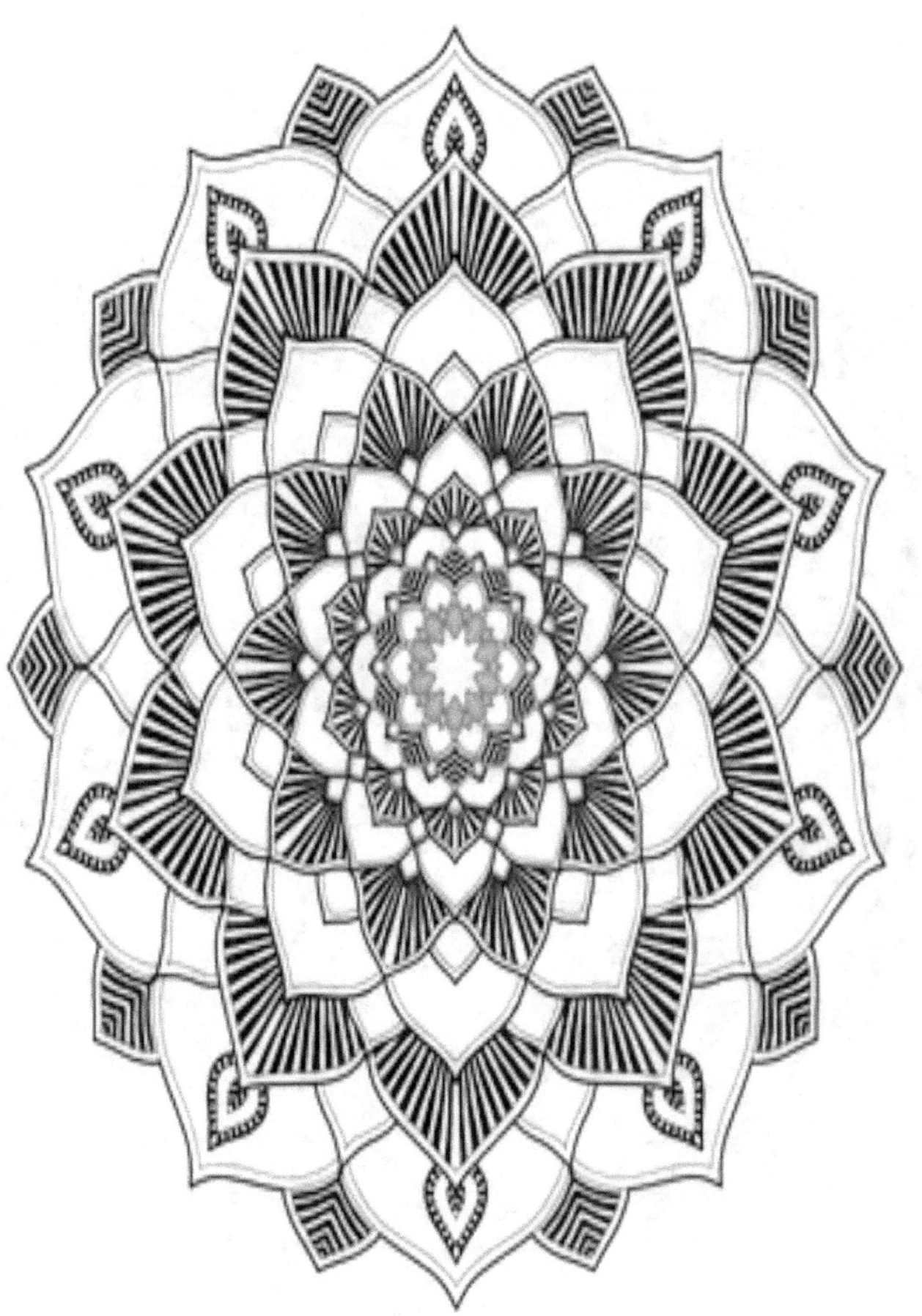

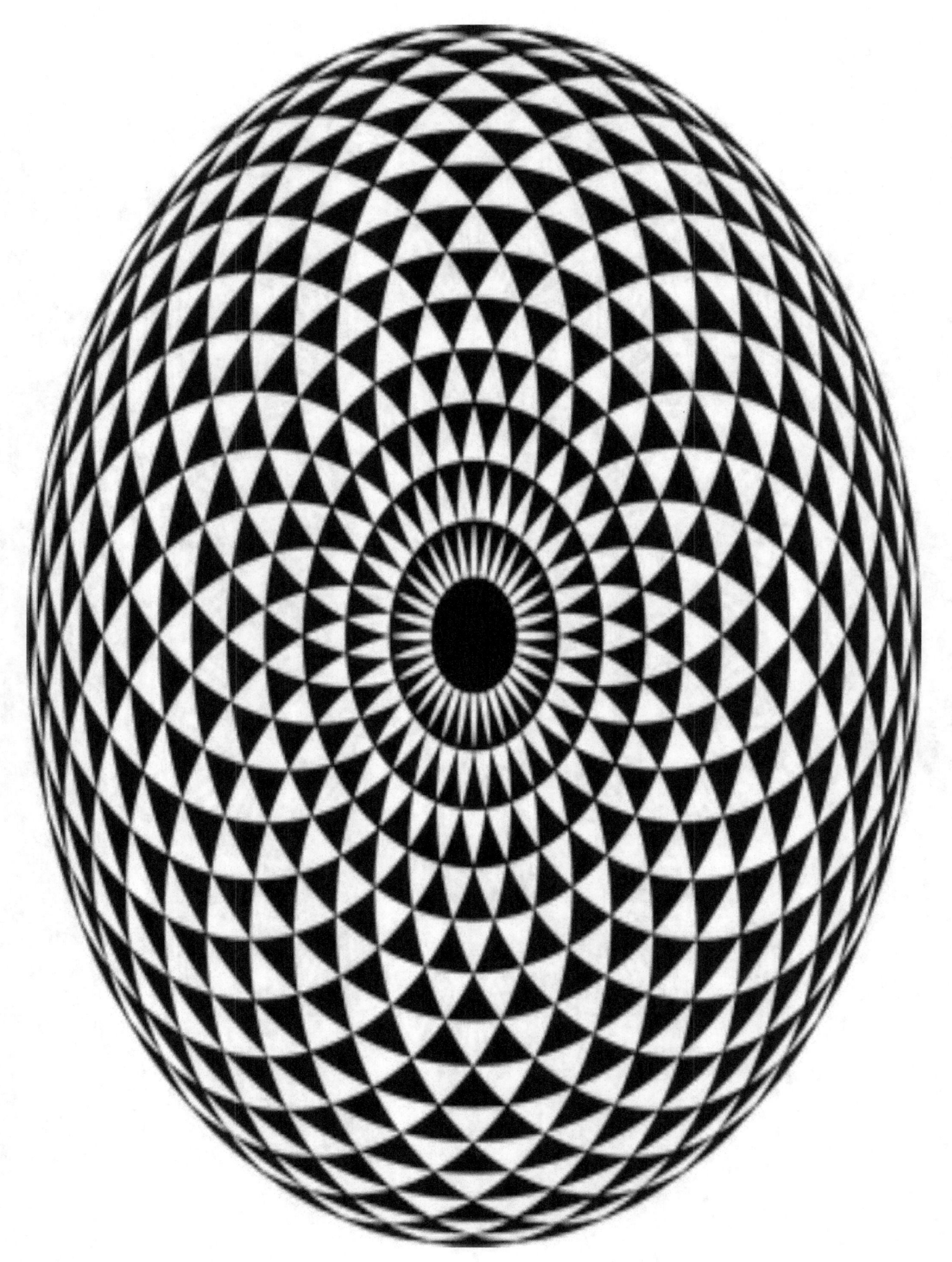

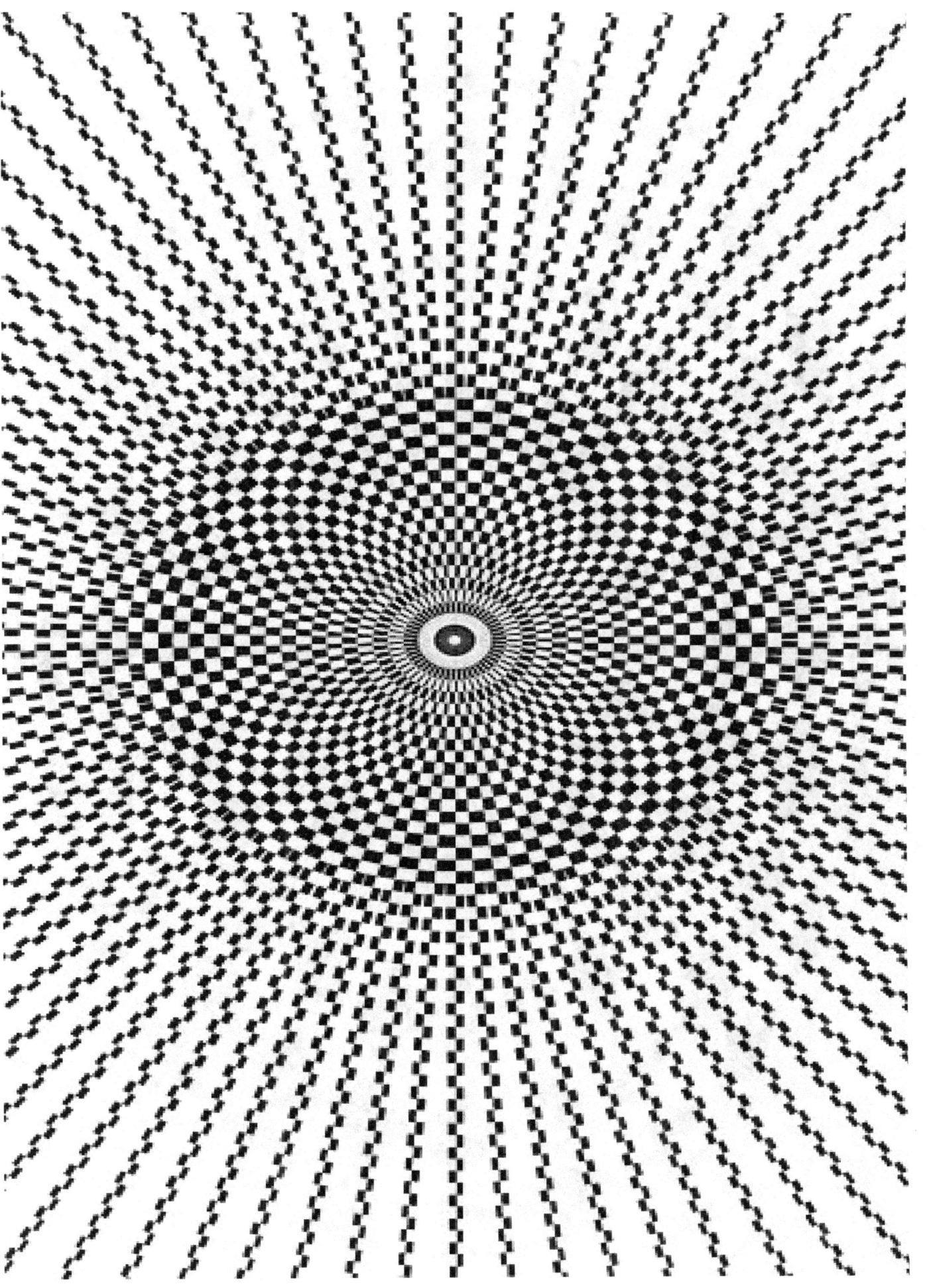

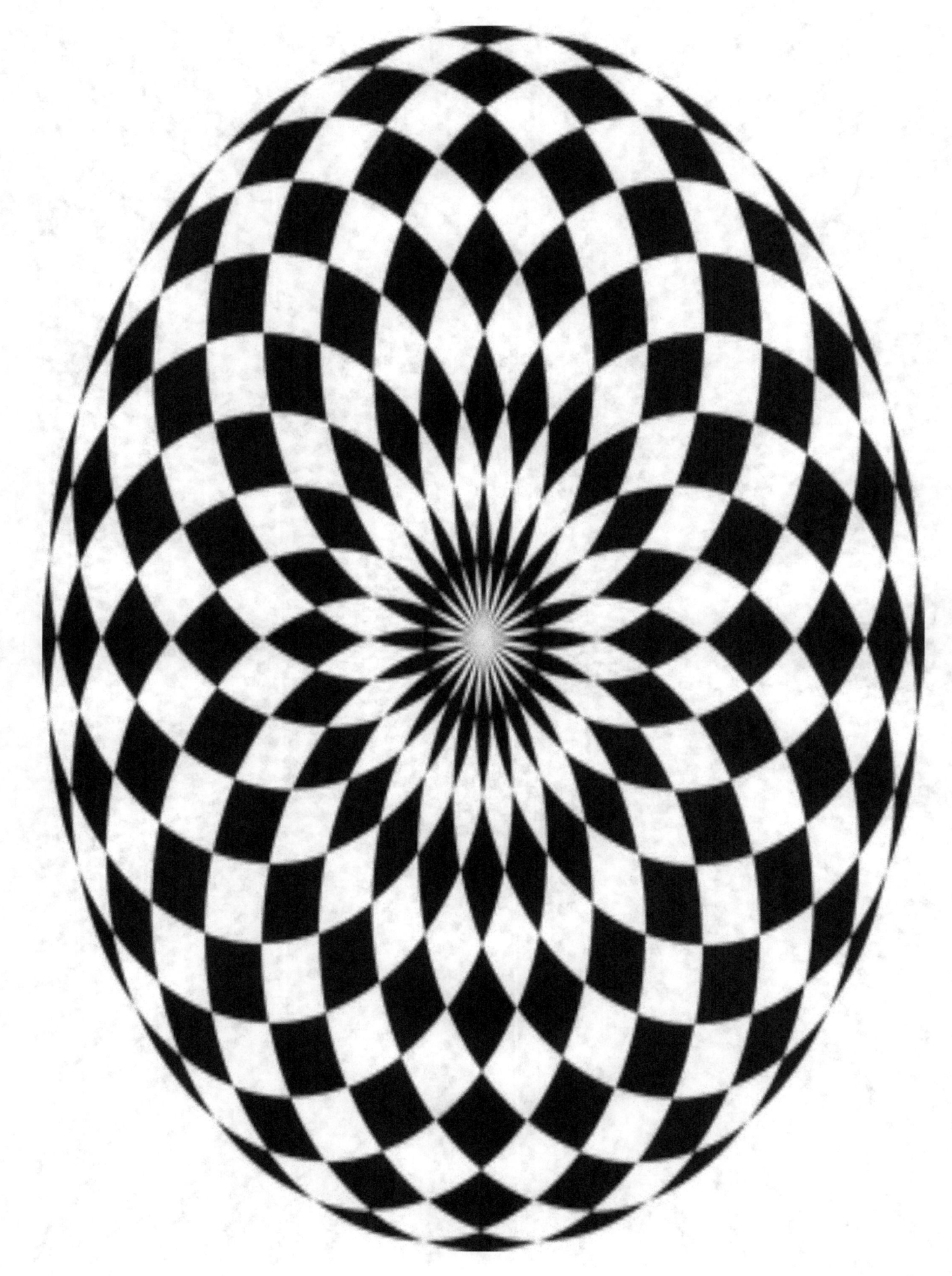

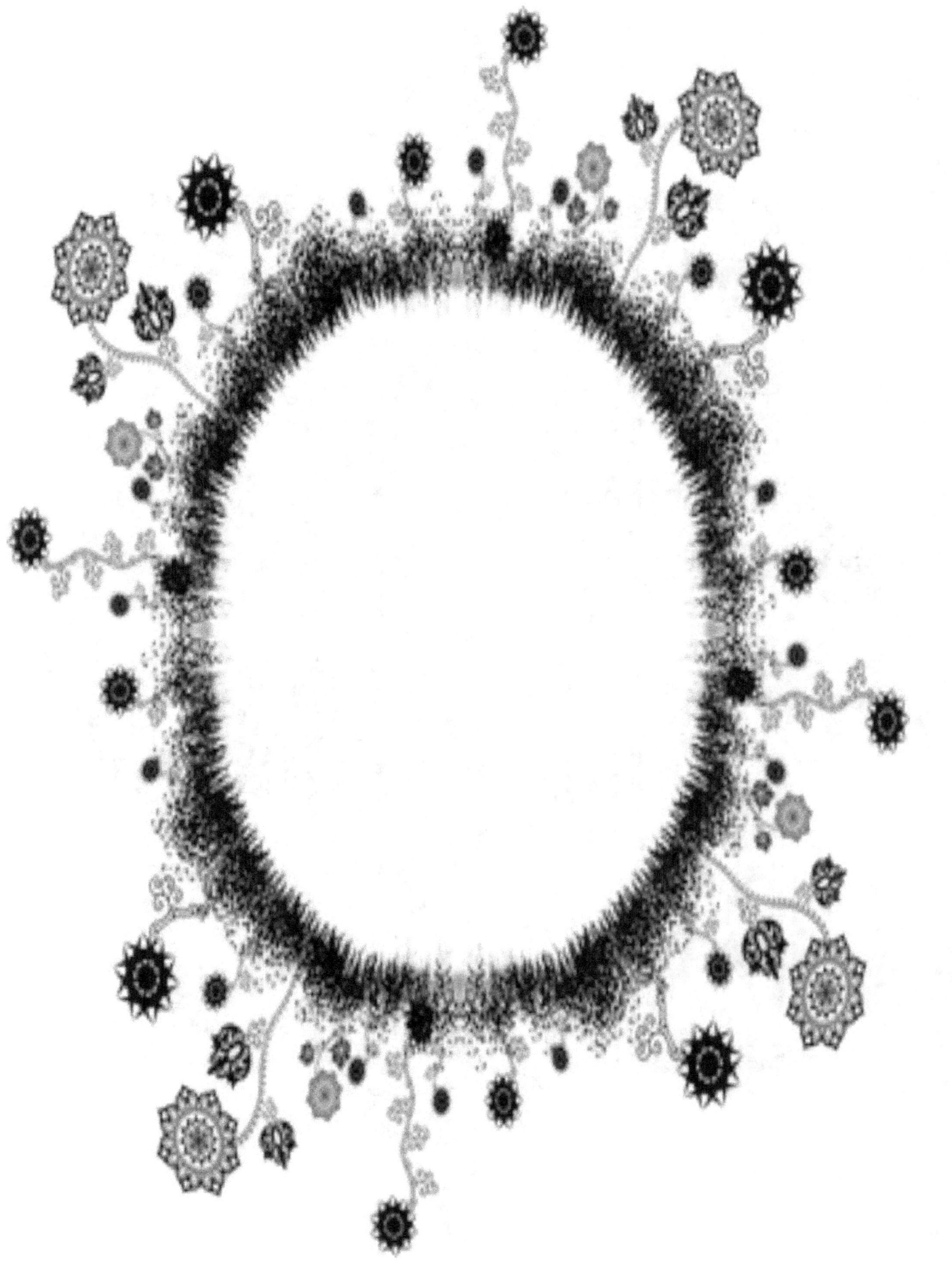

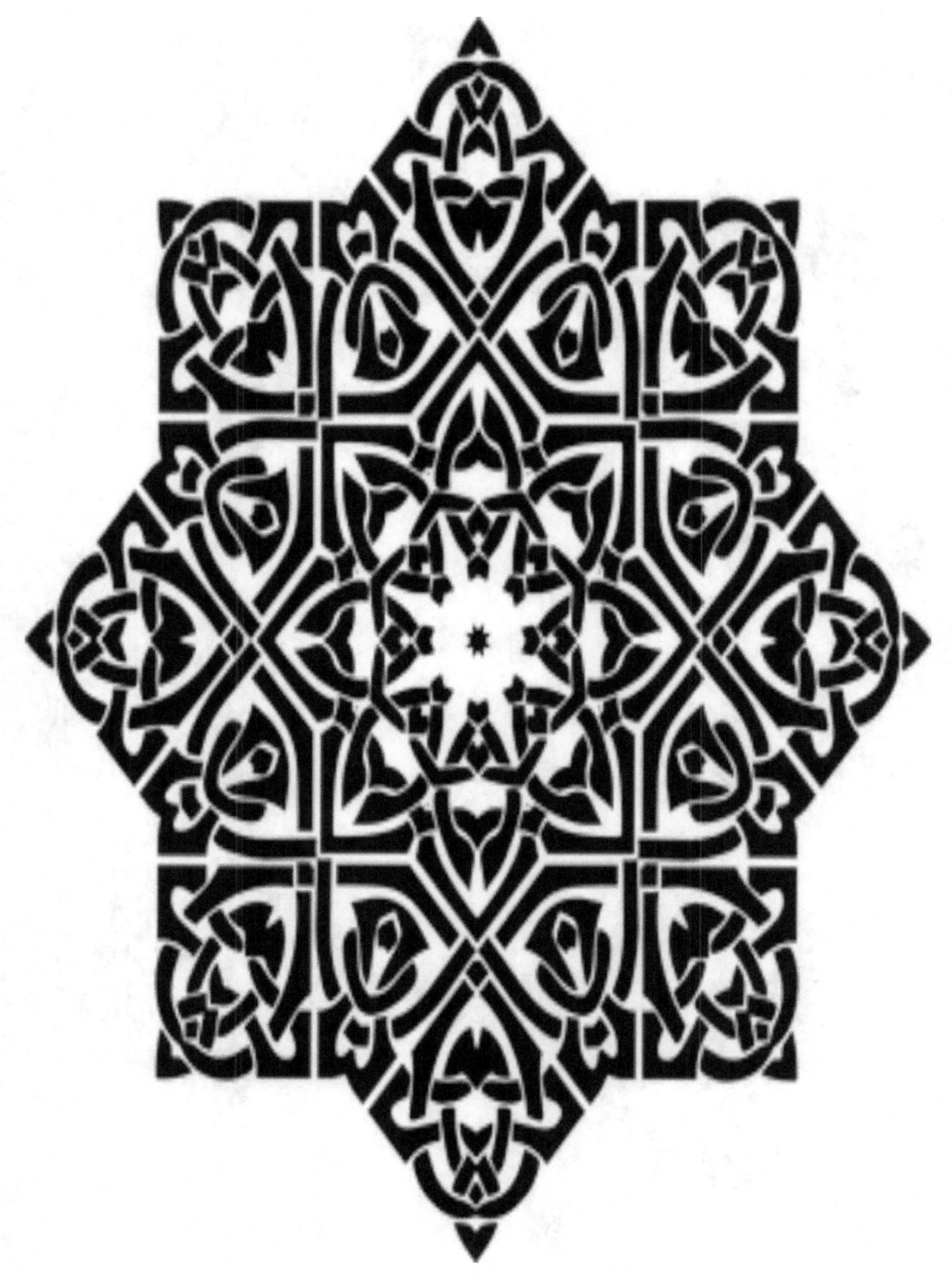

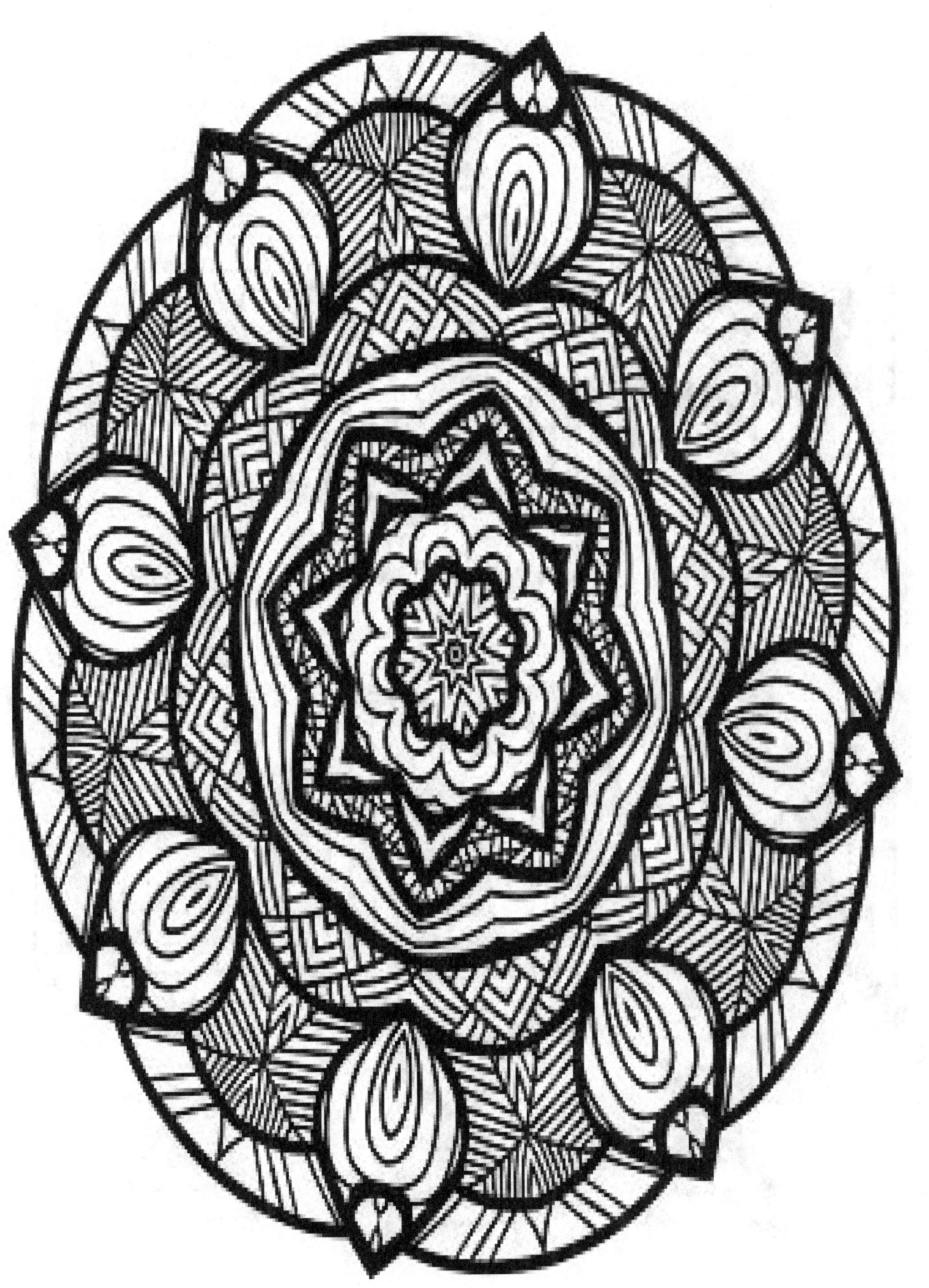

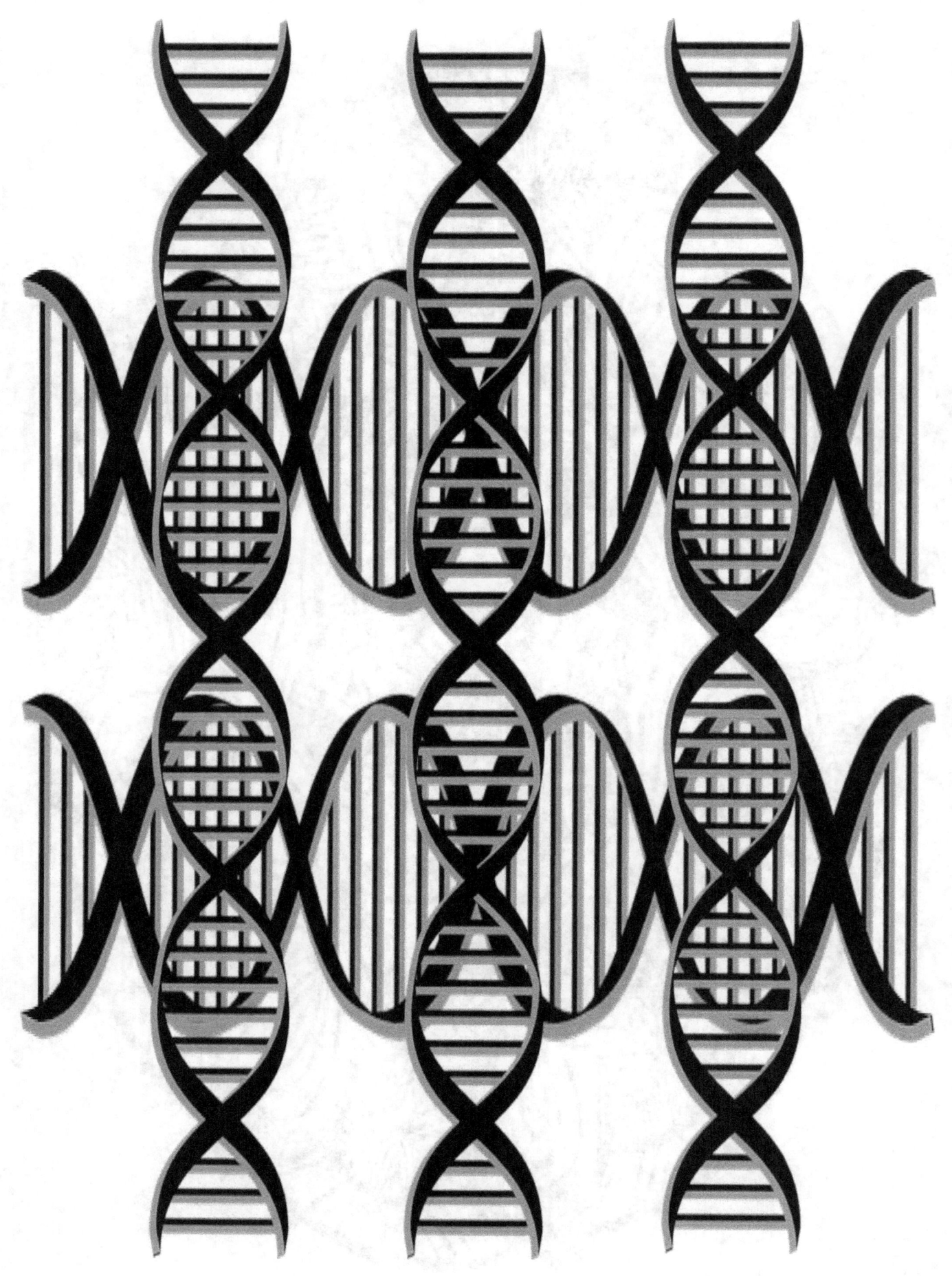

Just Your Luck

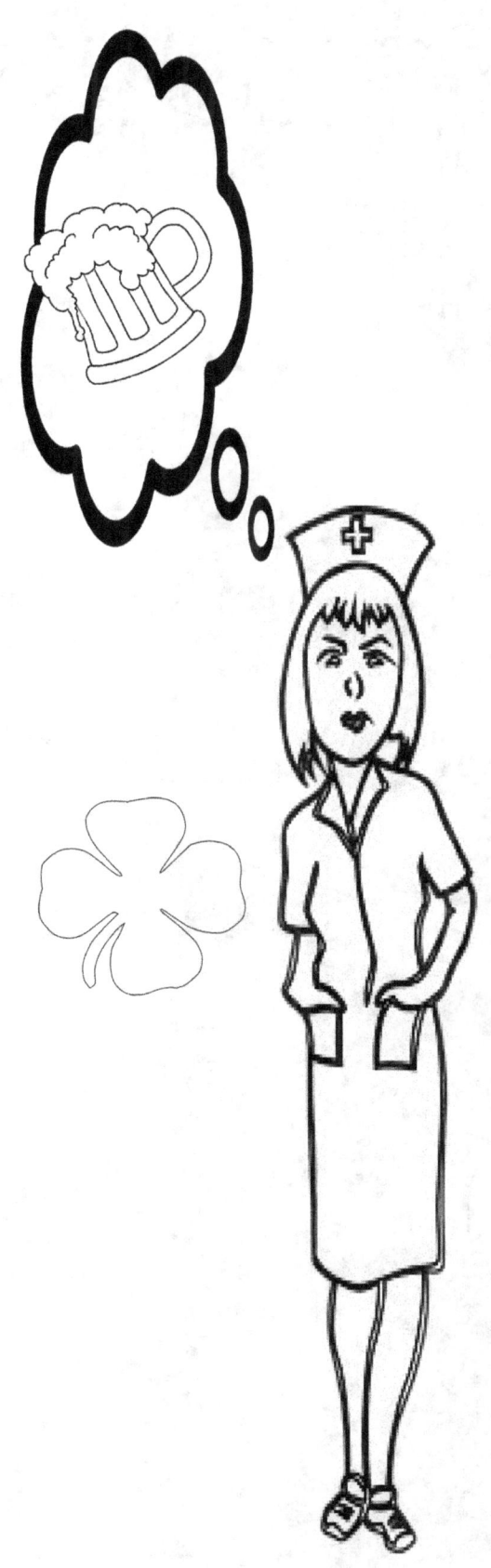

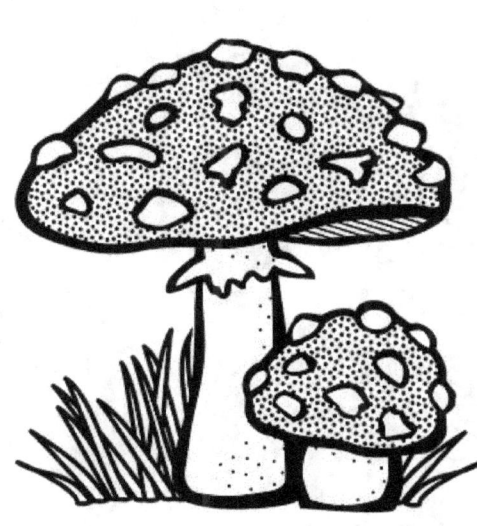

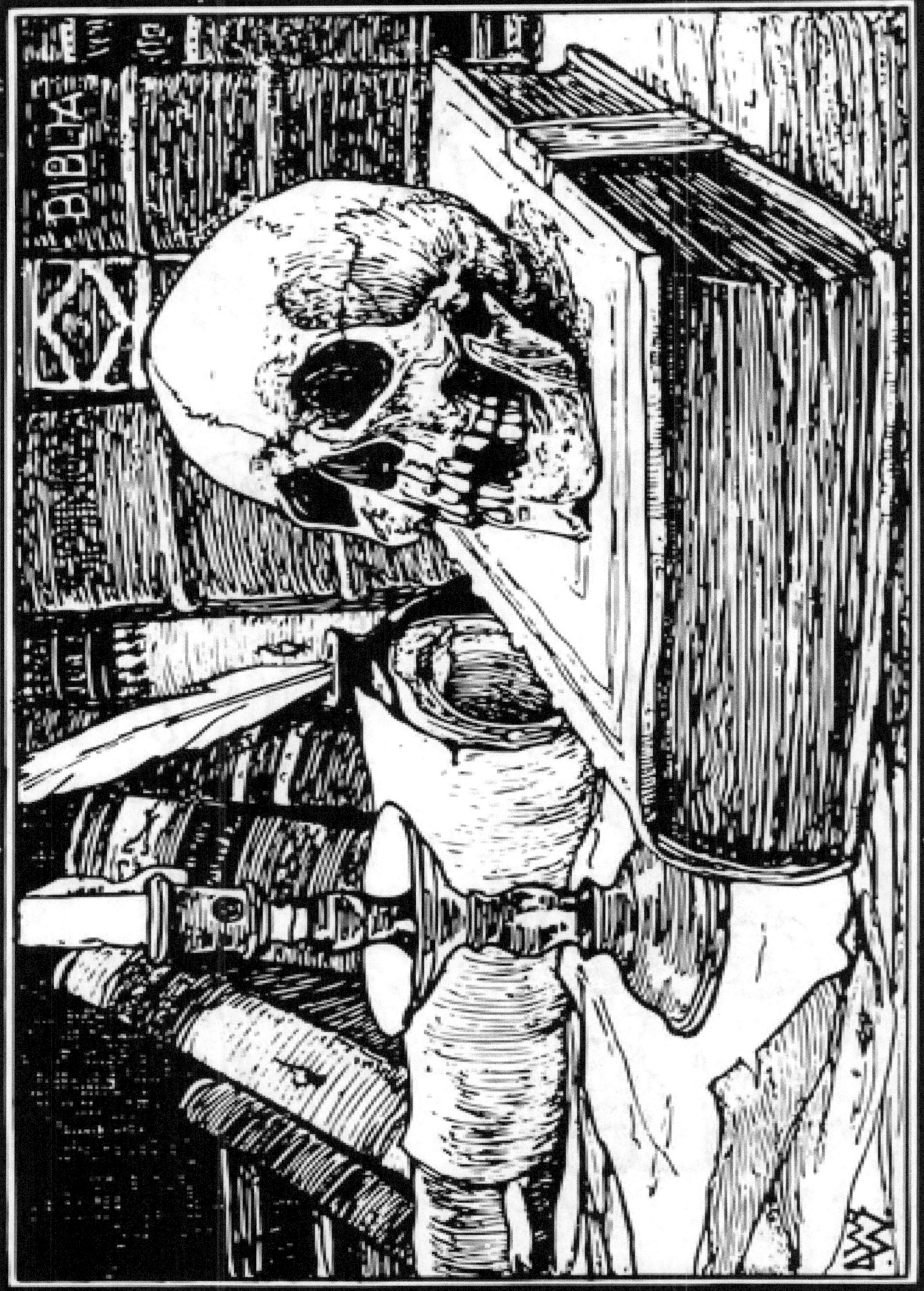

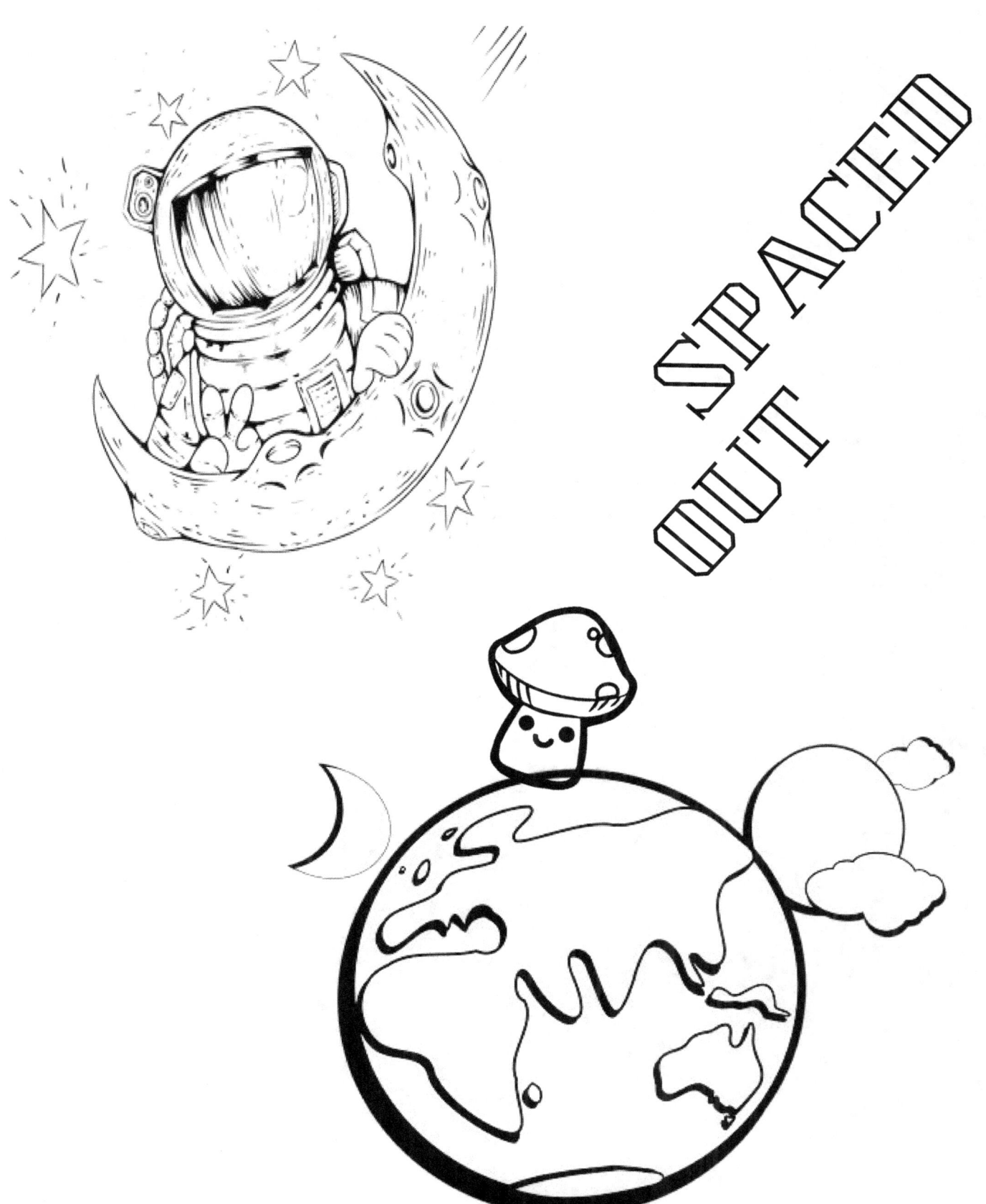

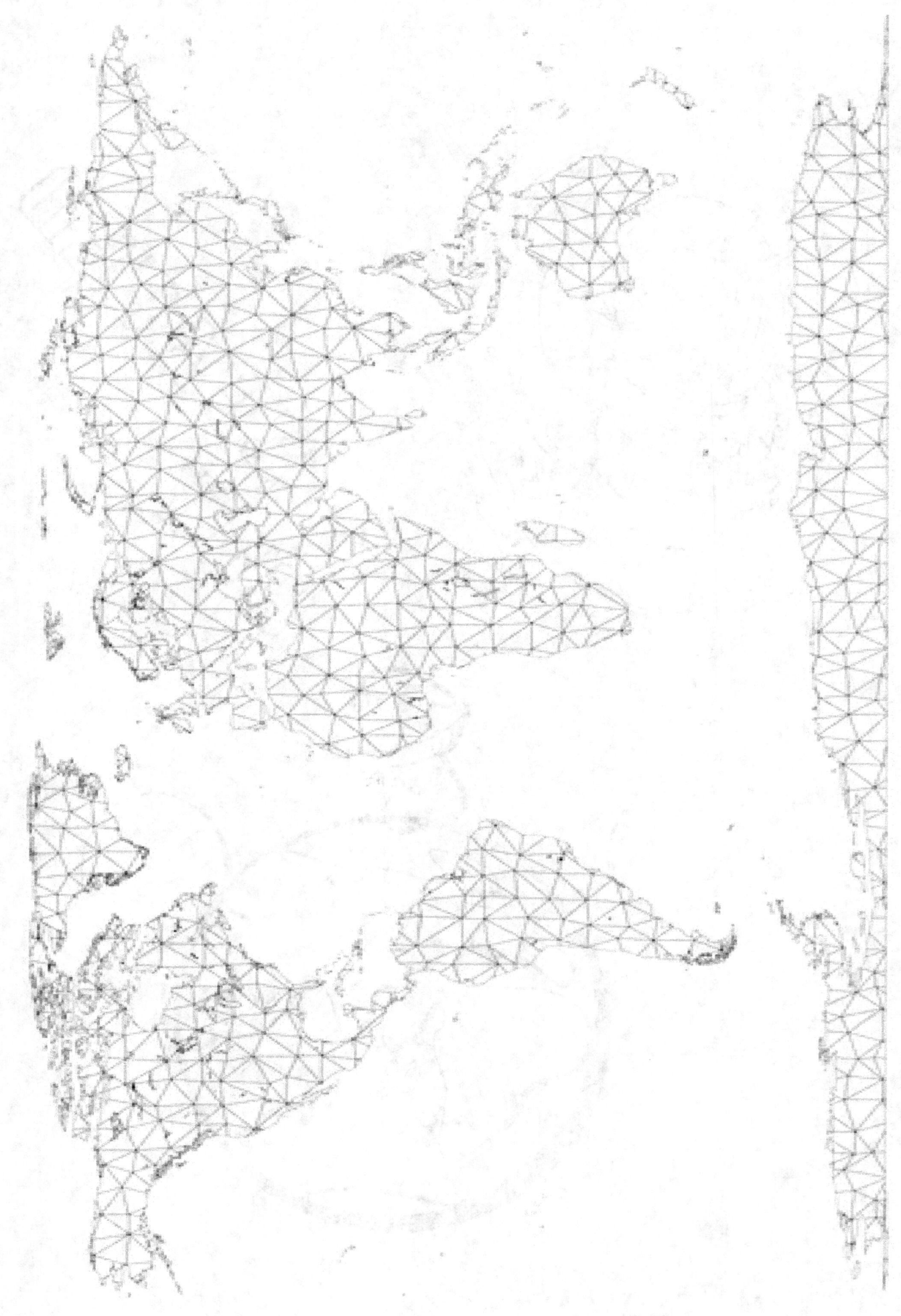

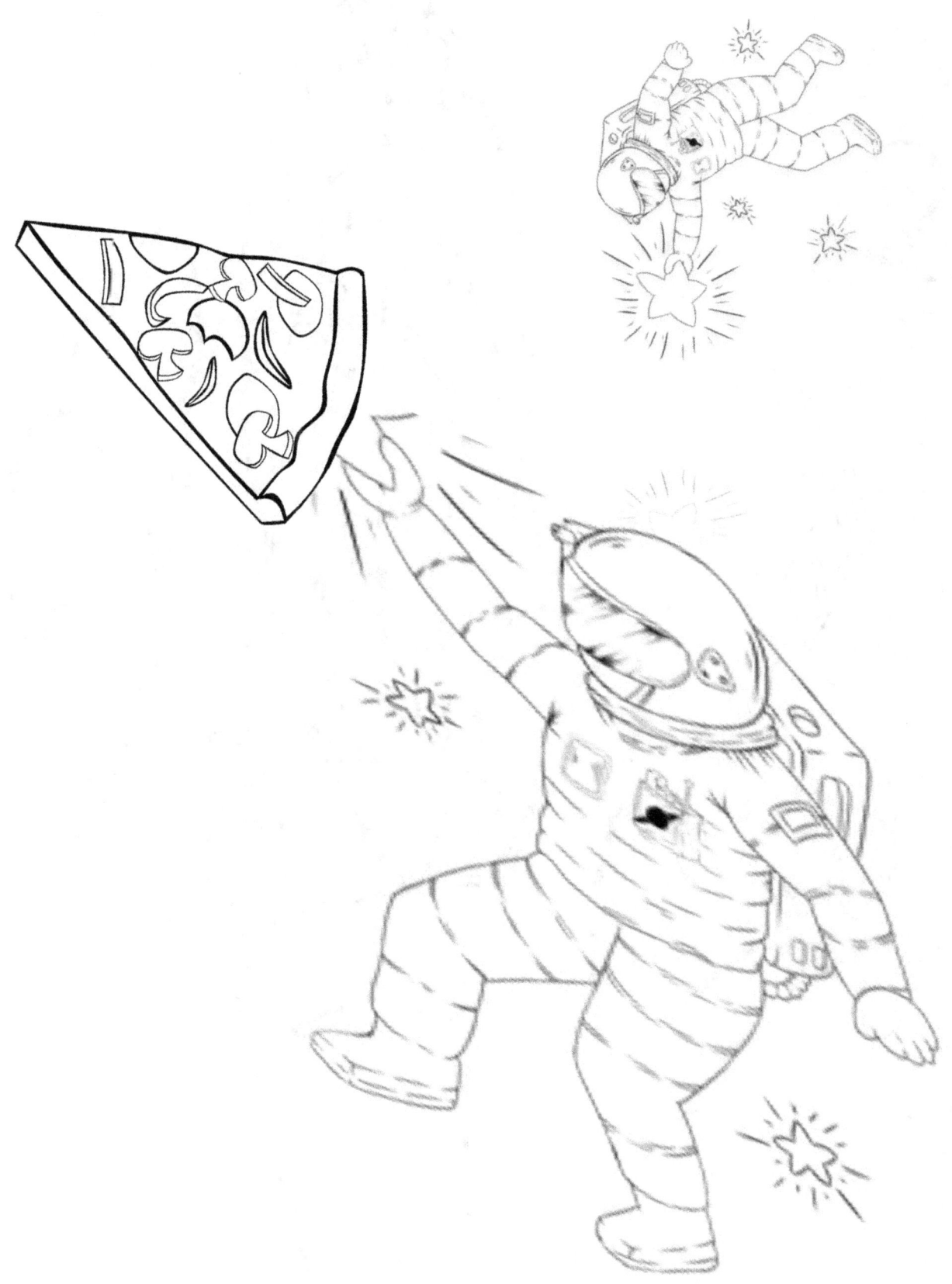

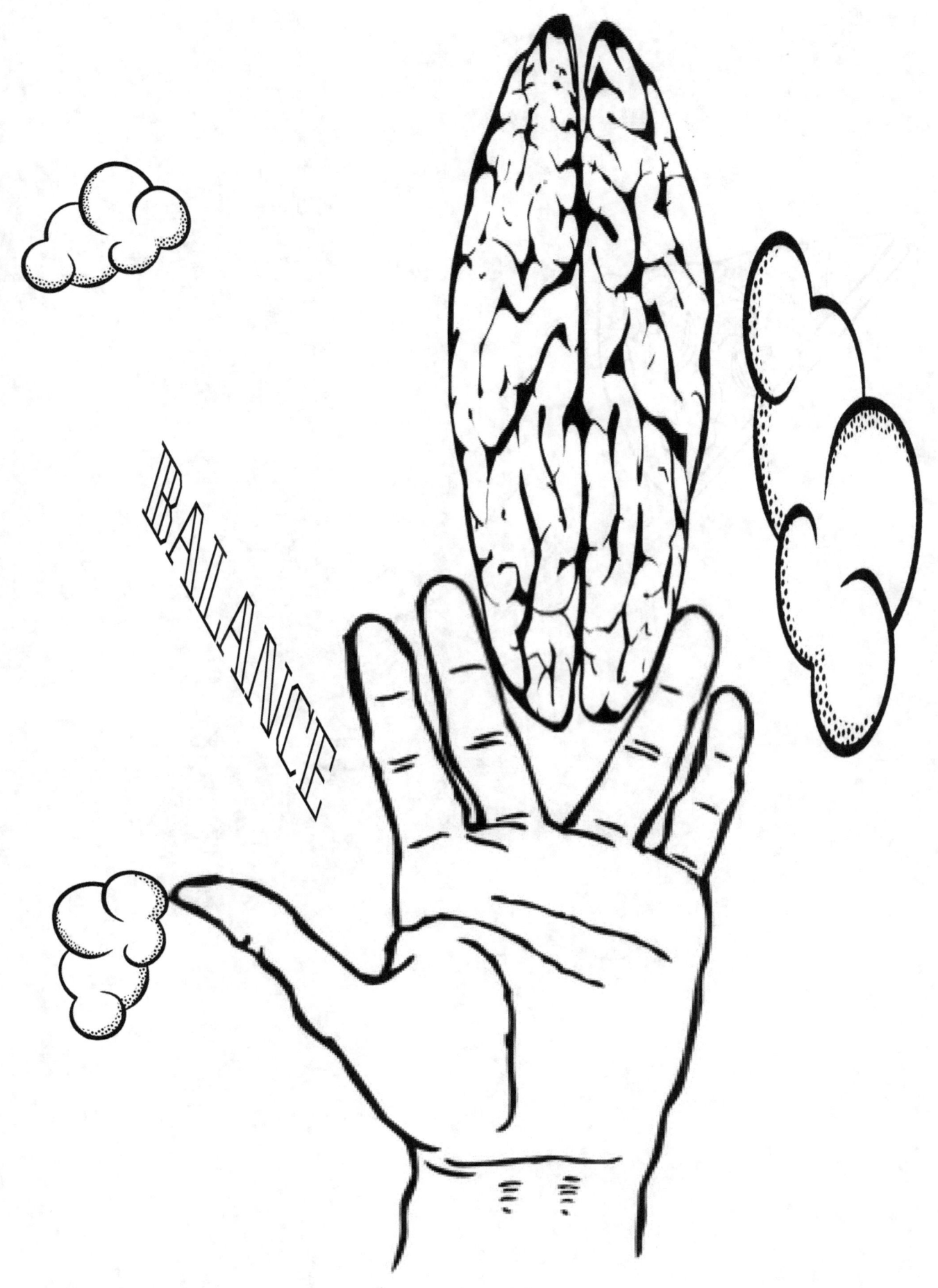

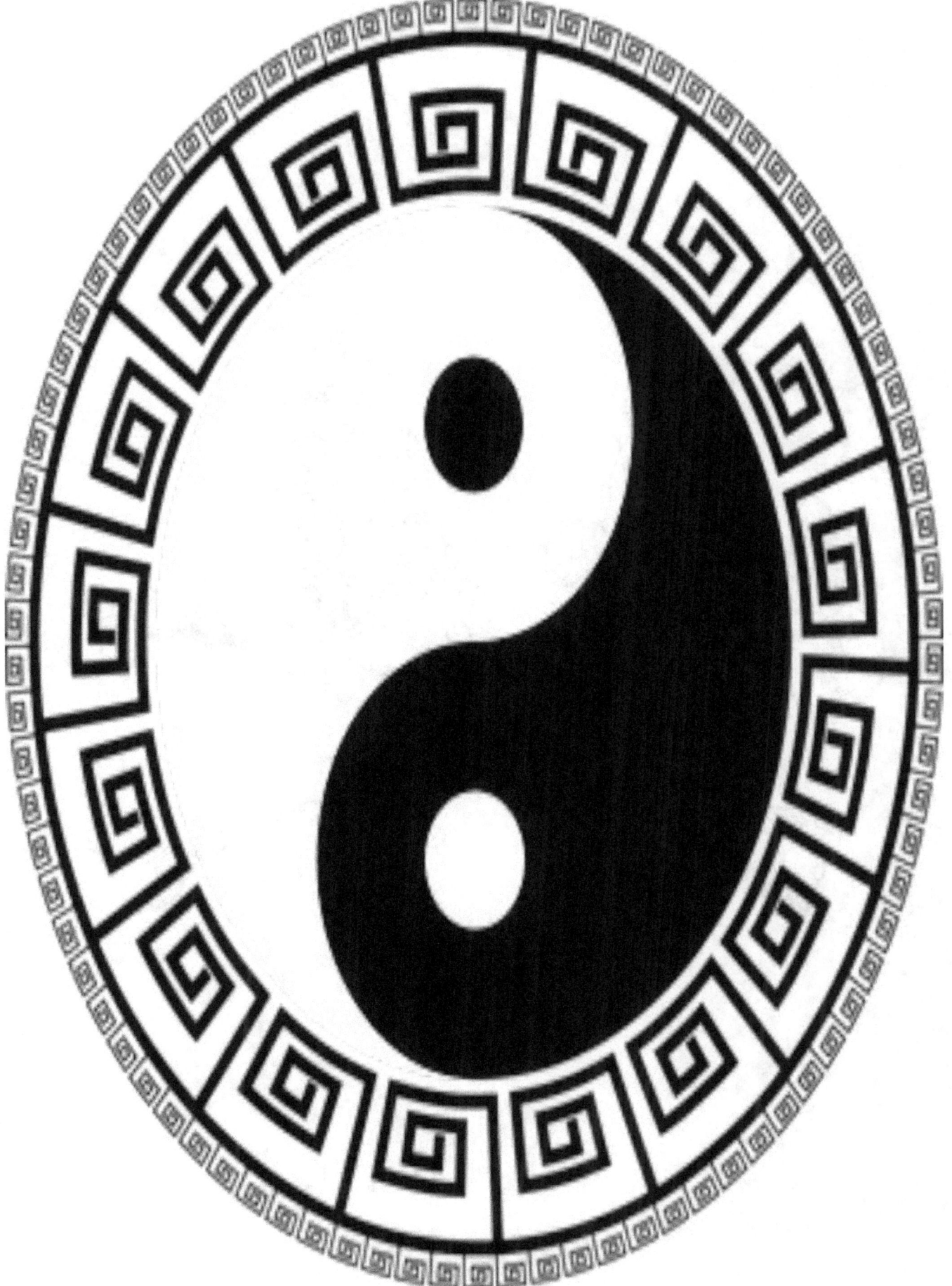

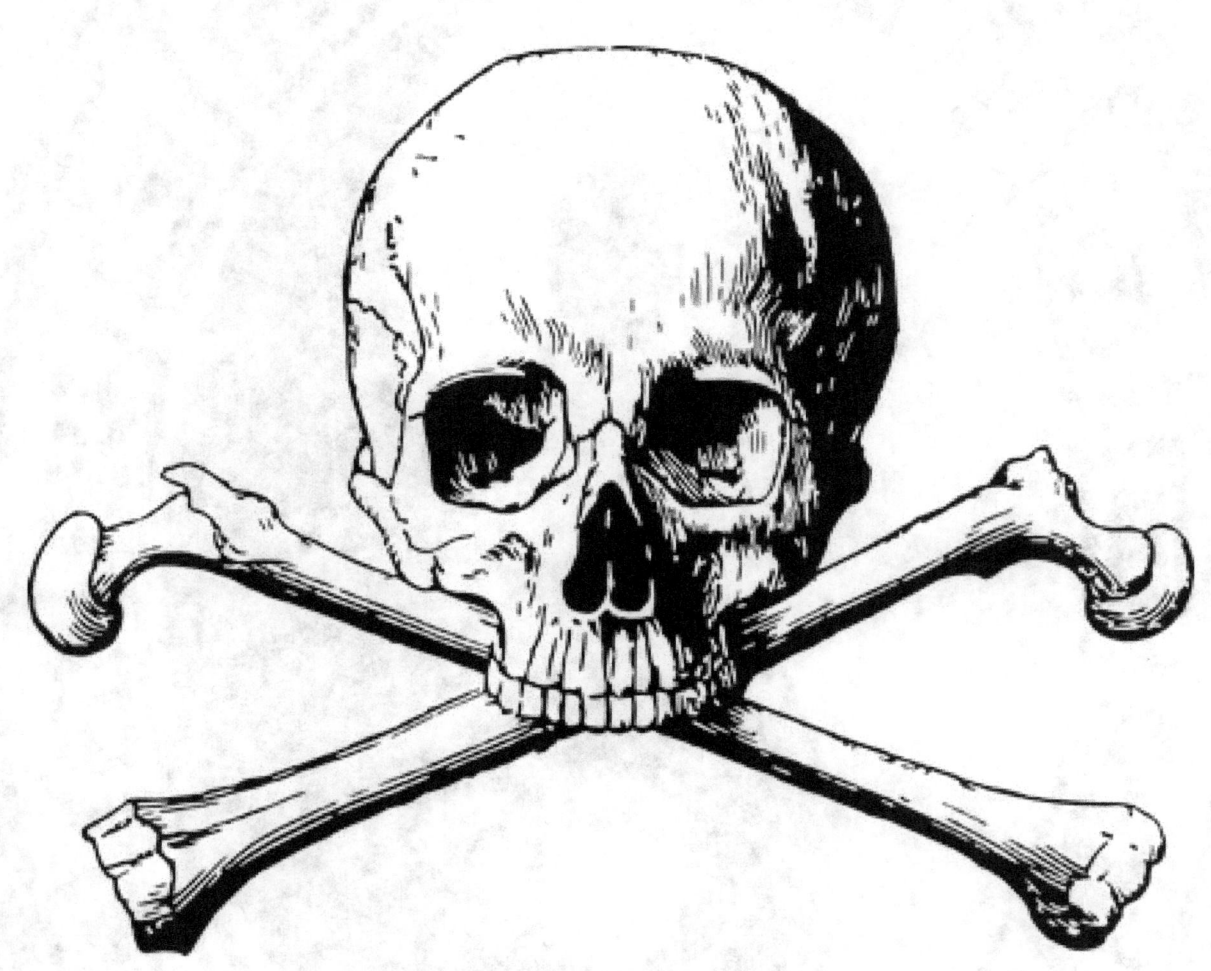

DEATH

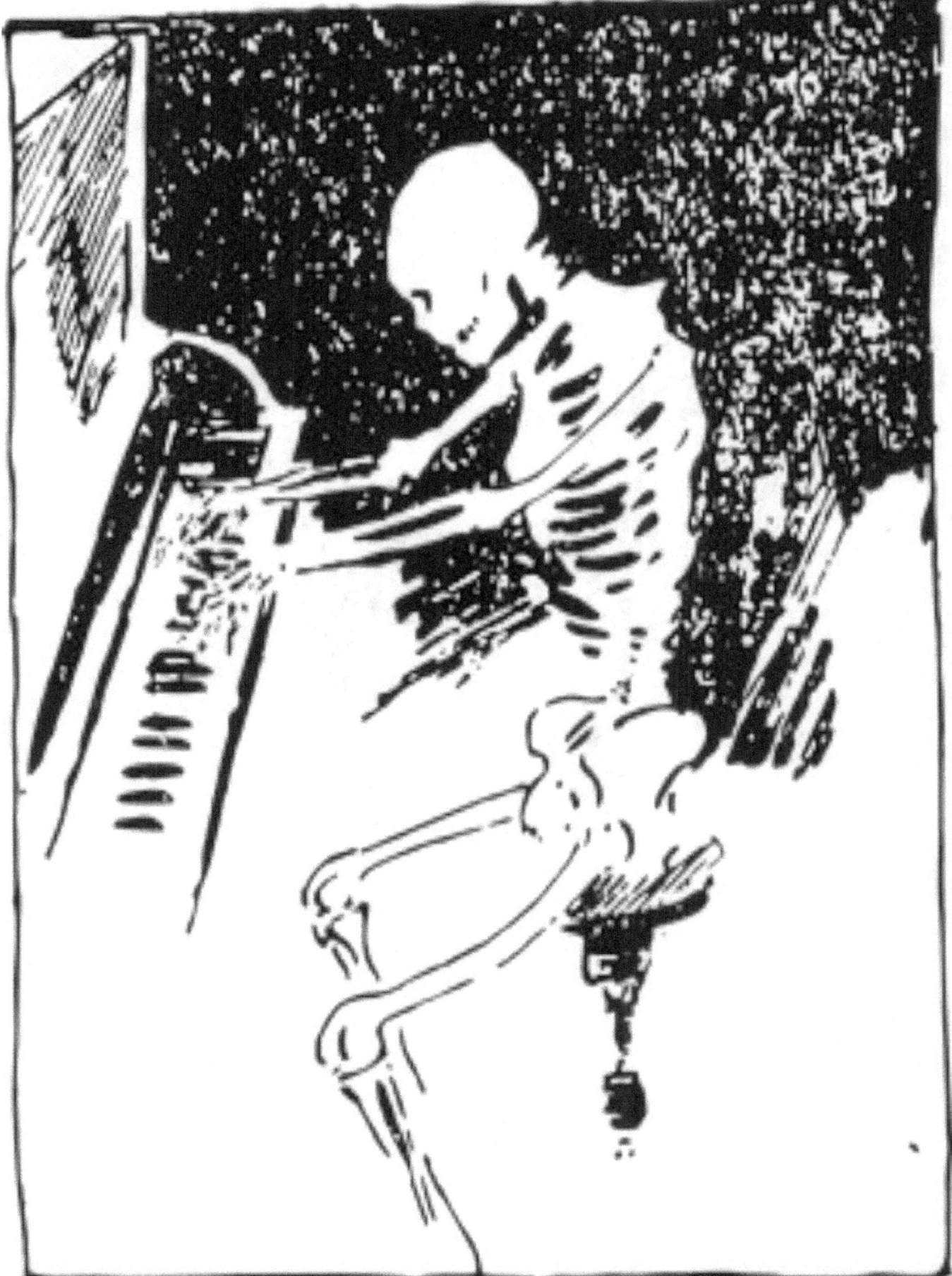

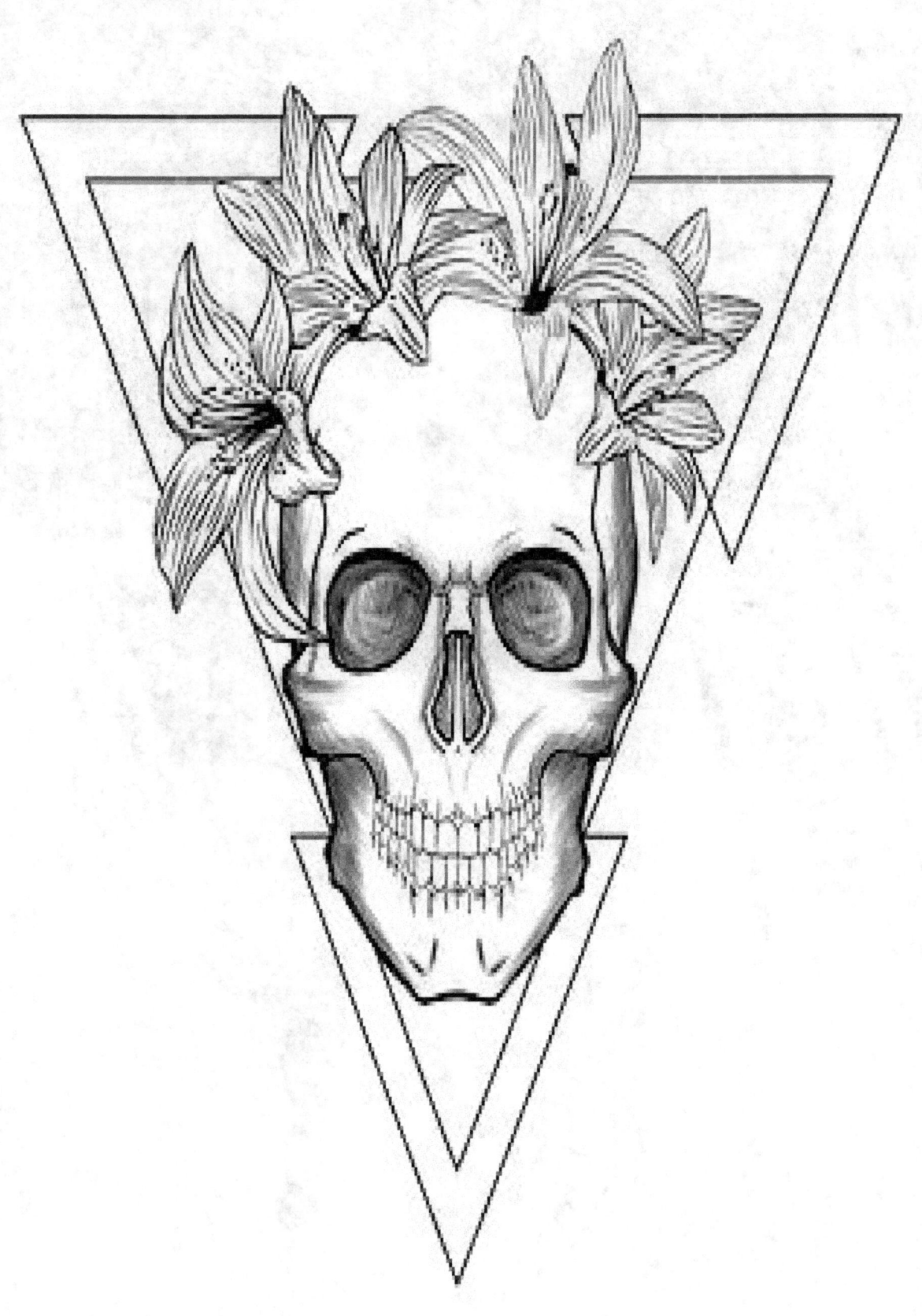

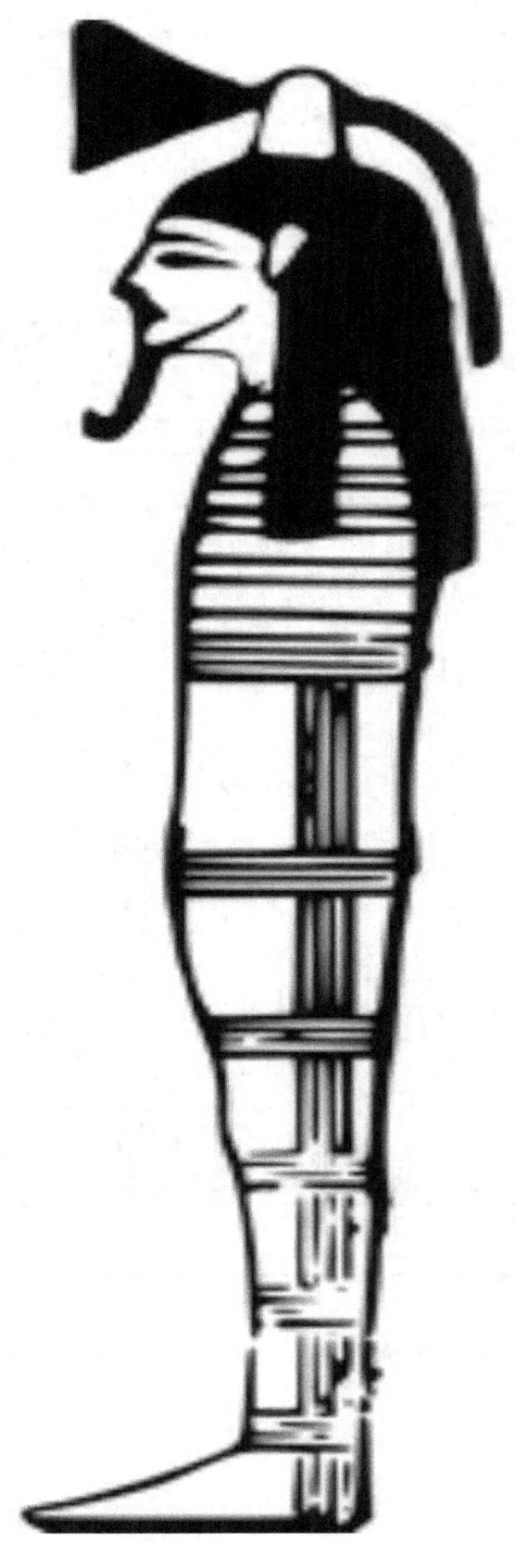

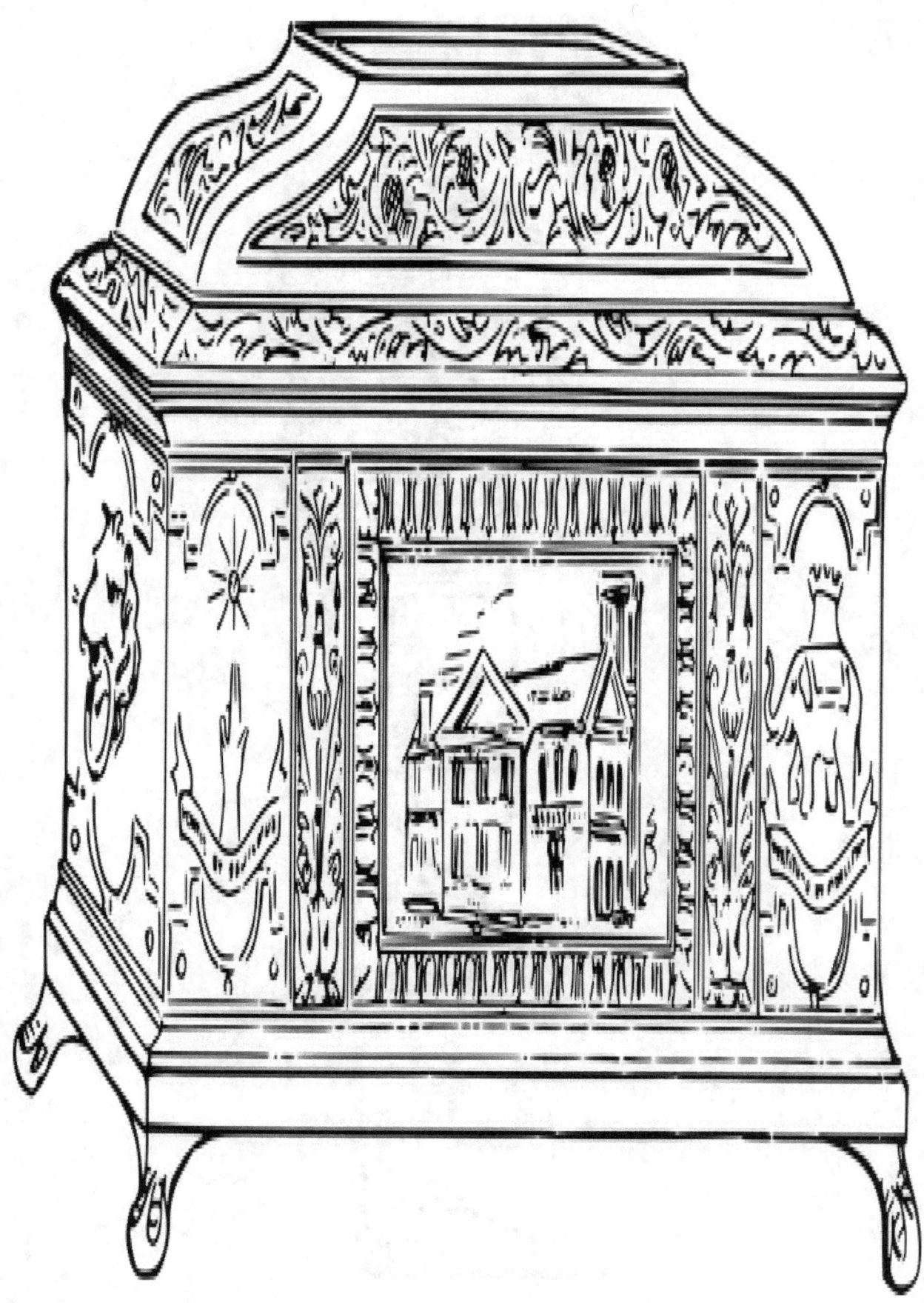

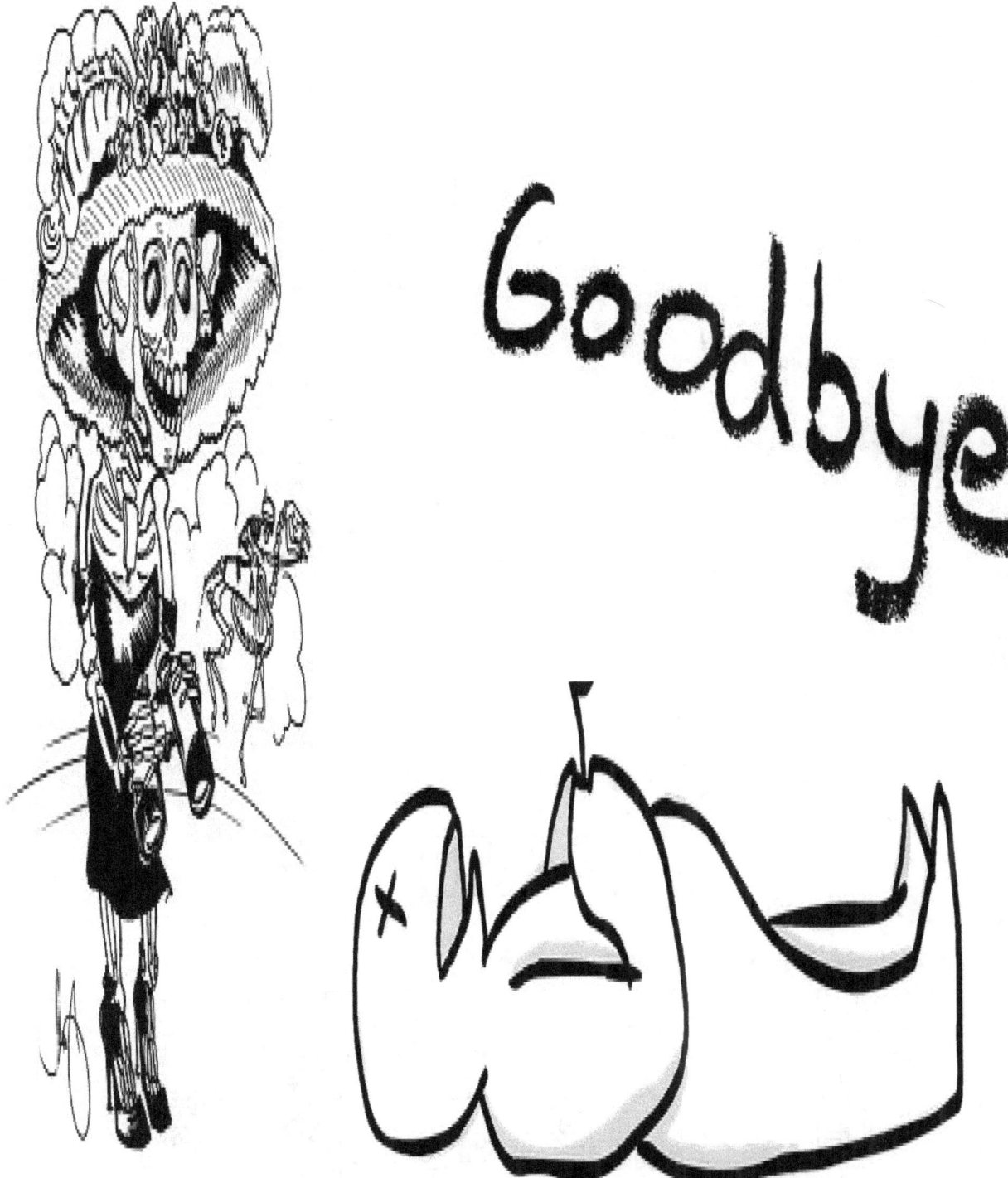

Goodbye

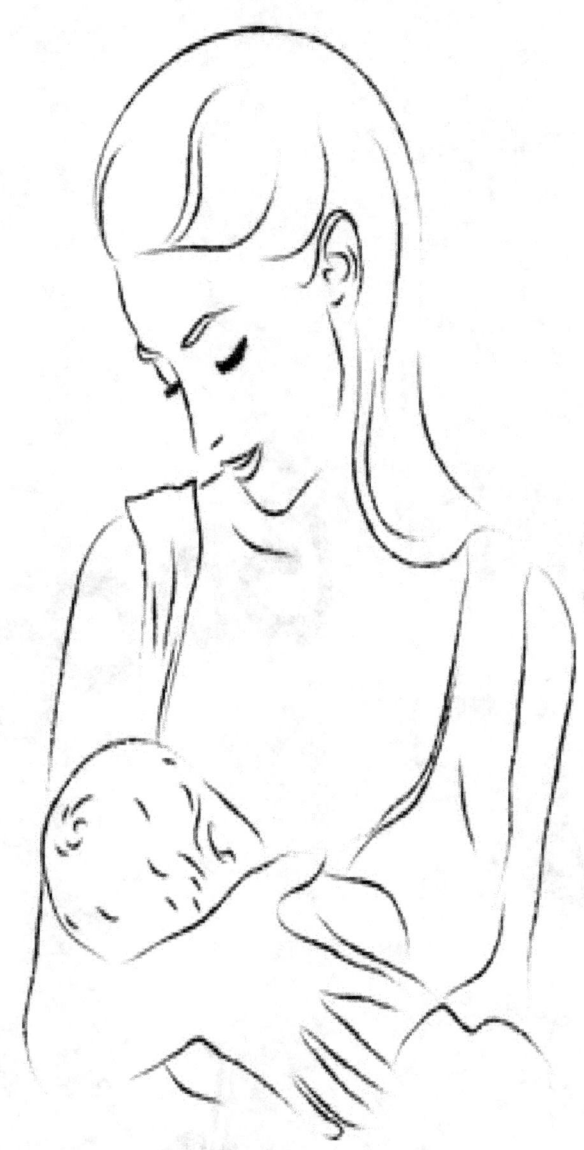

AND

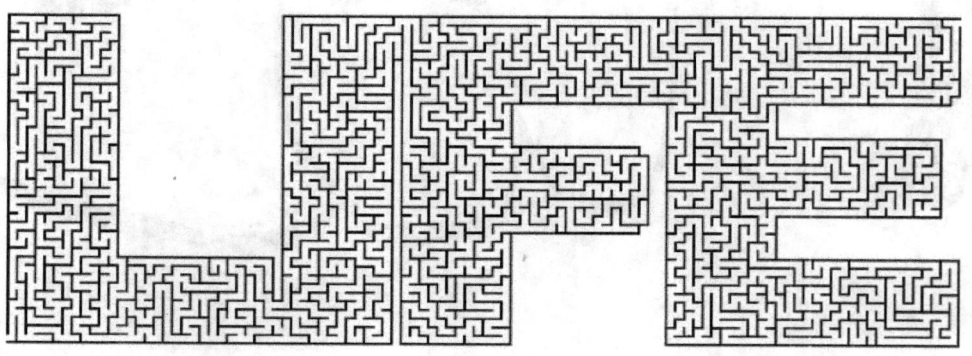

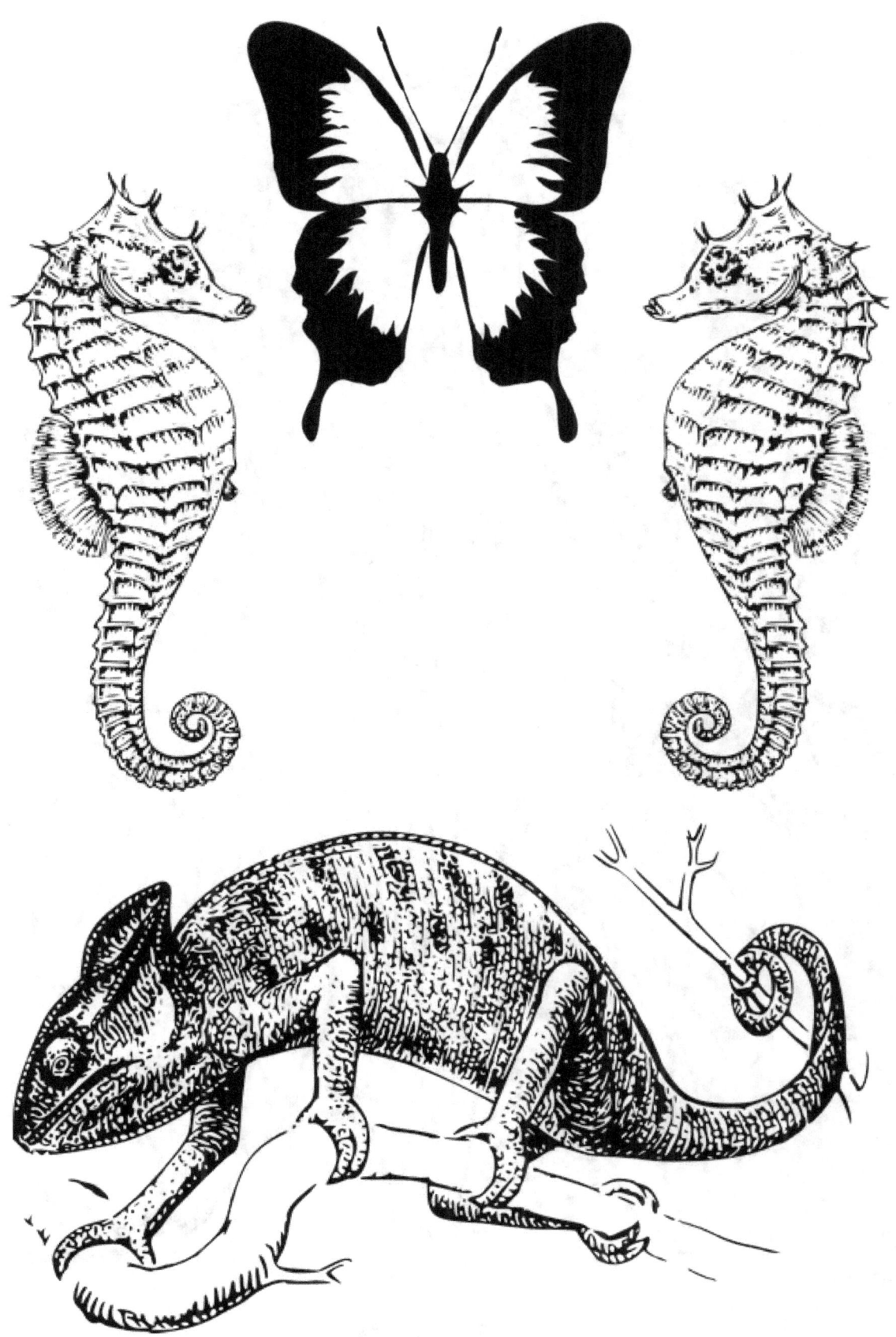

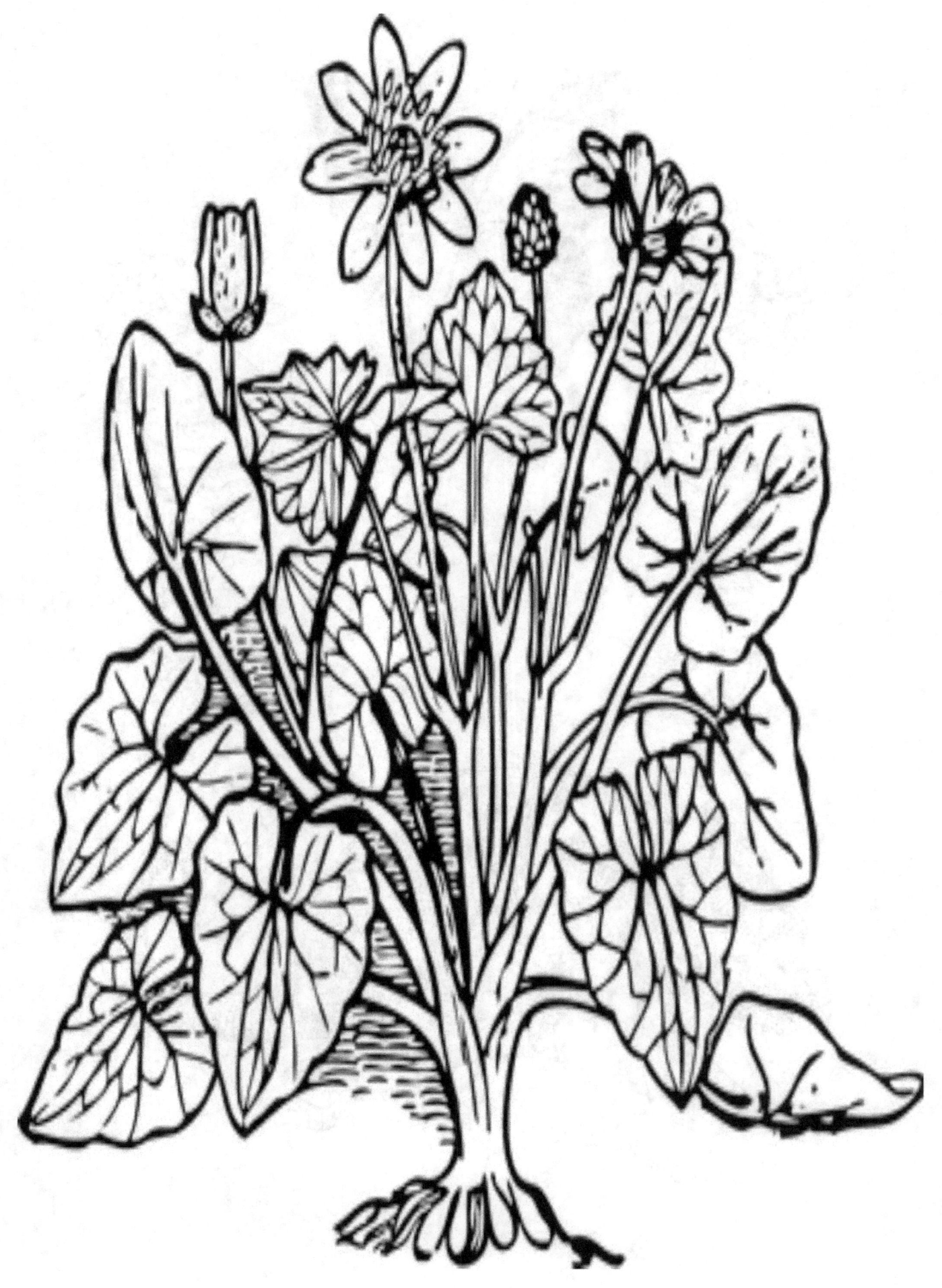

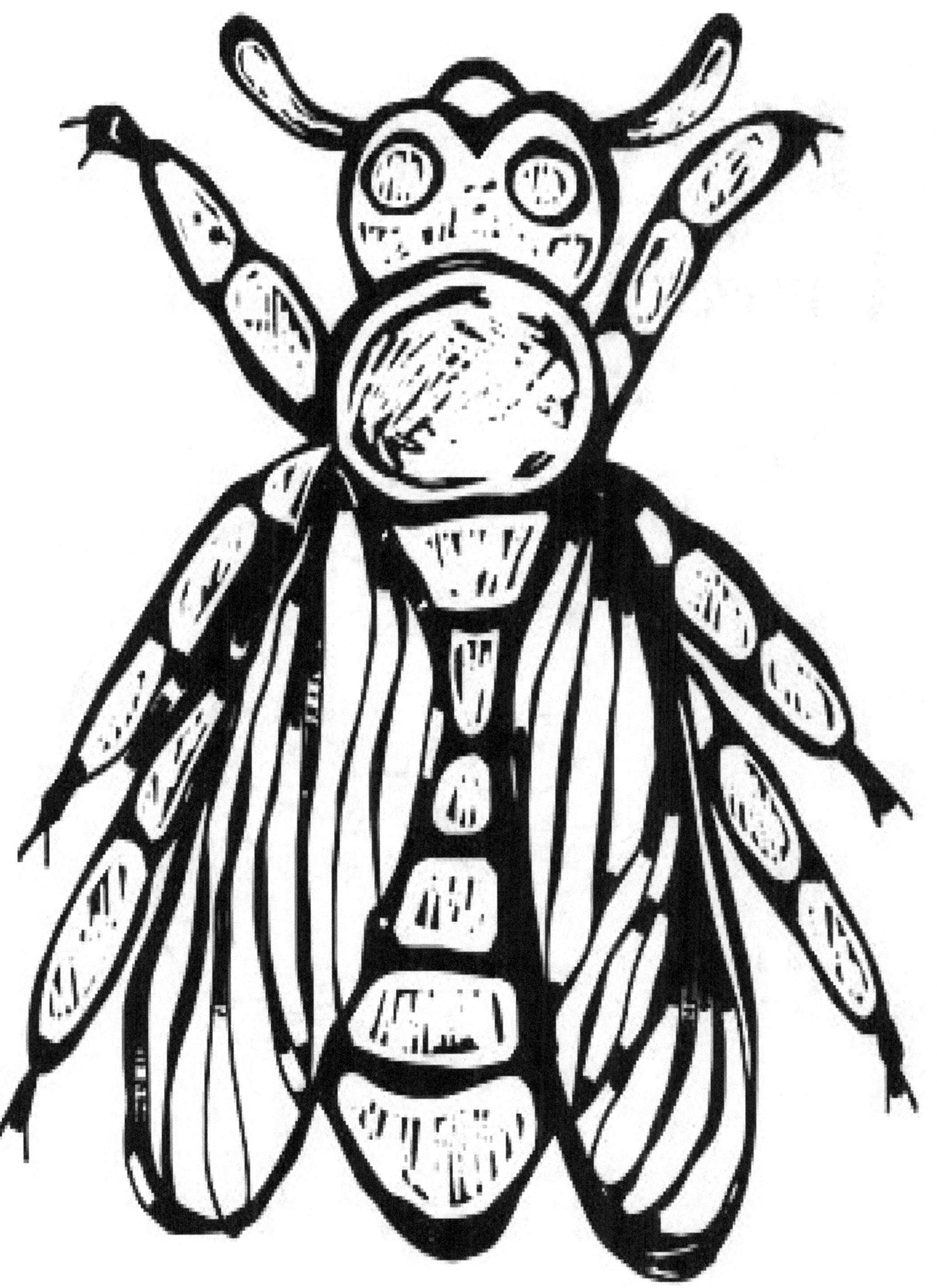

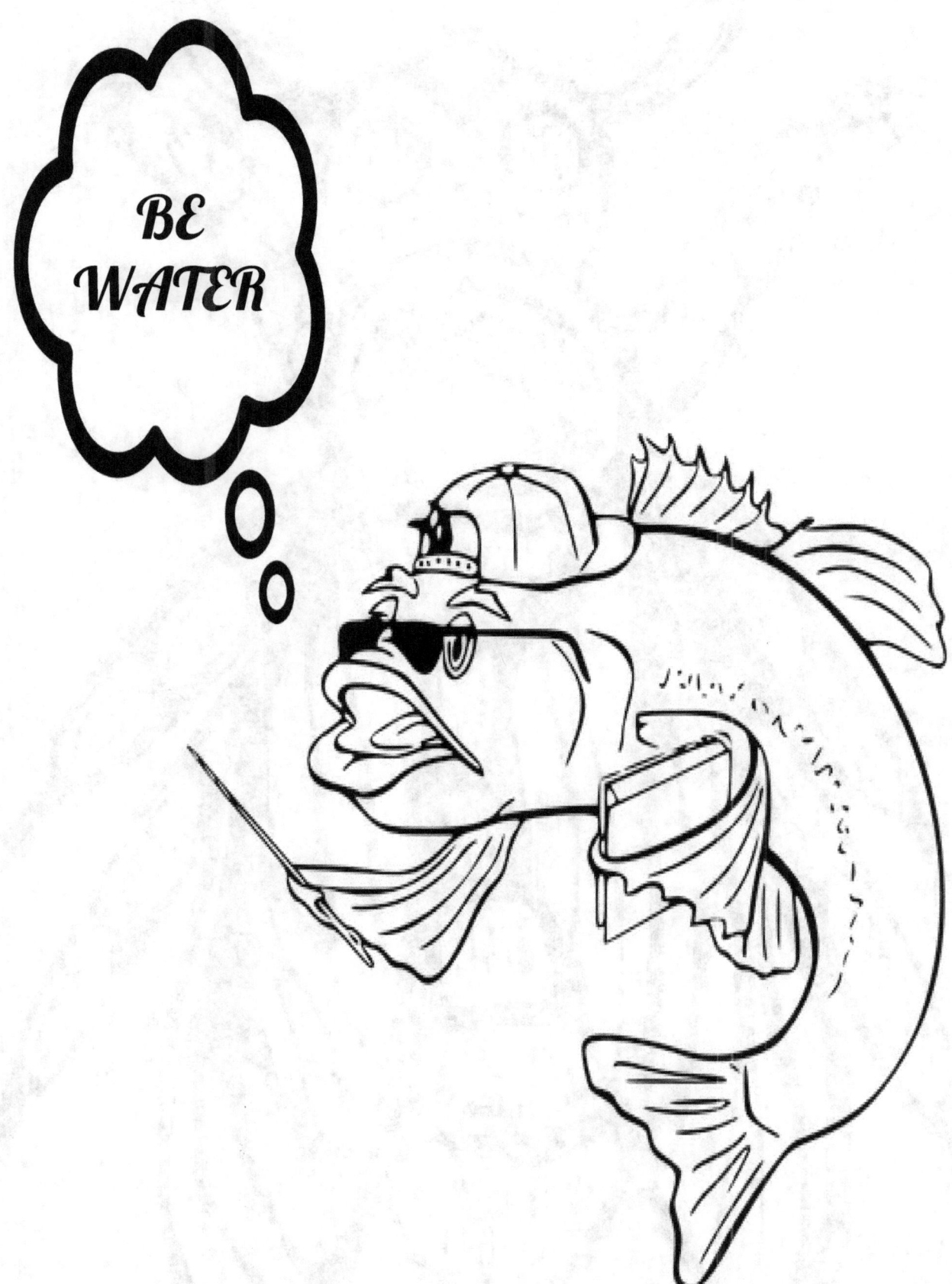

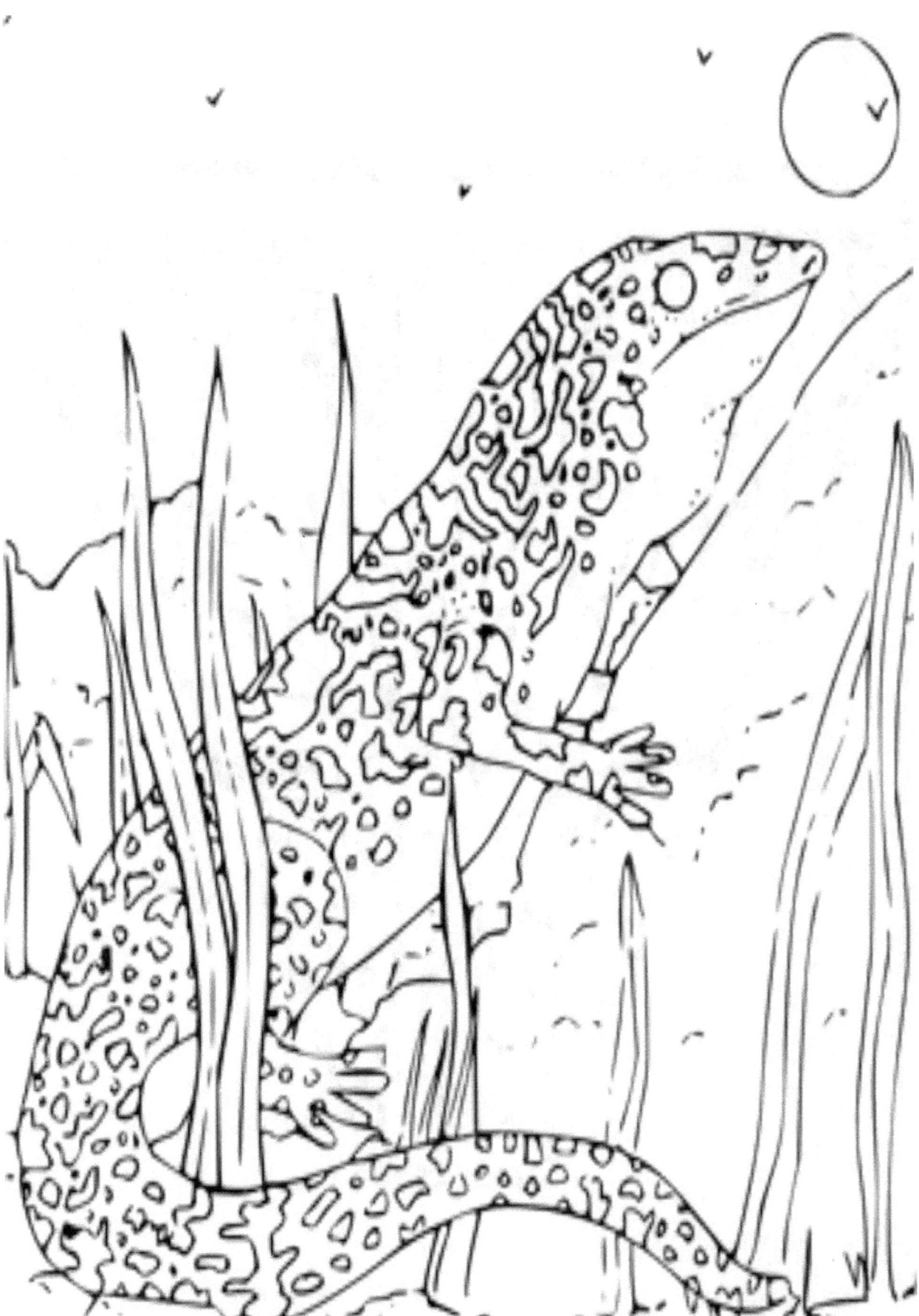

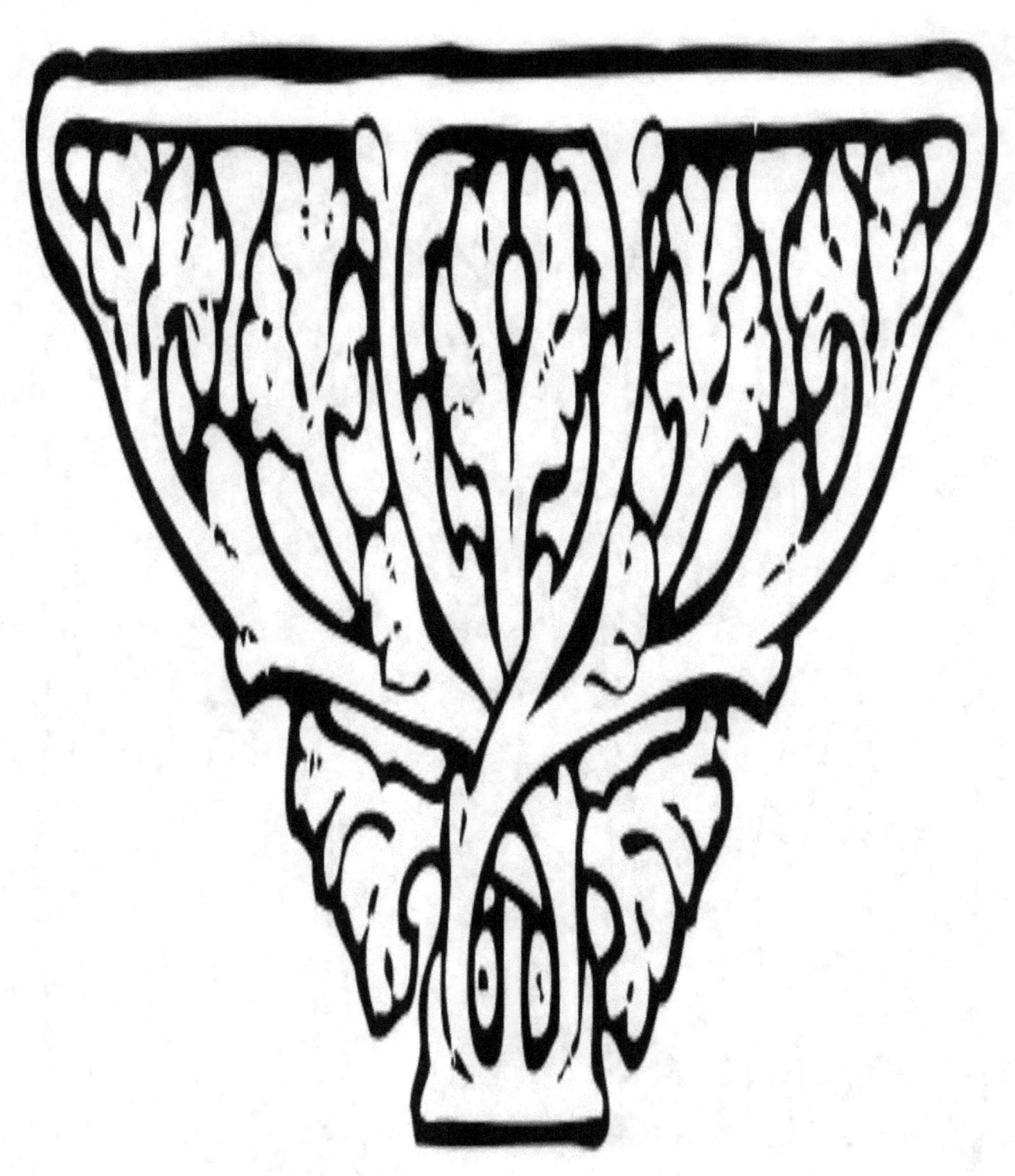

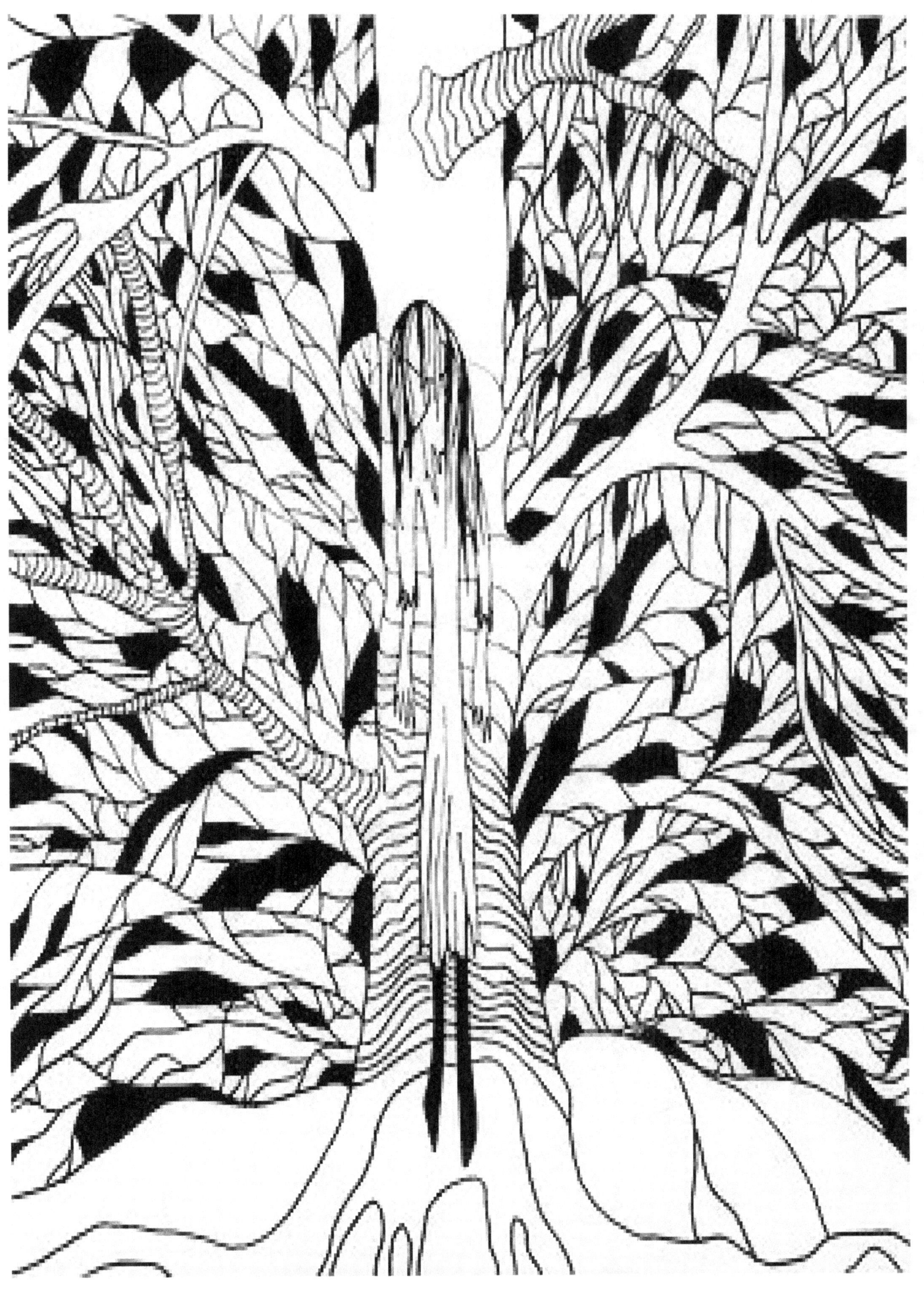

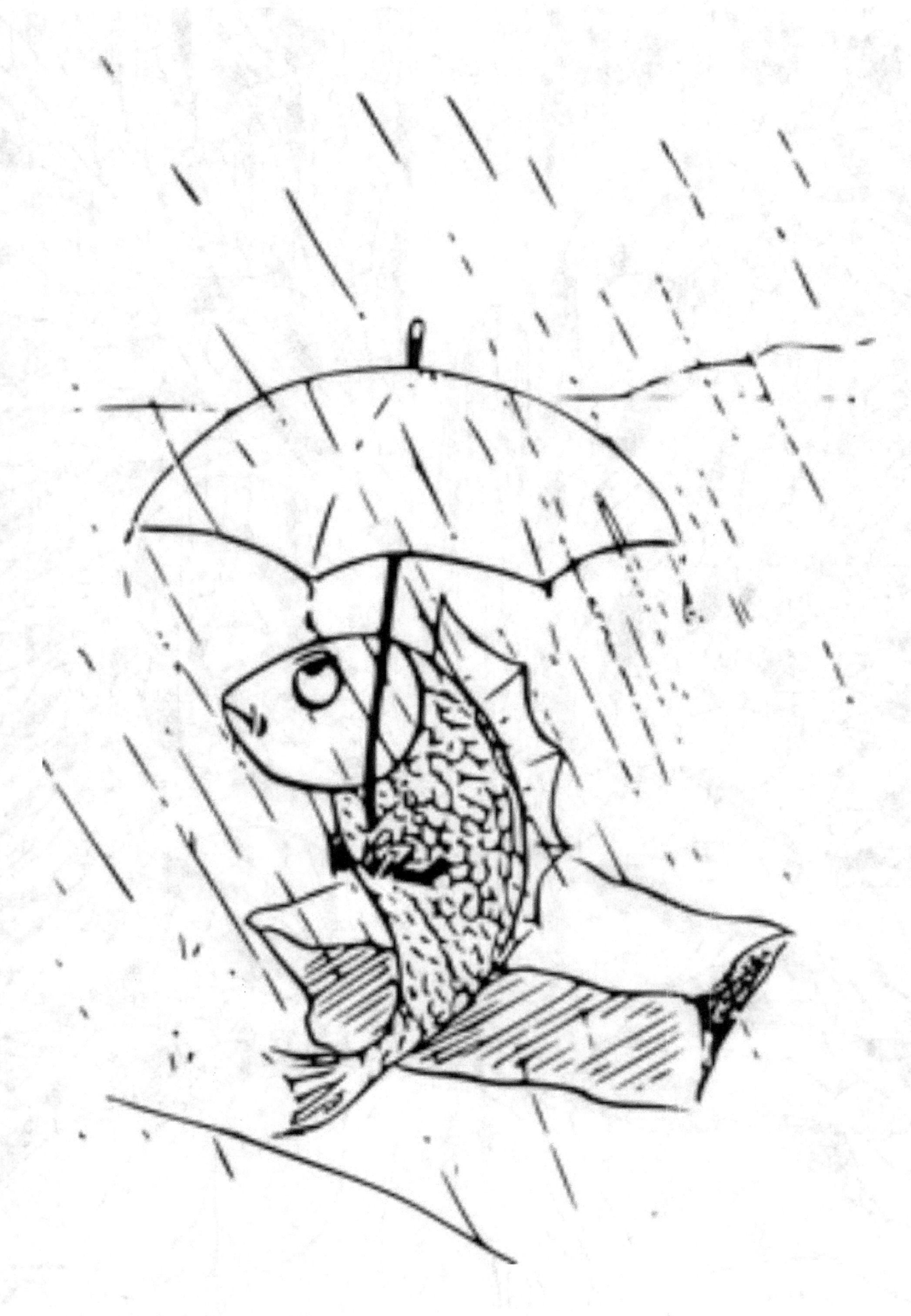

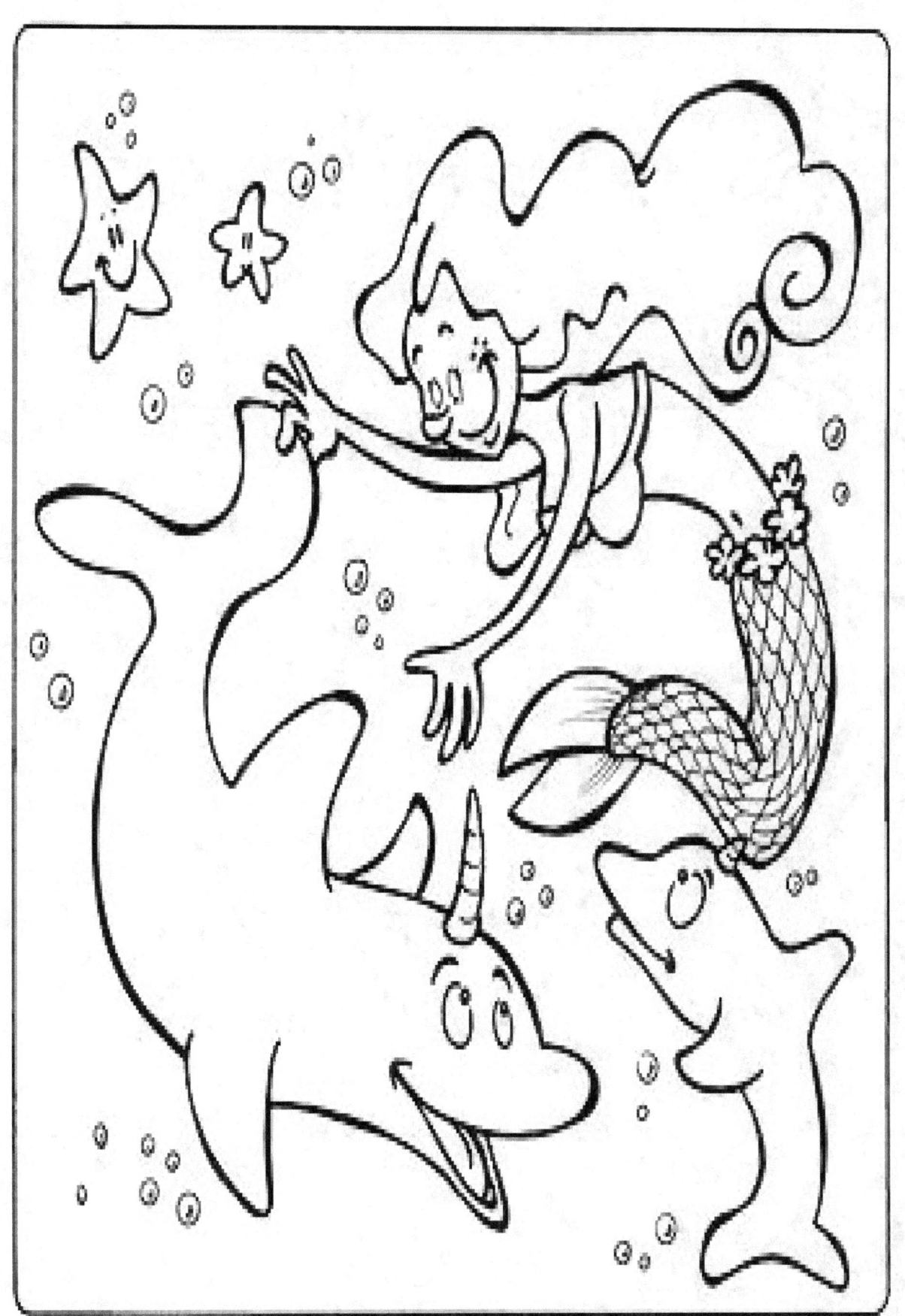

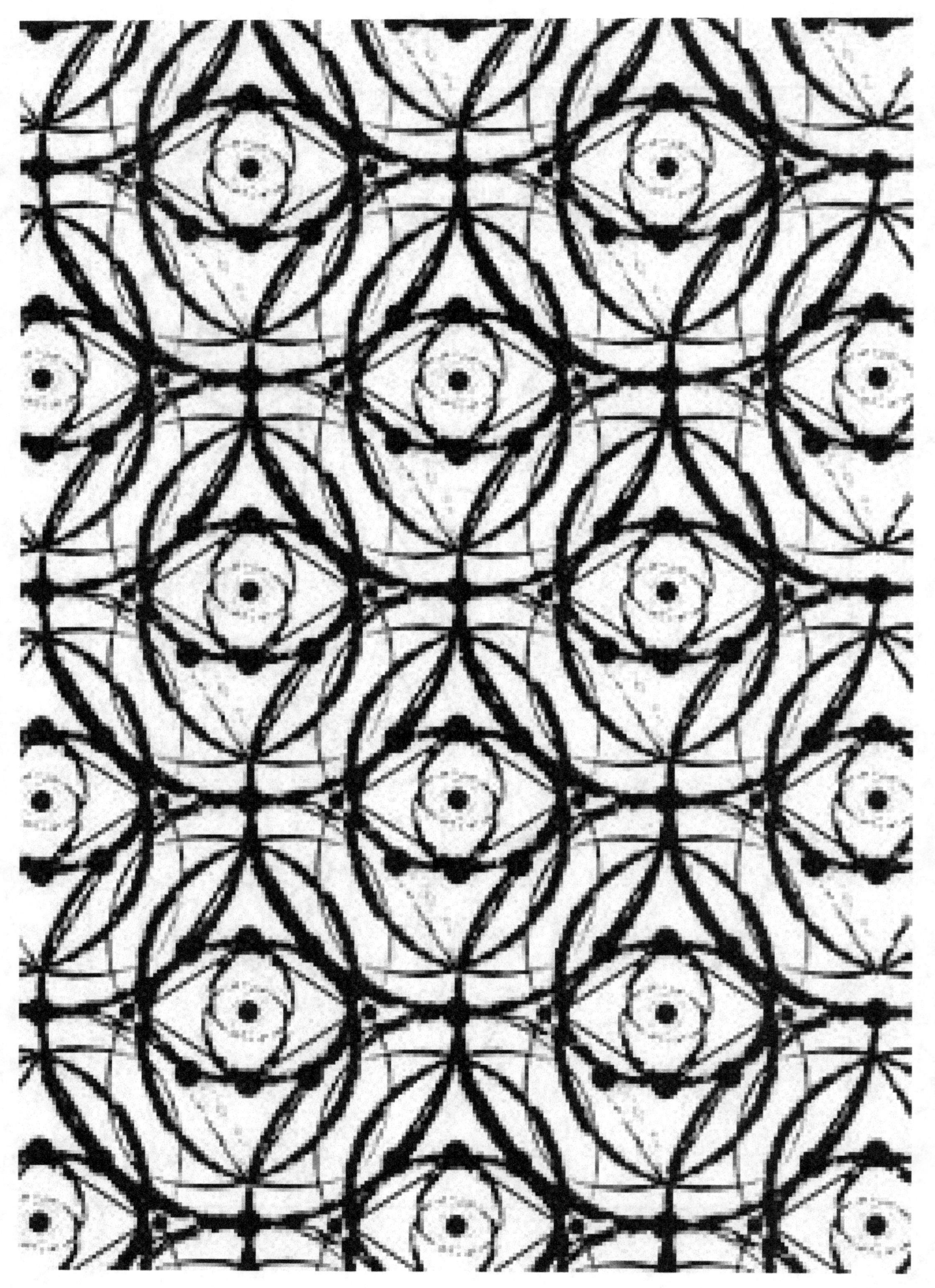

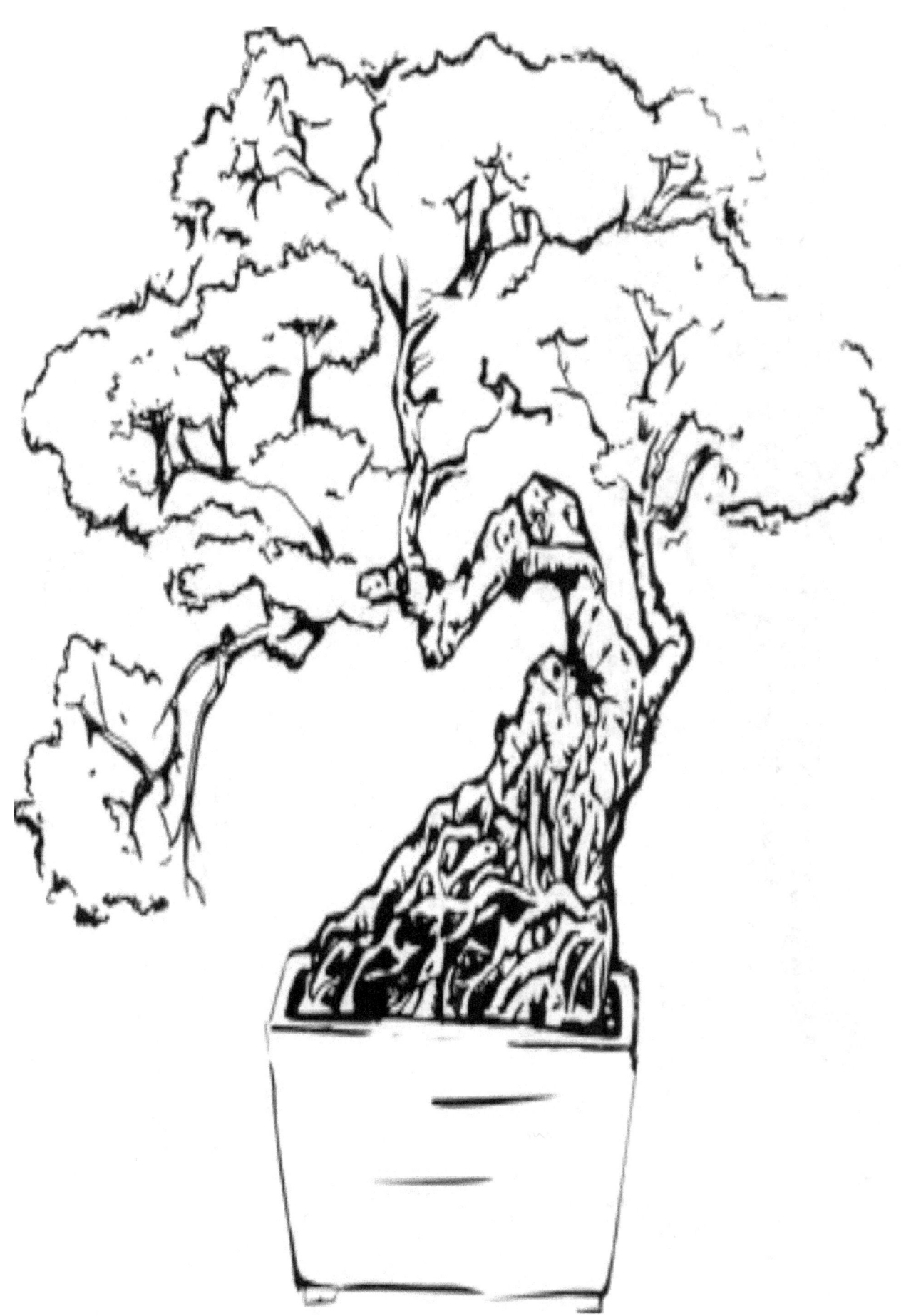

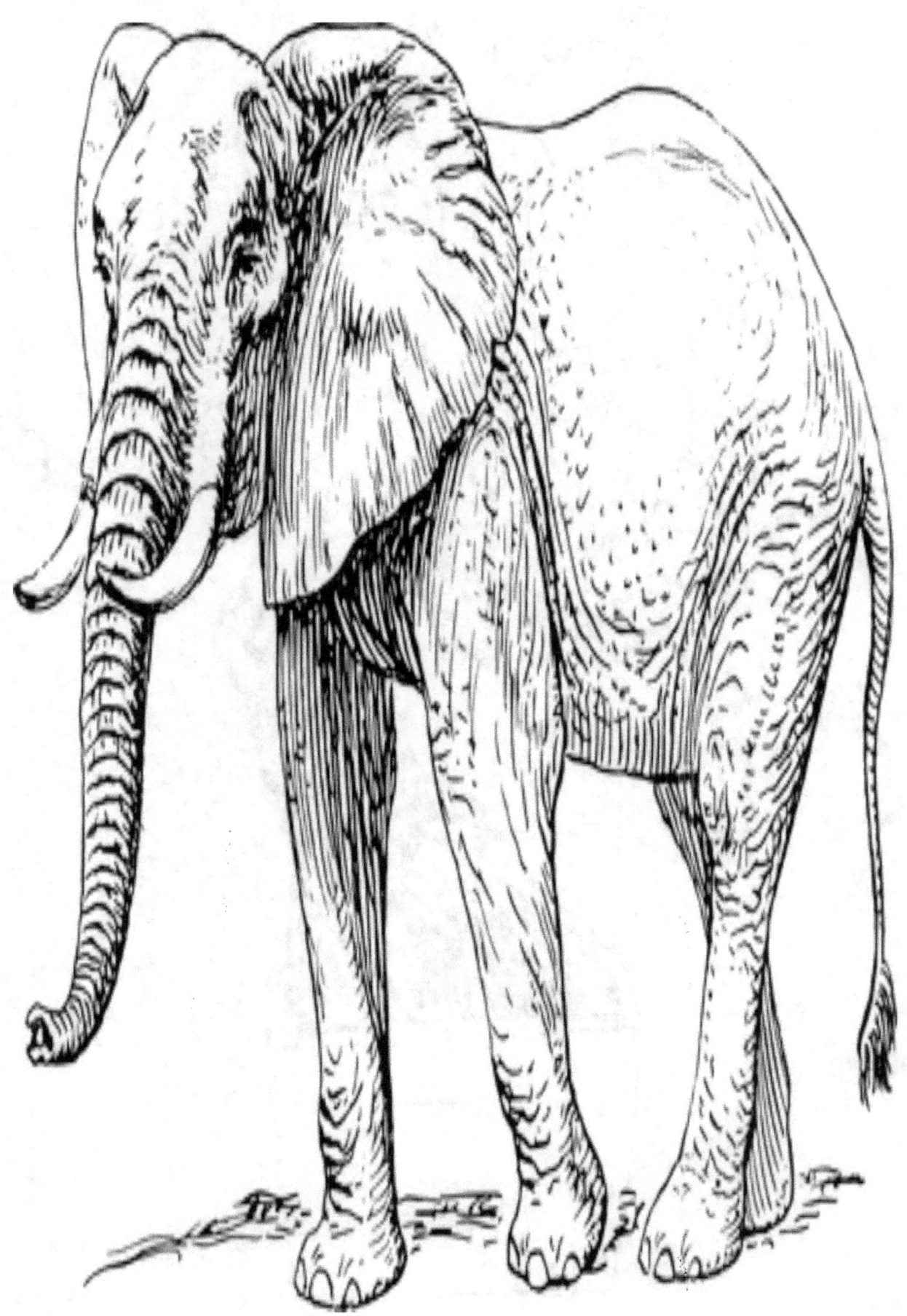

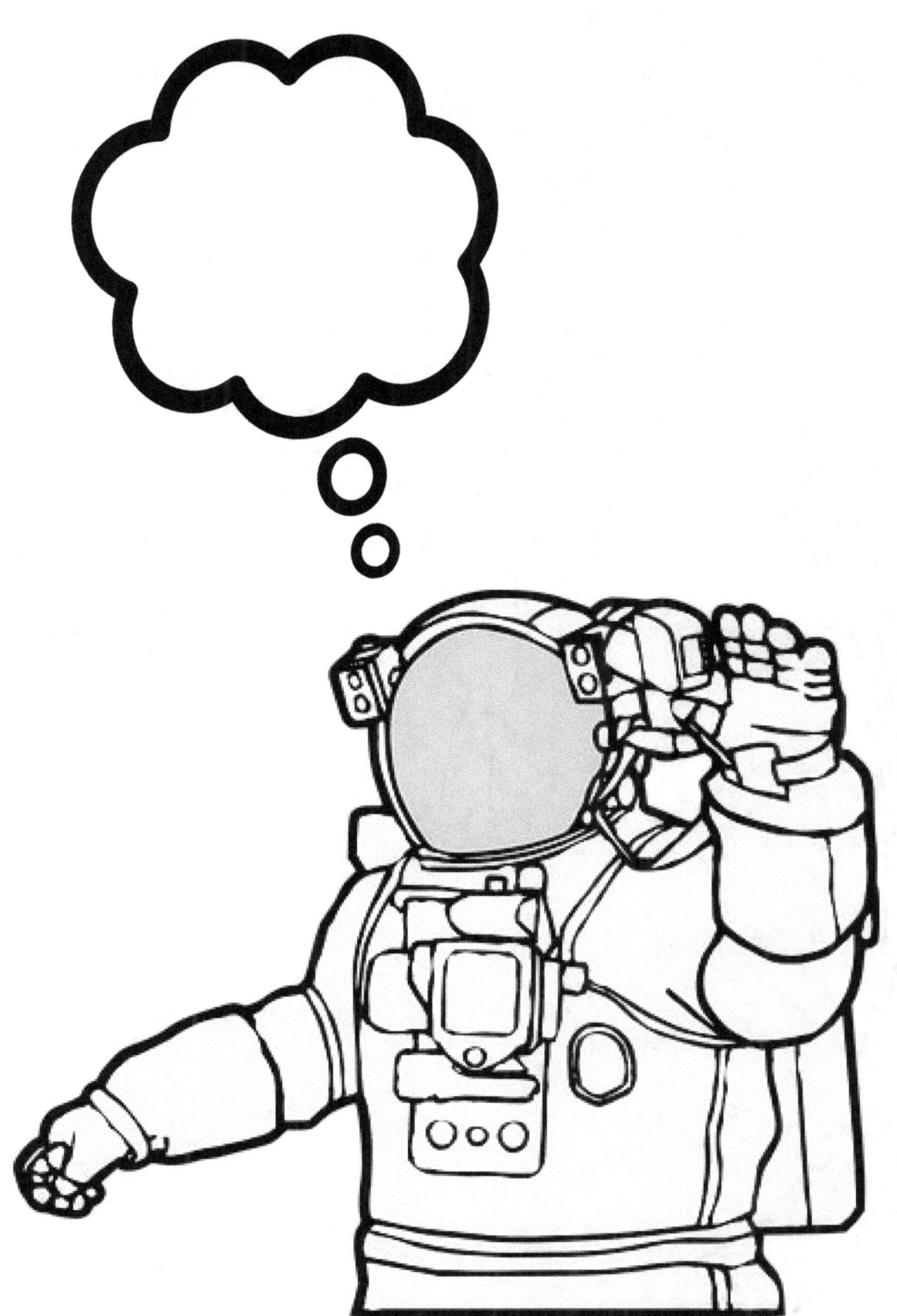

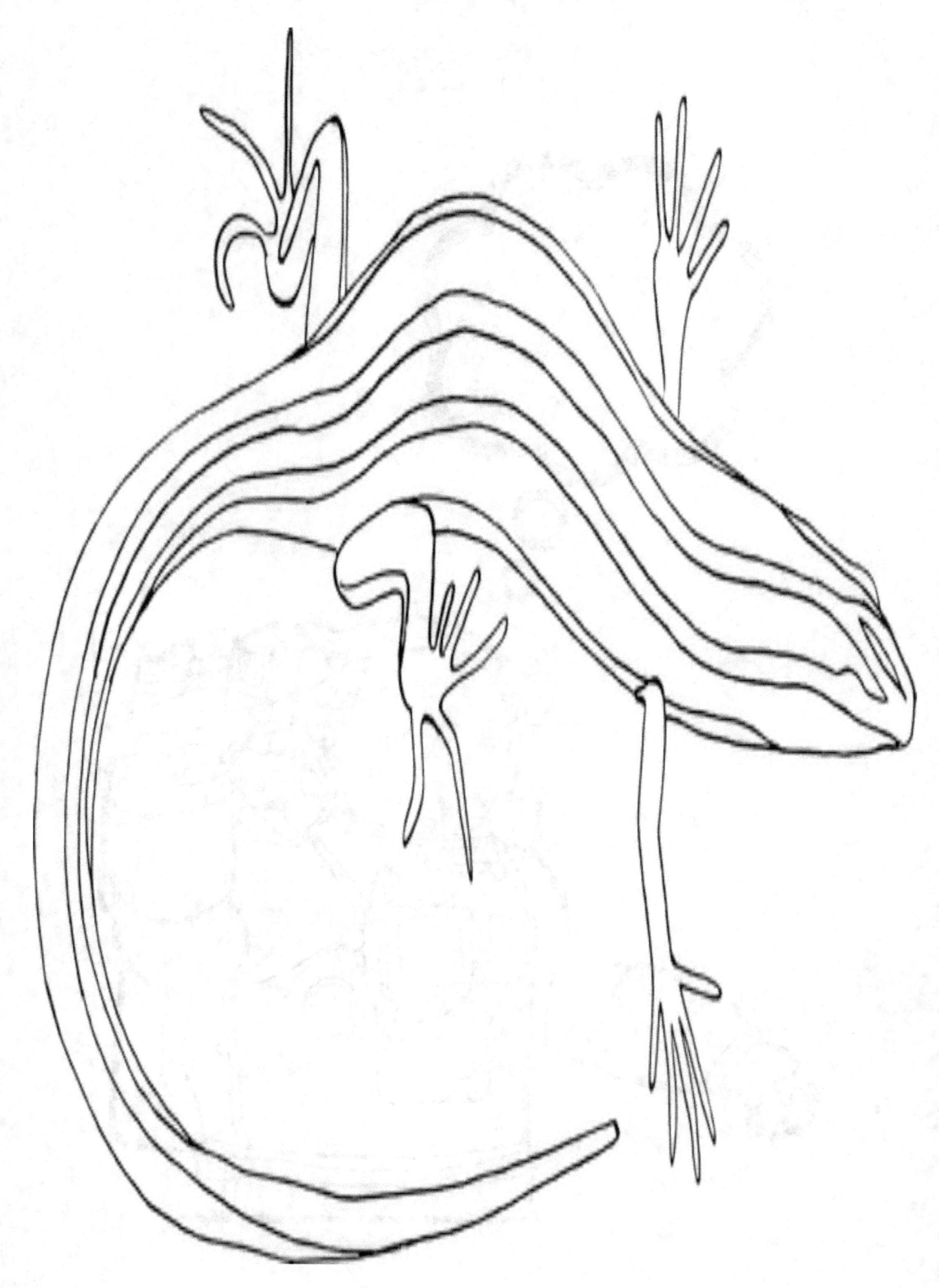

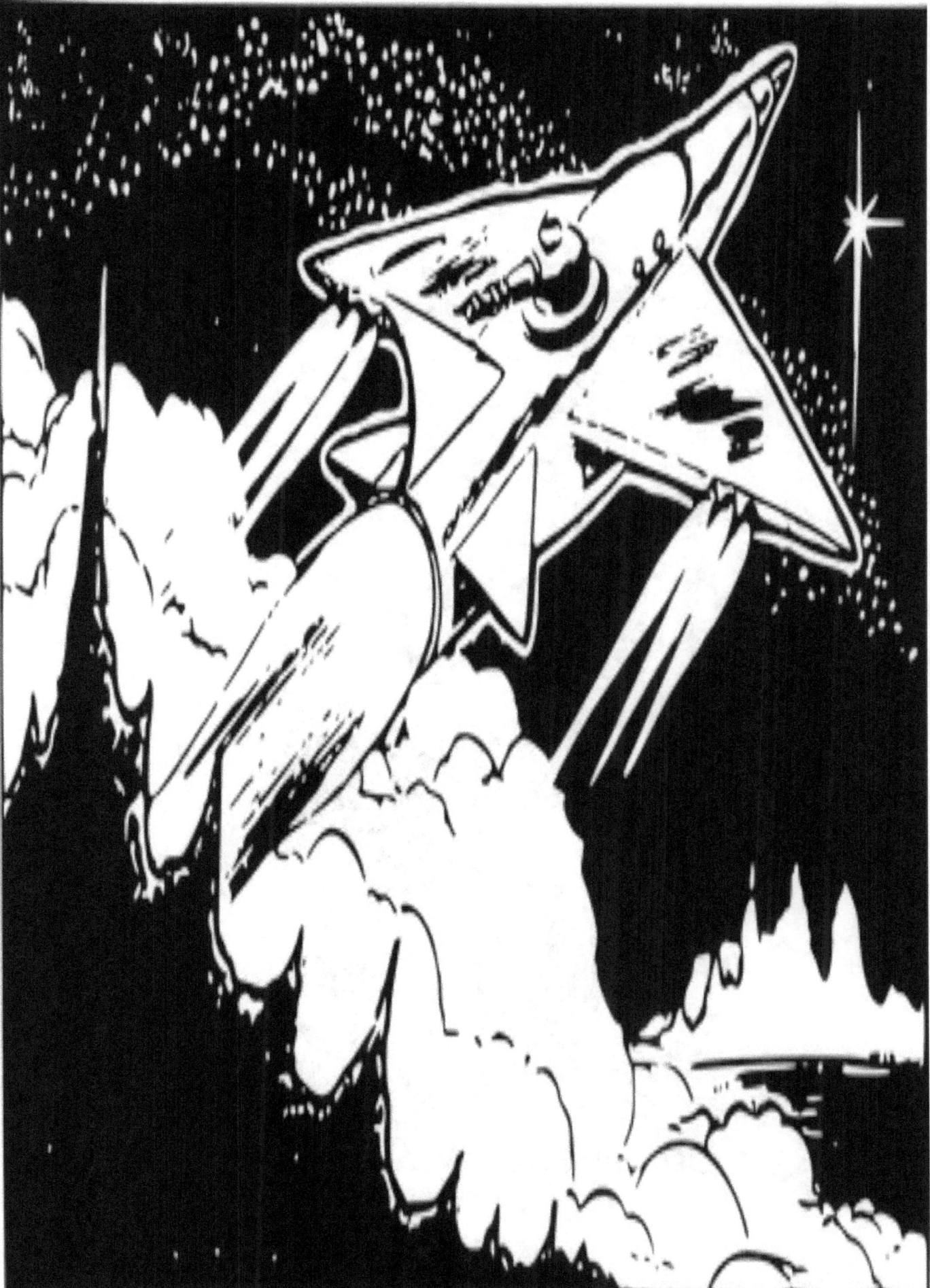

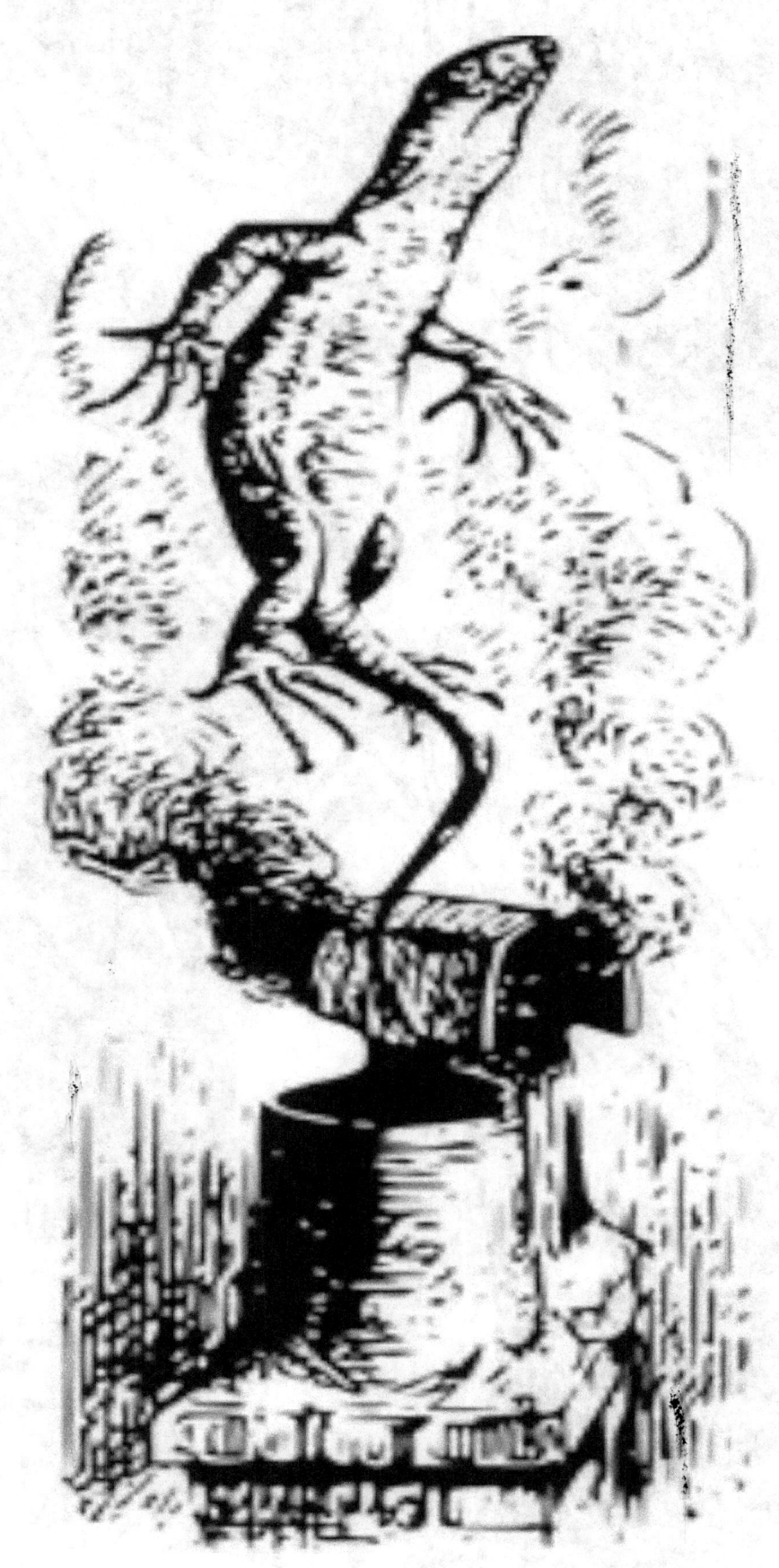

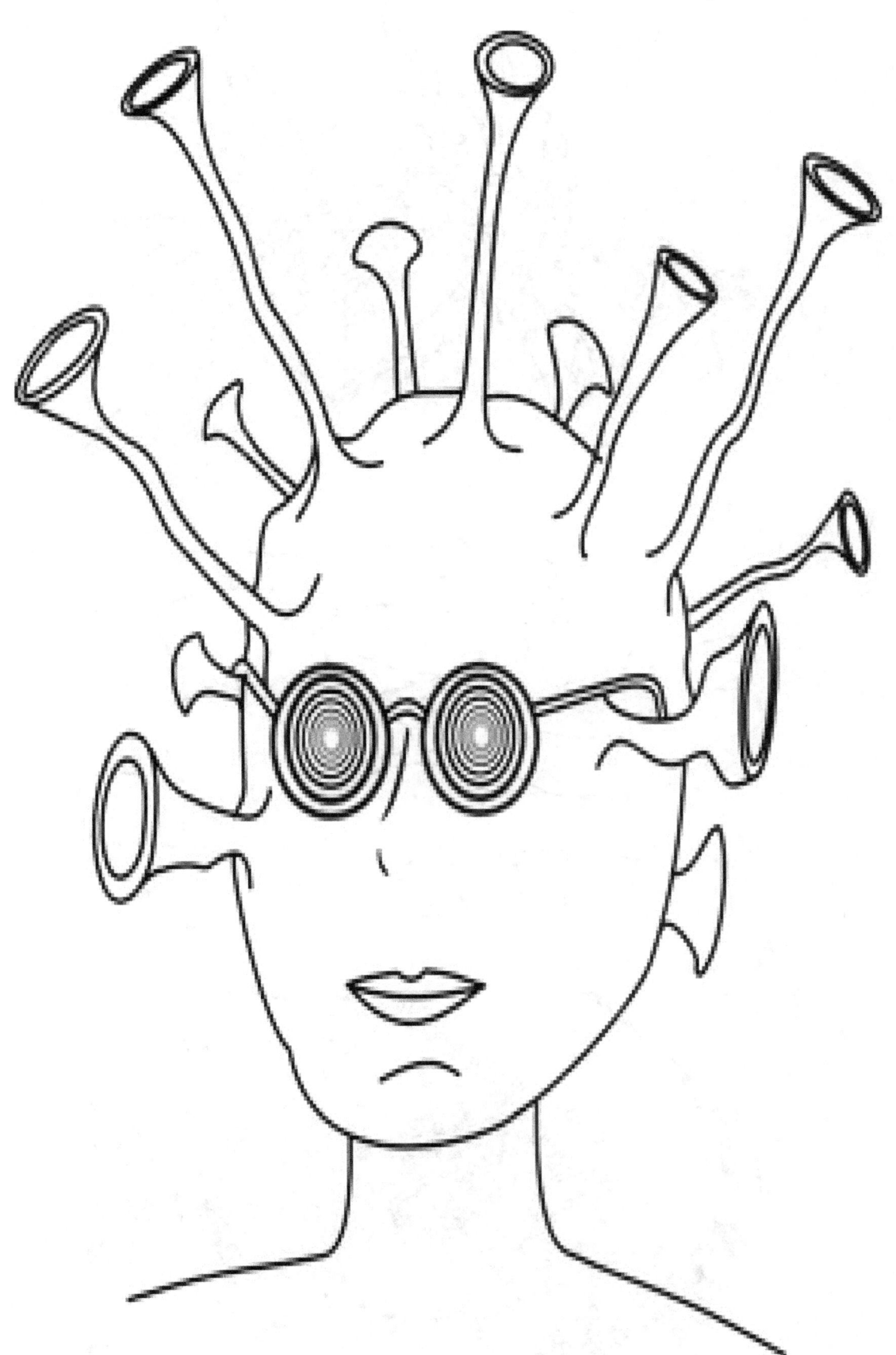

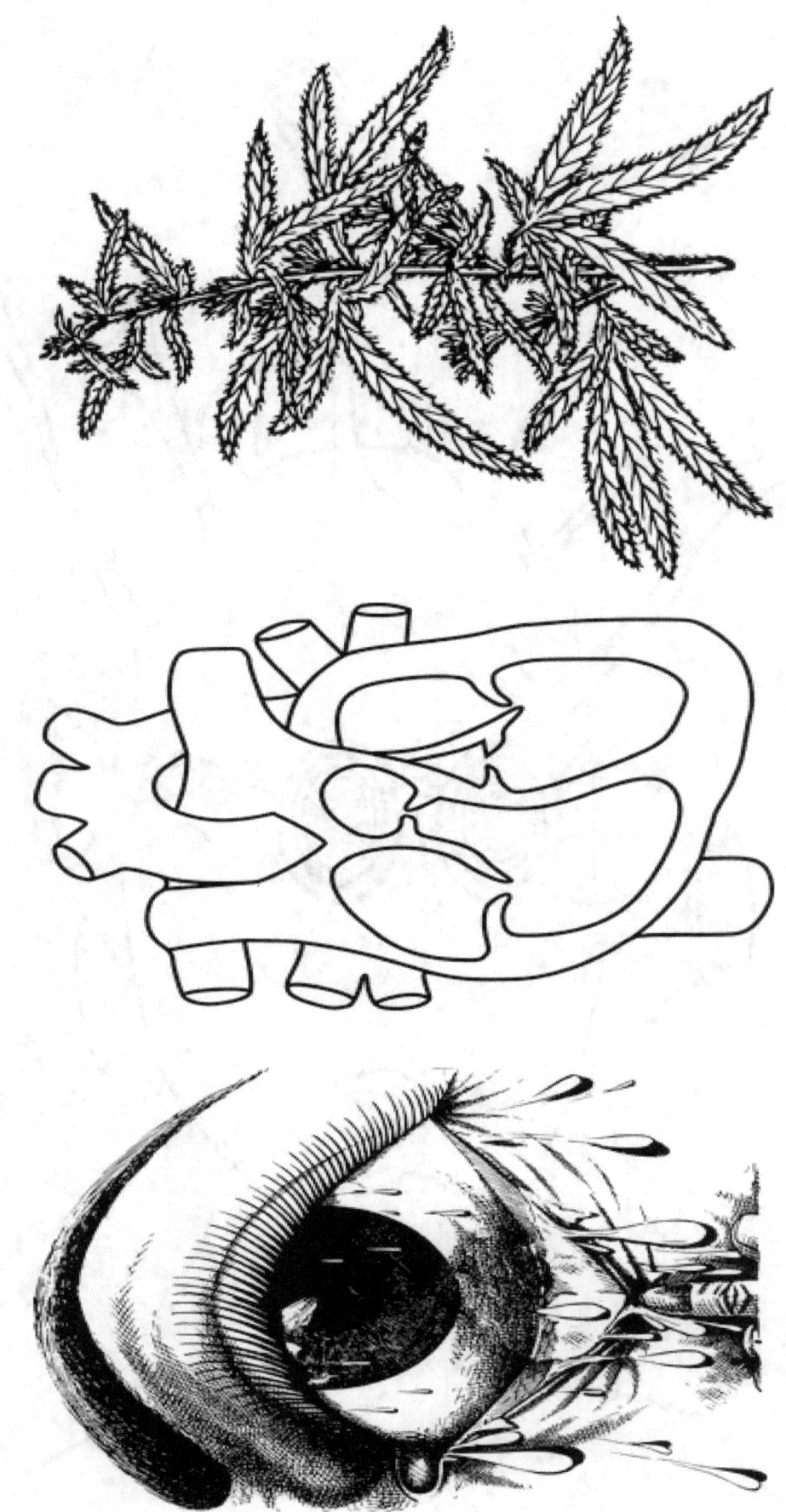

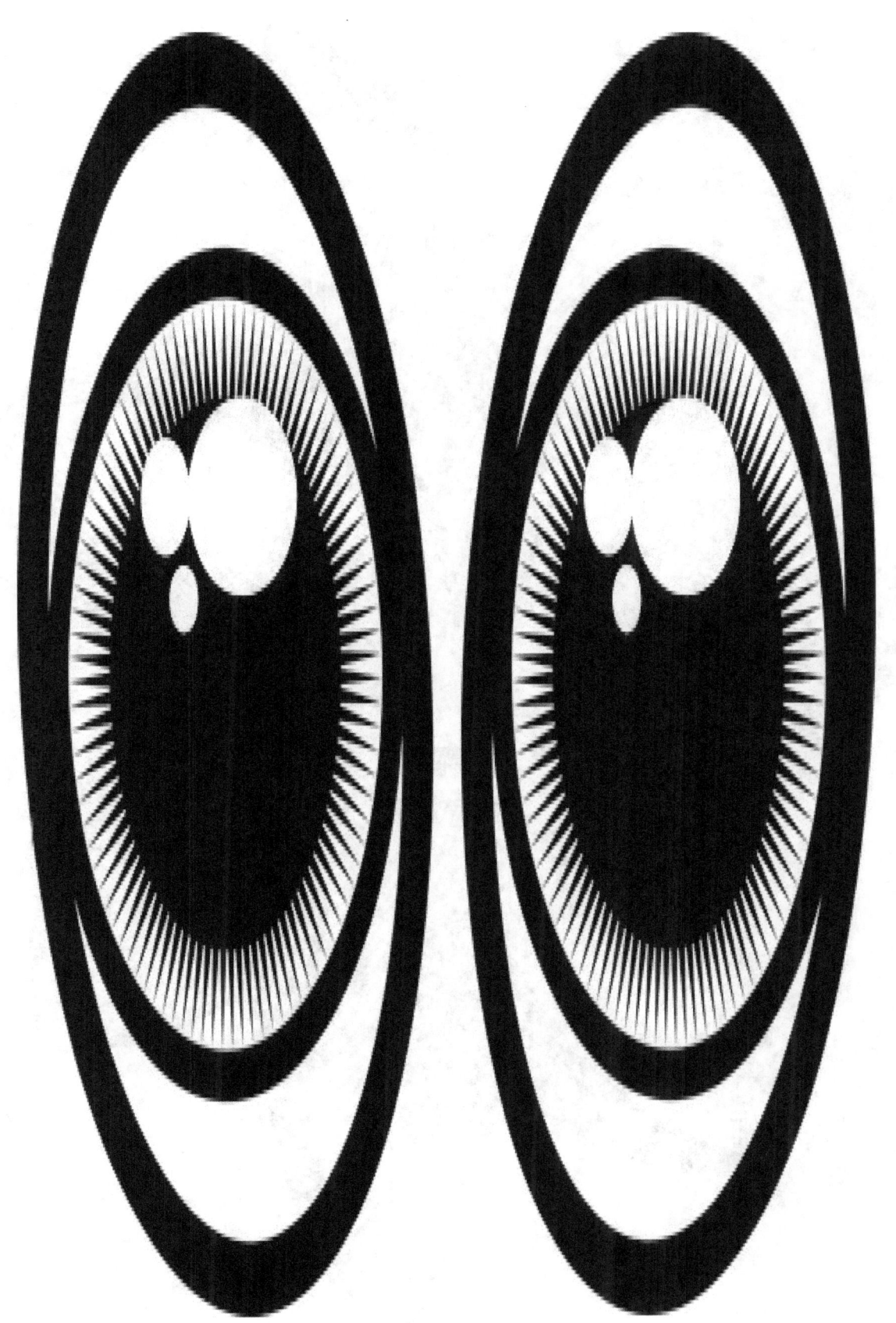

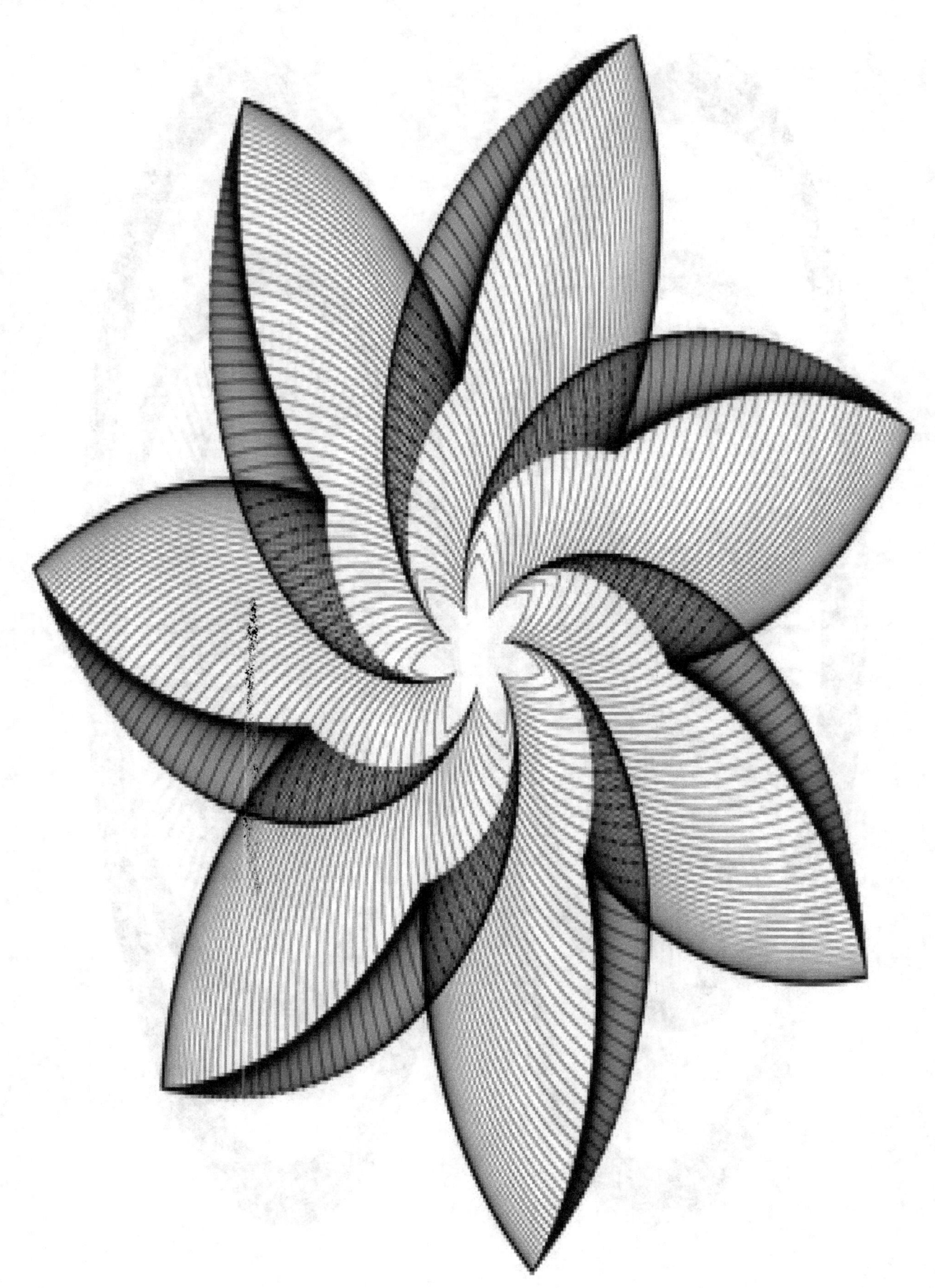

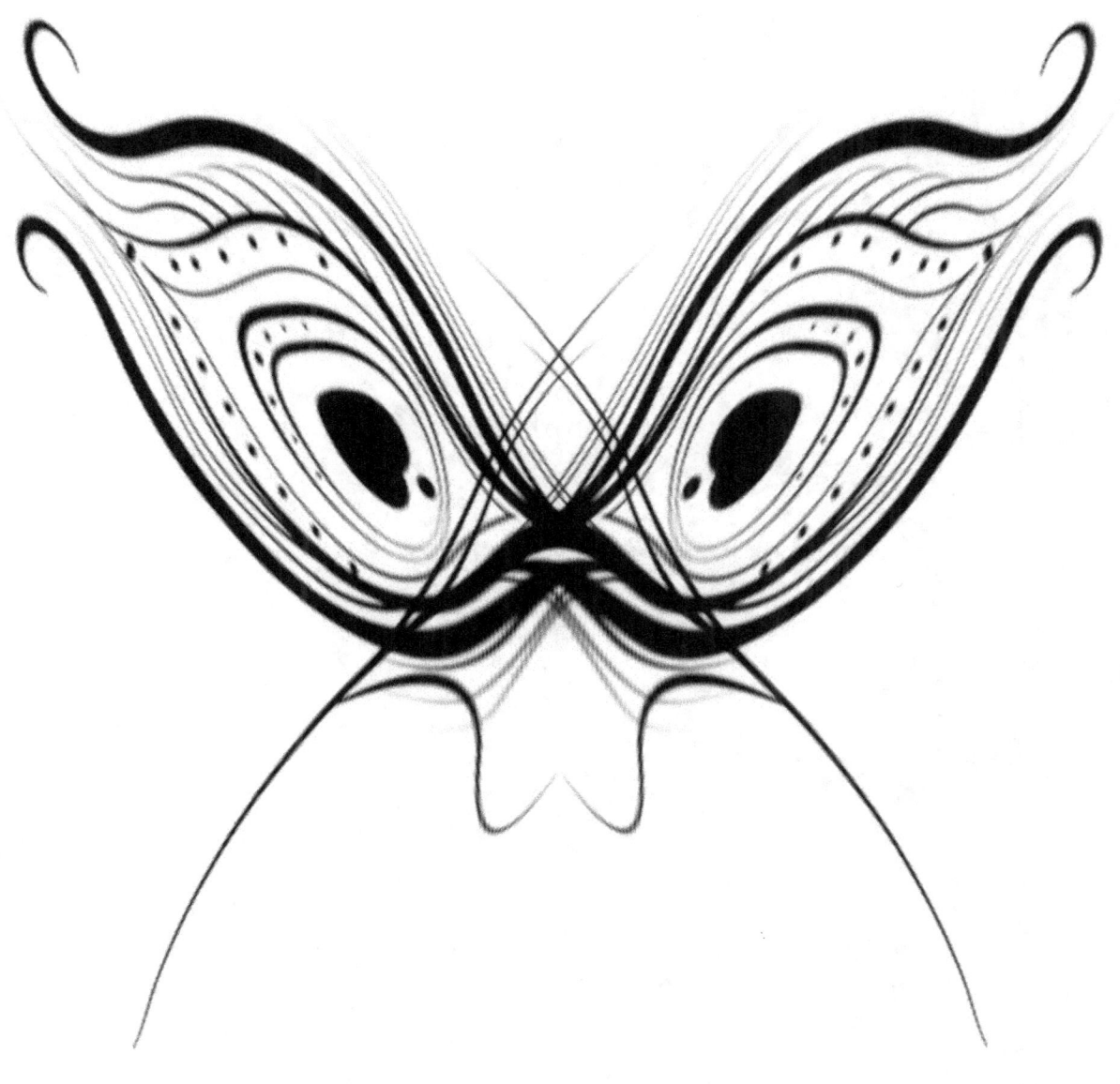

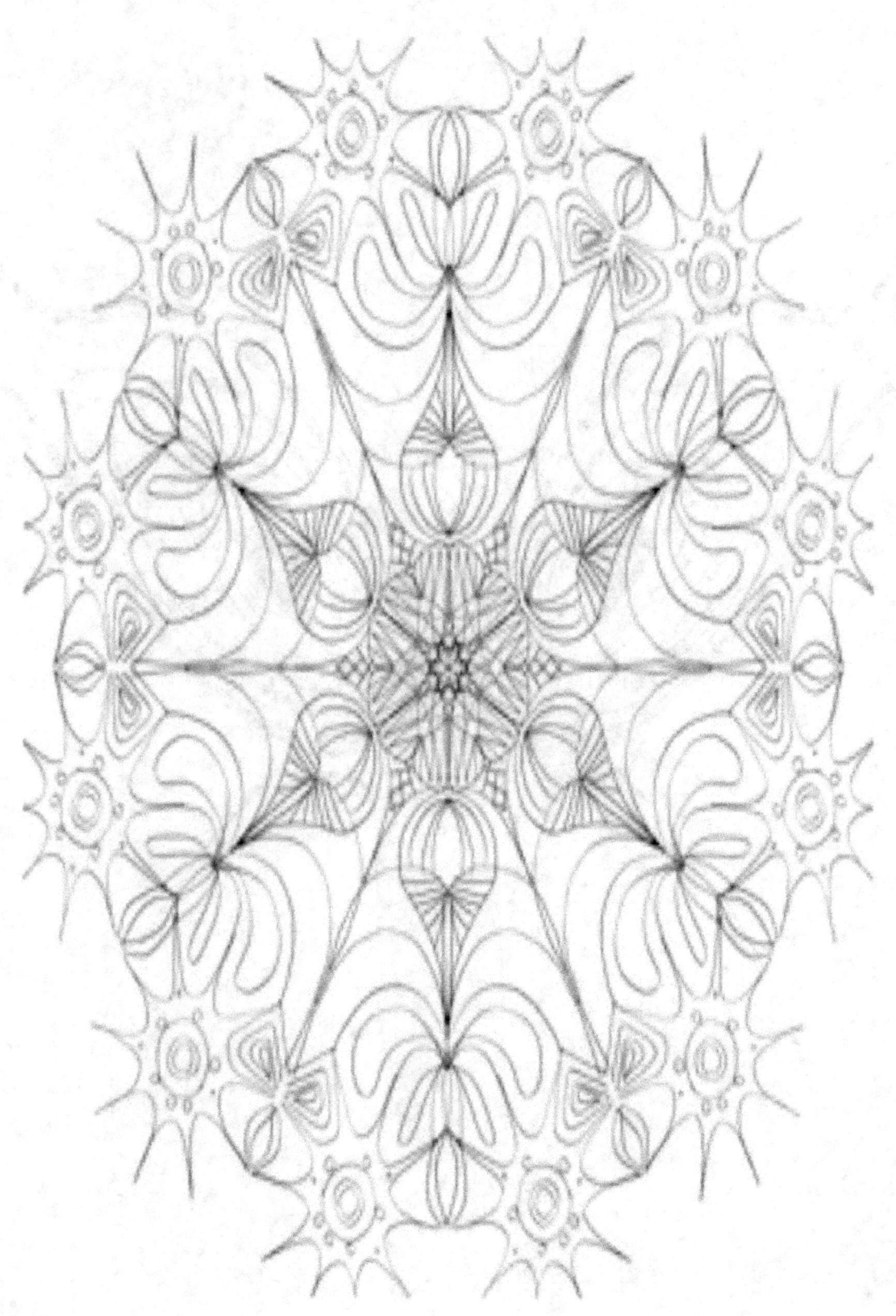

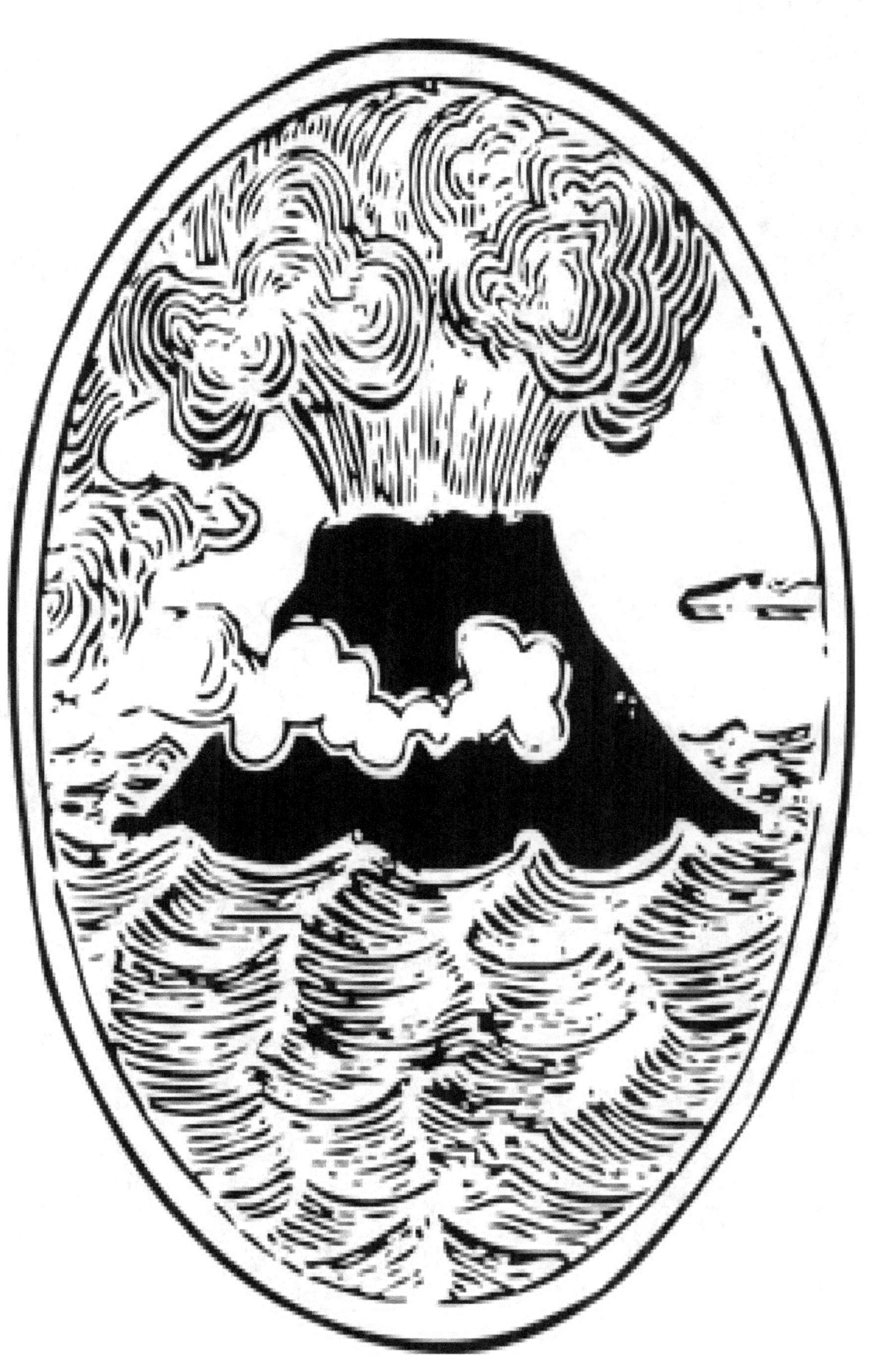

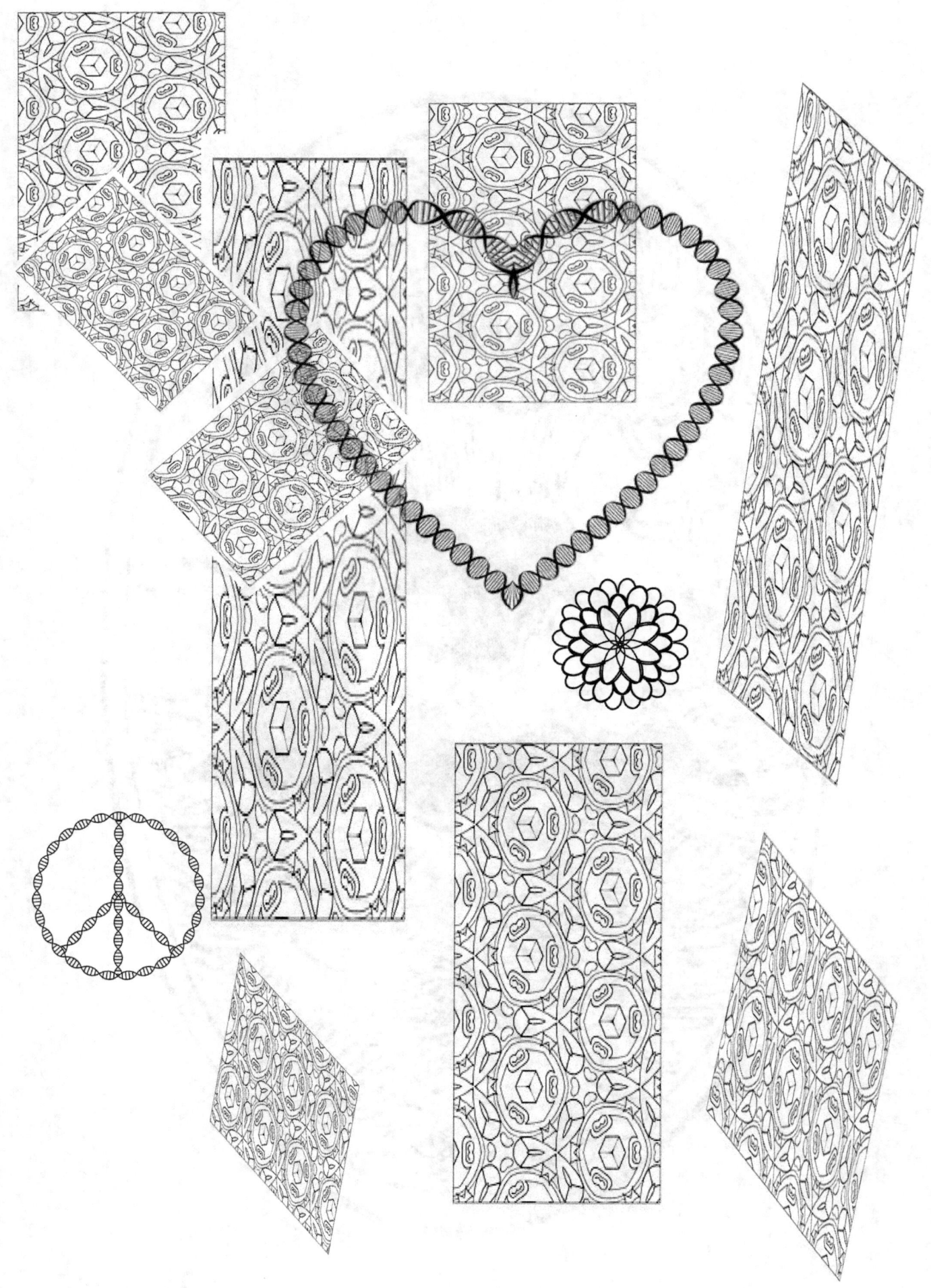

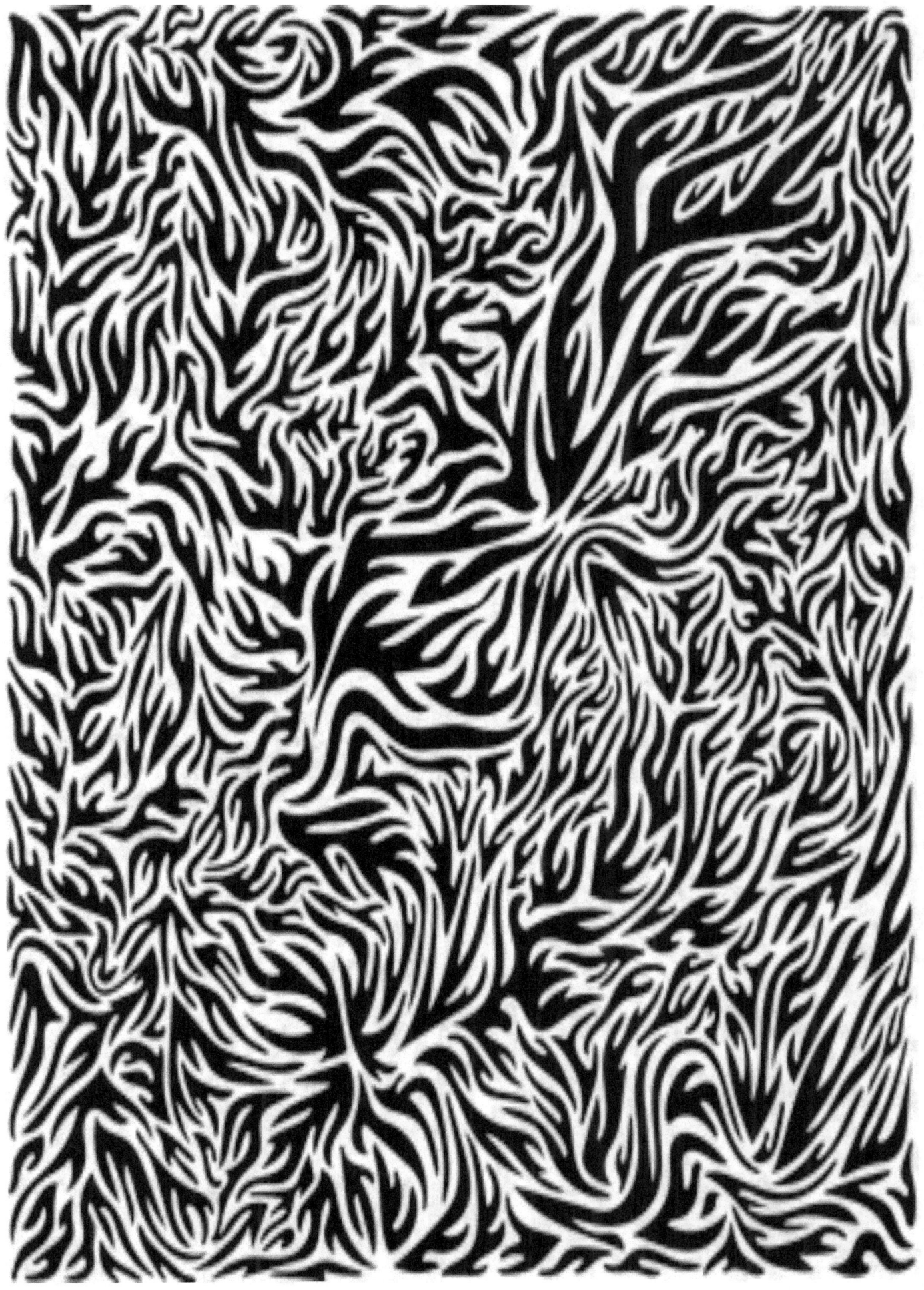

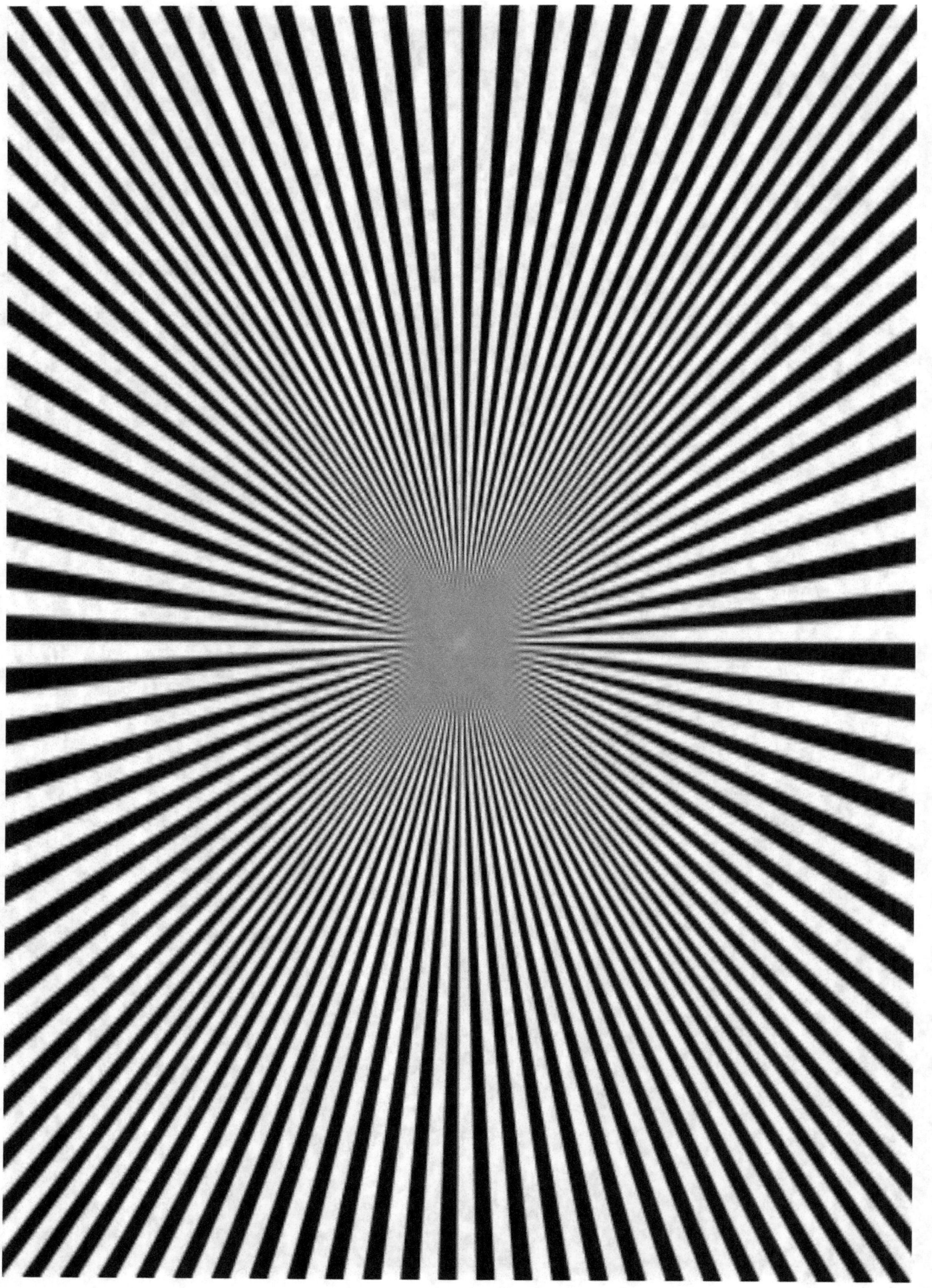

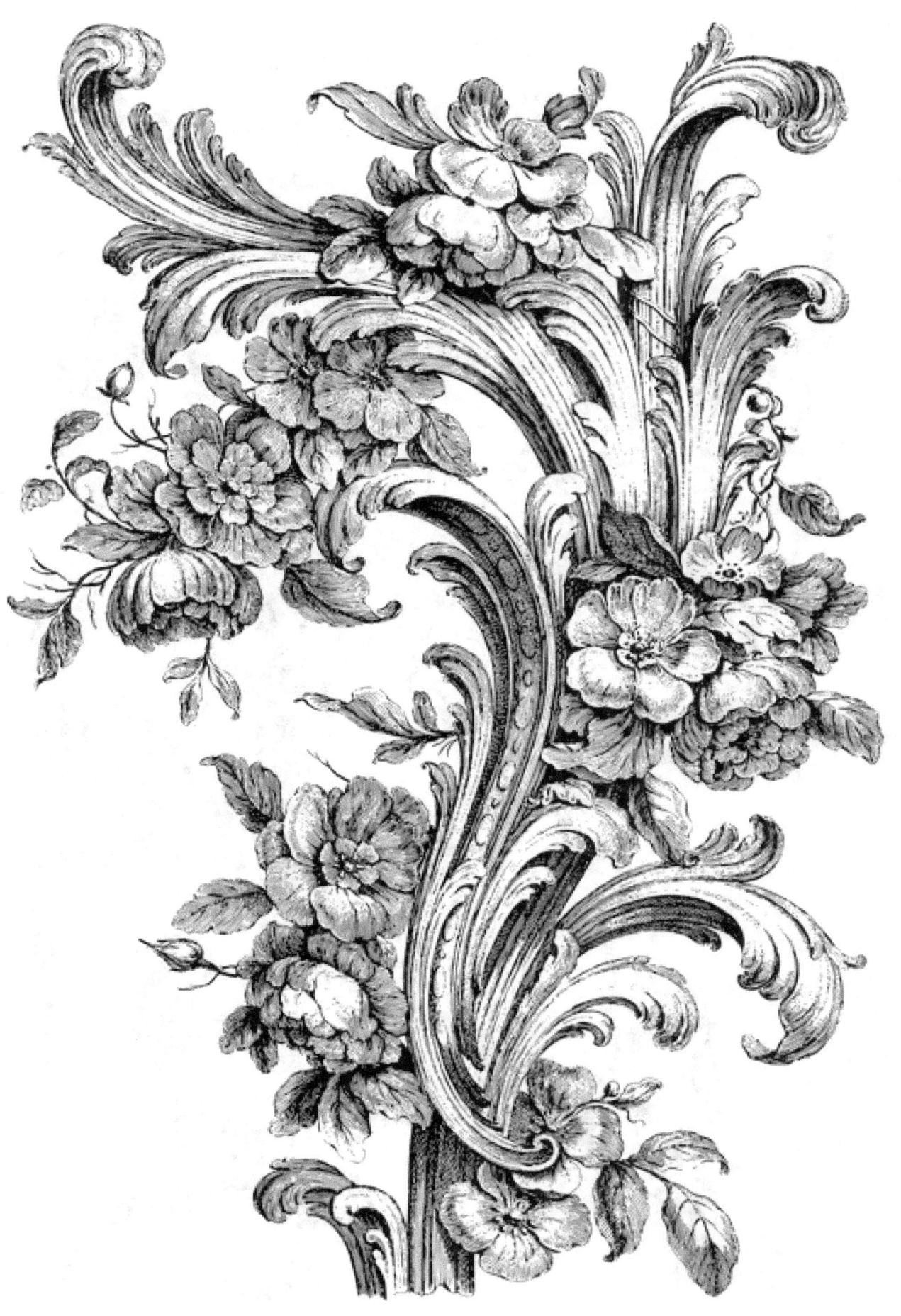

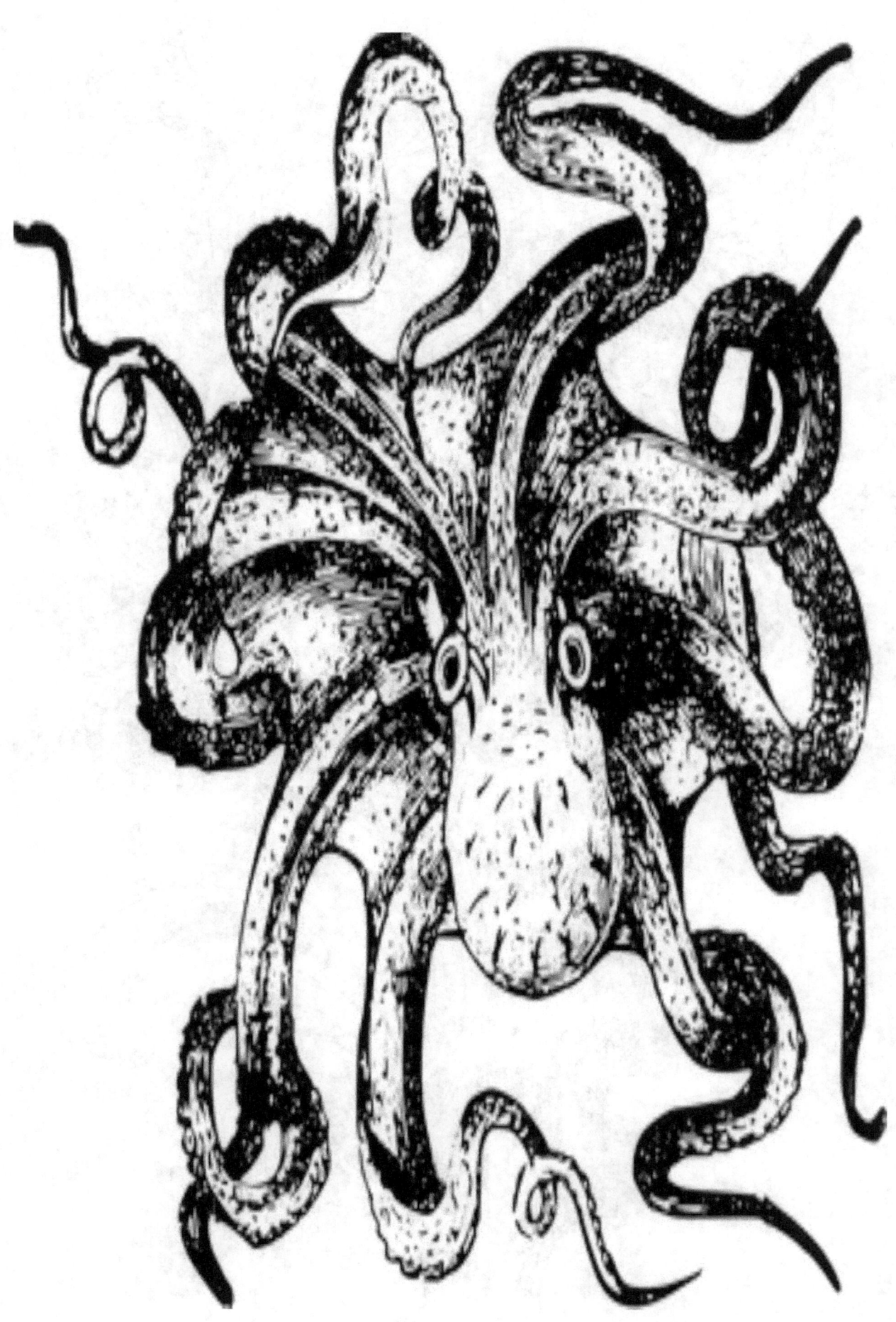

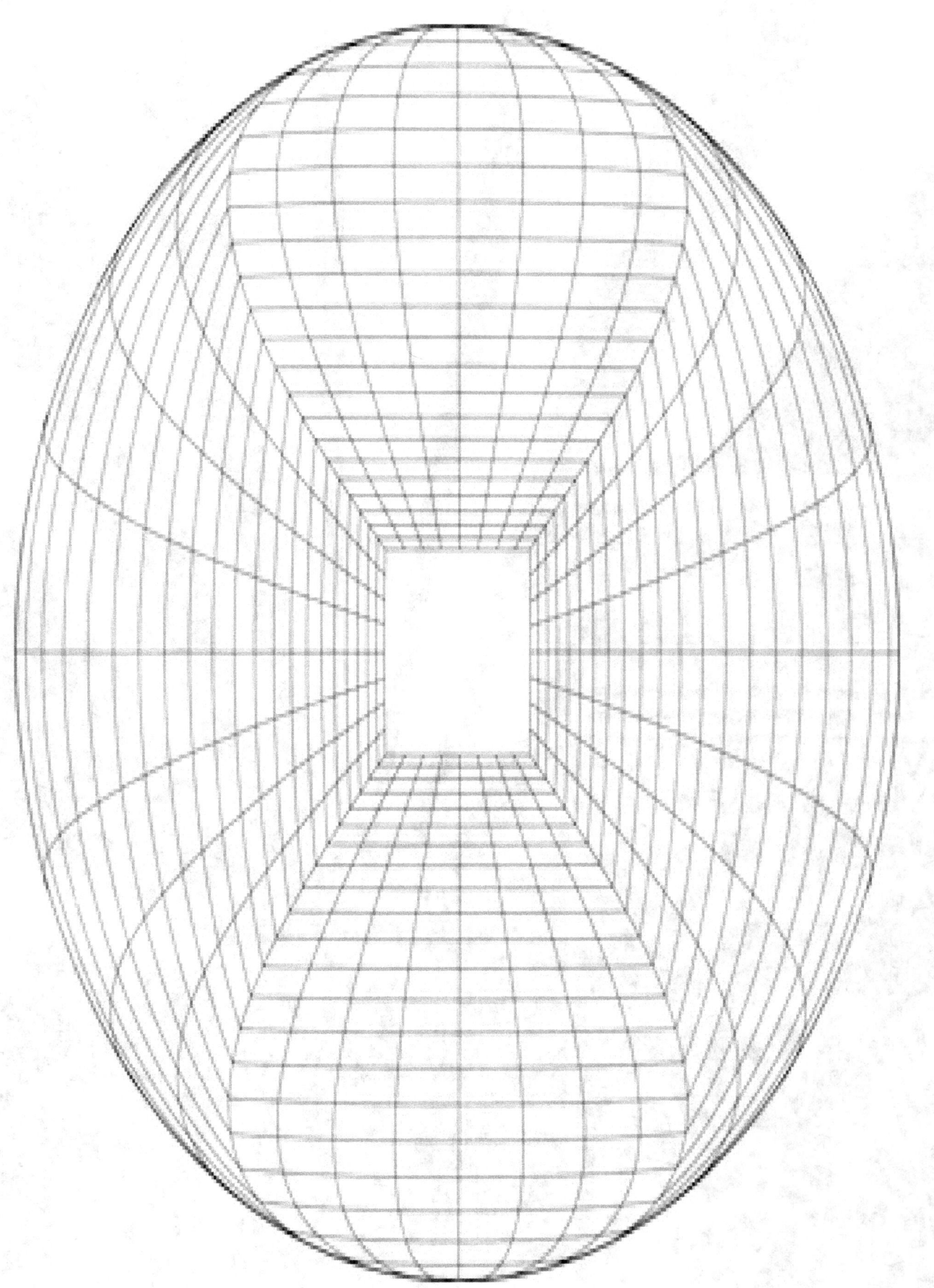

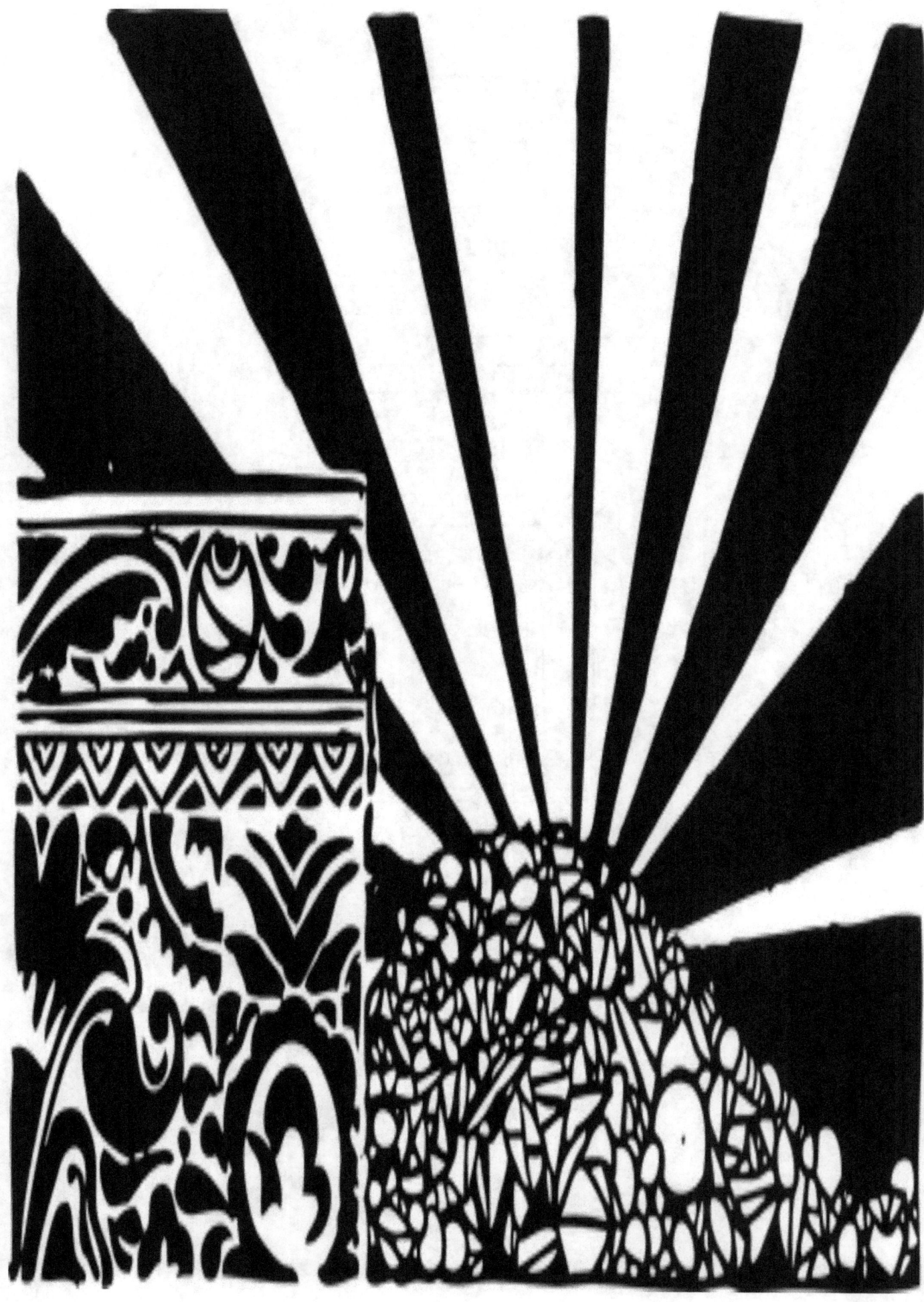

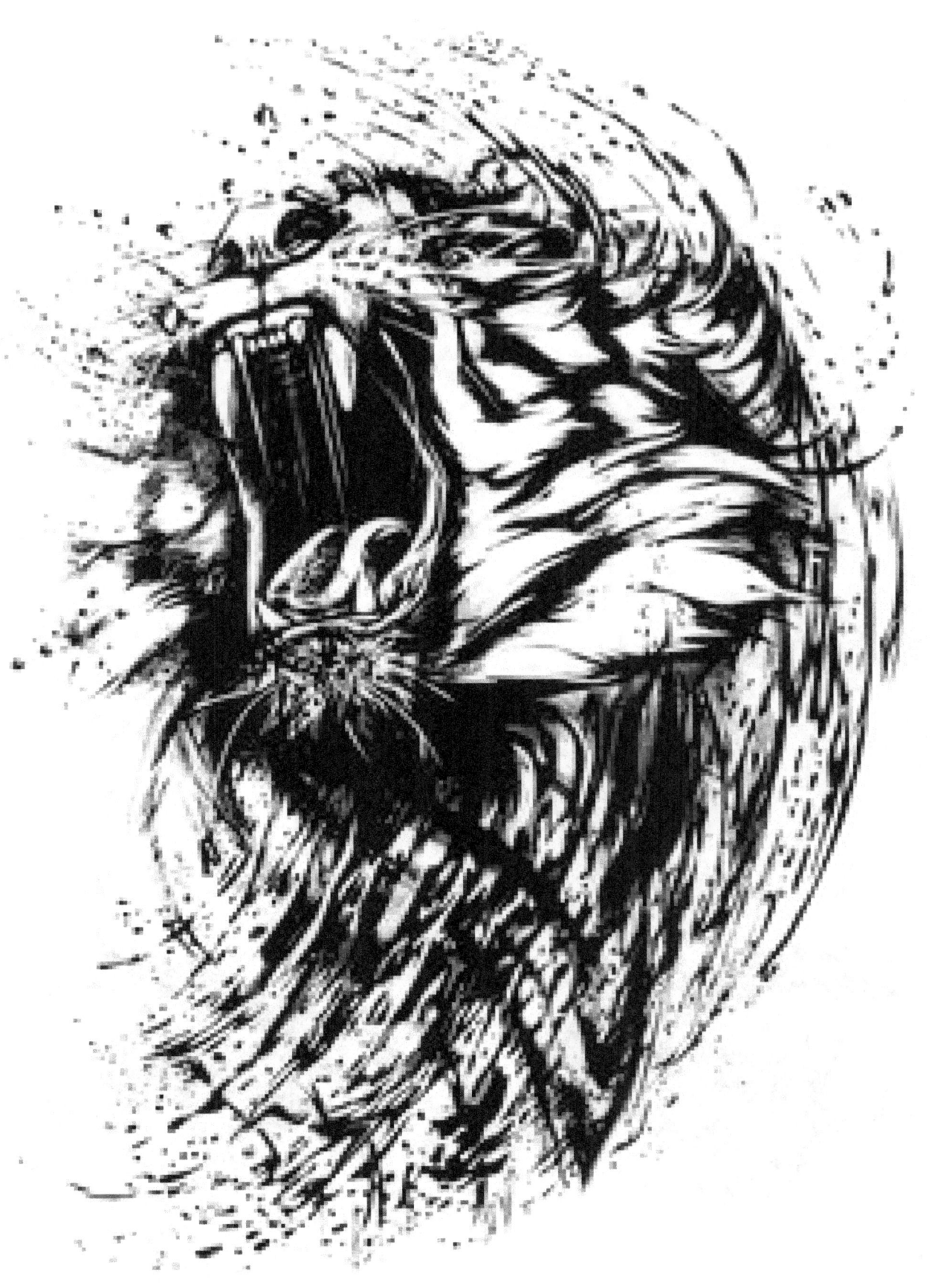

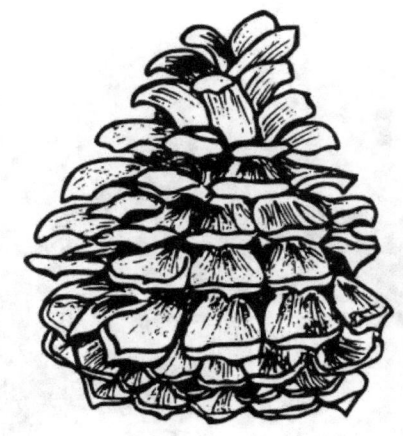

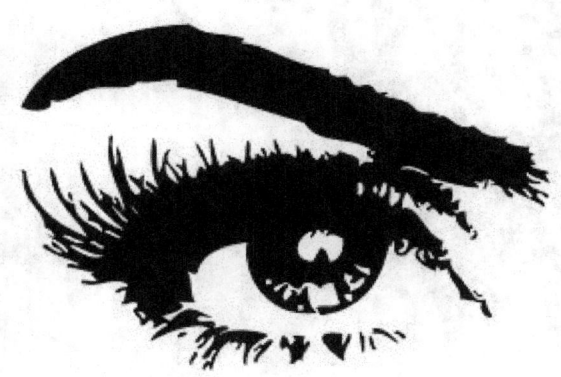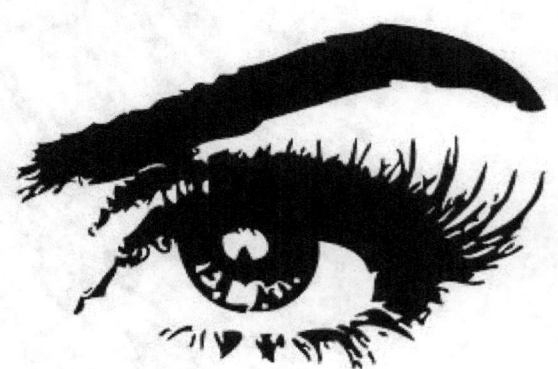

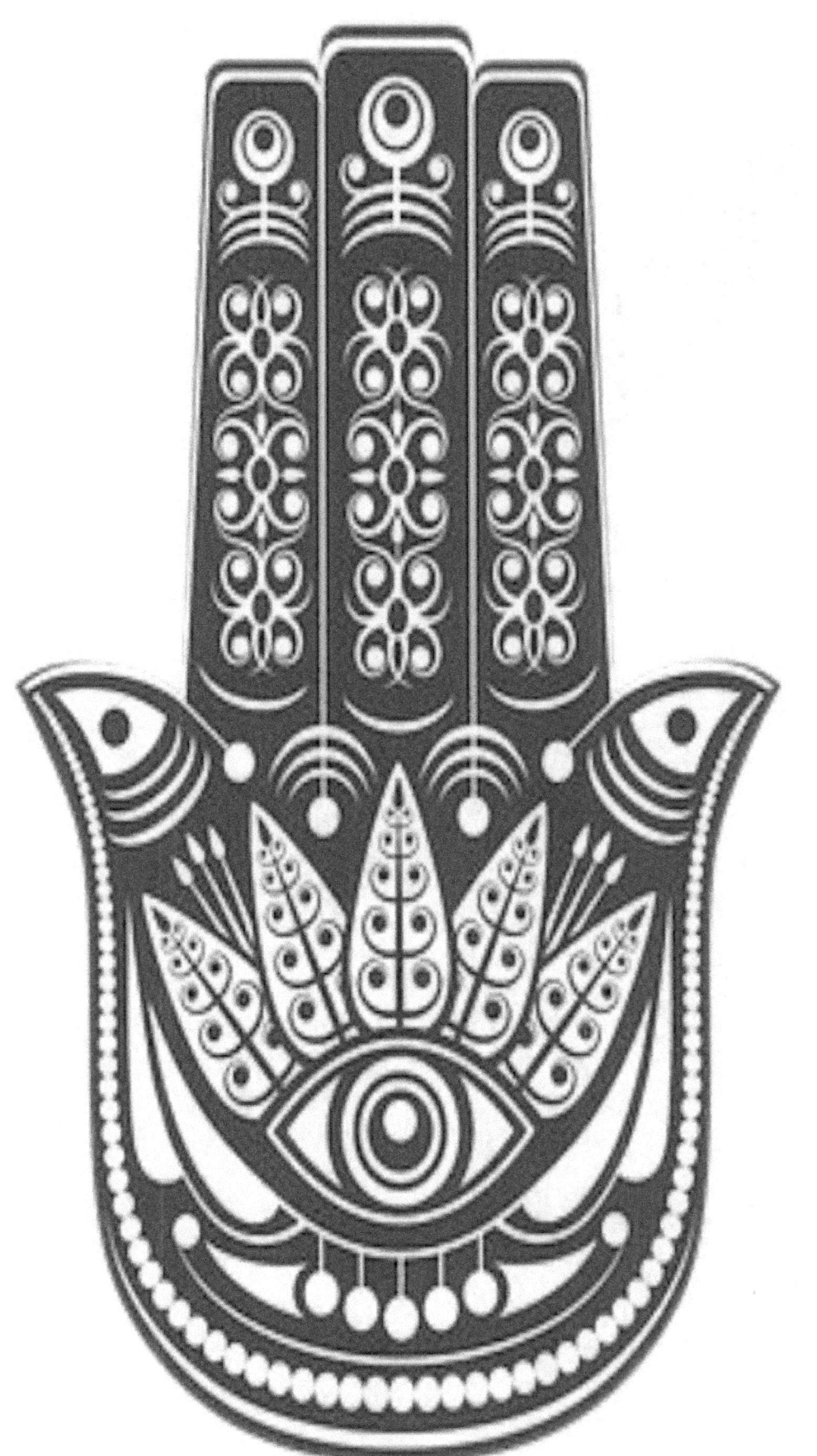

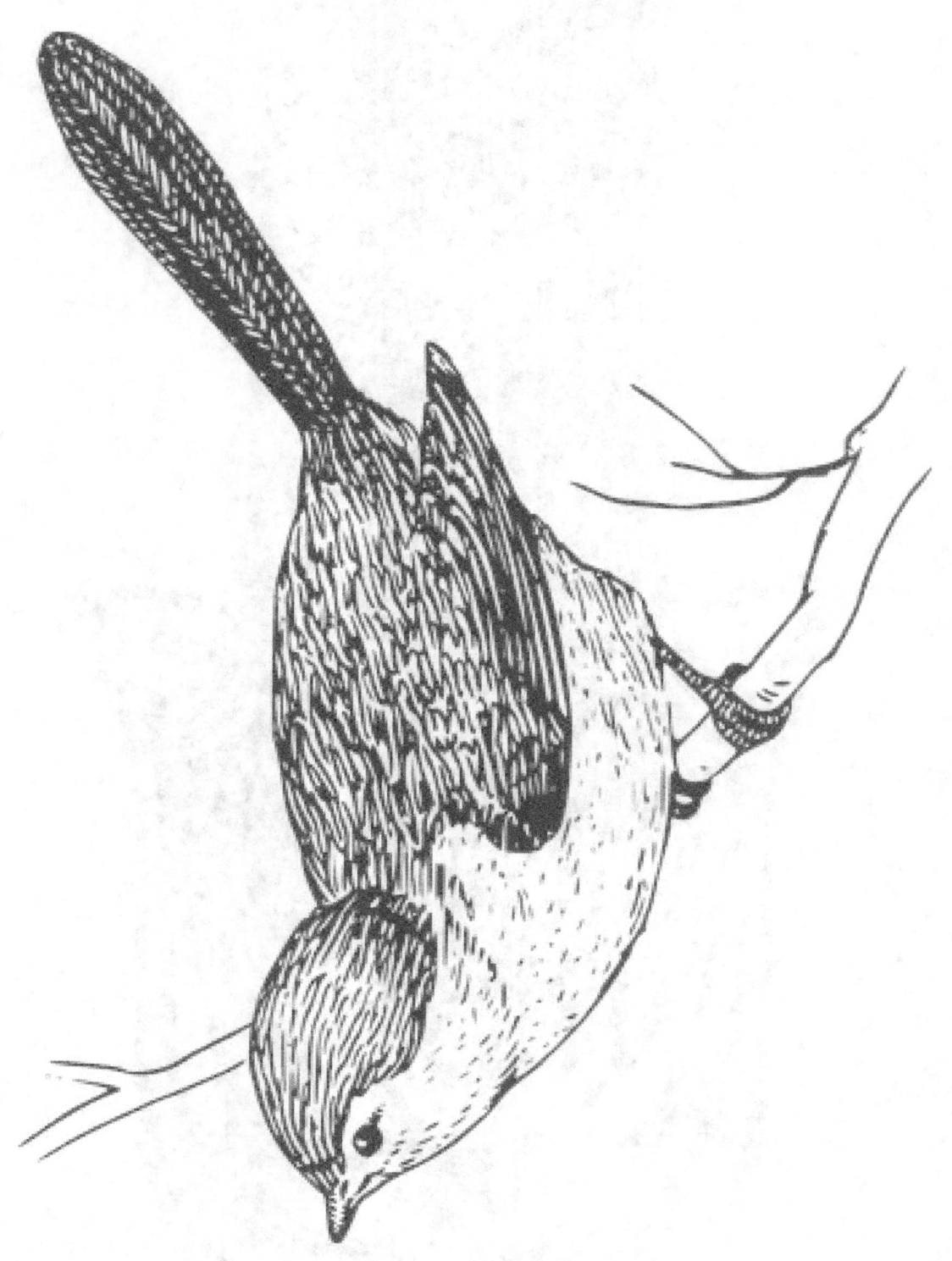

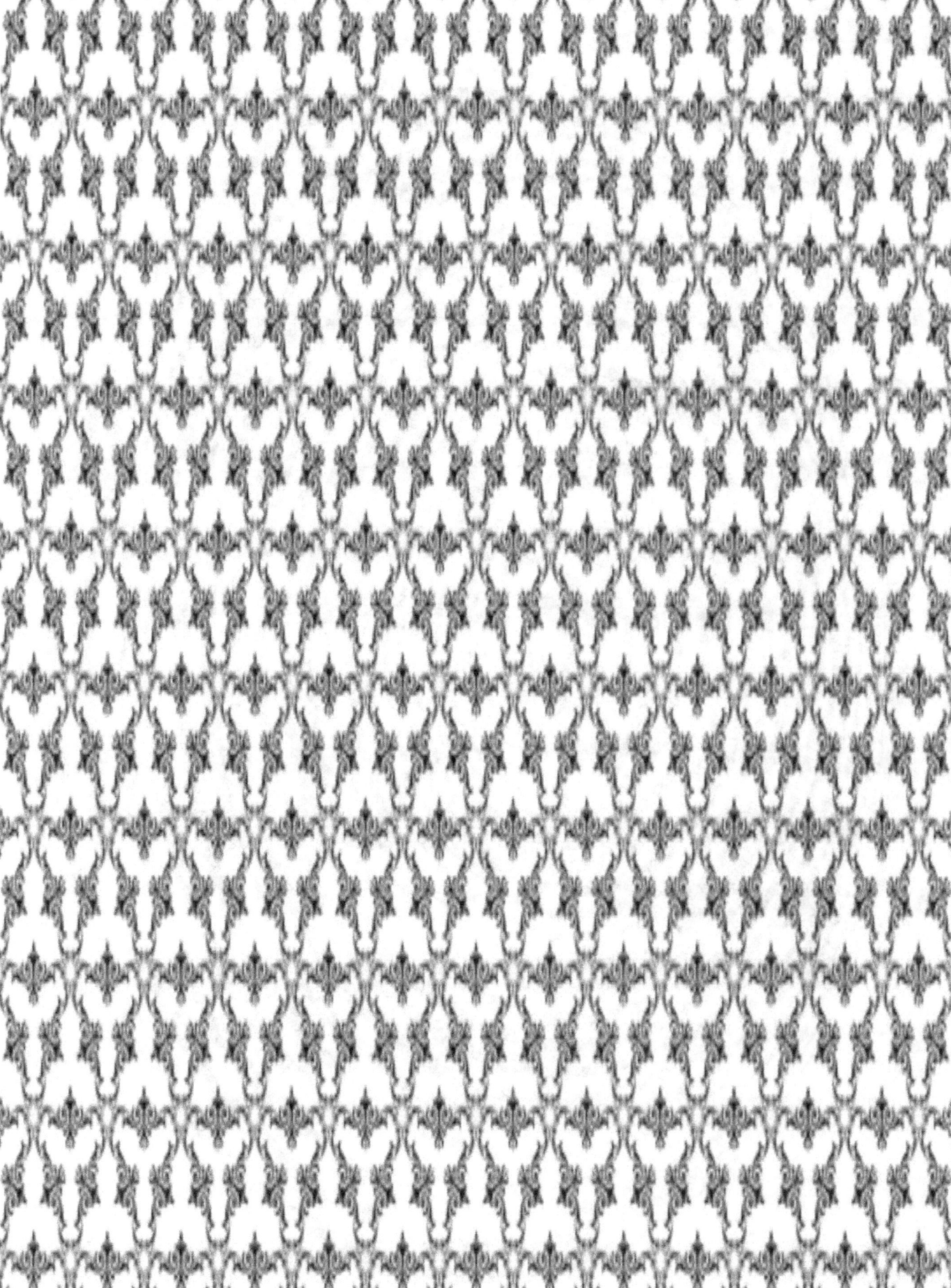

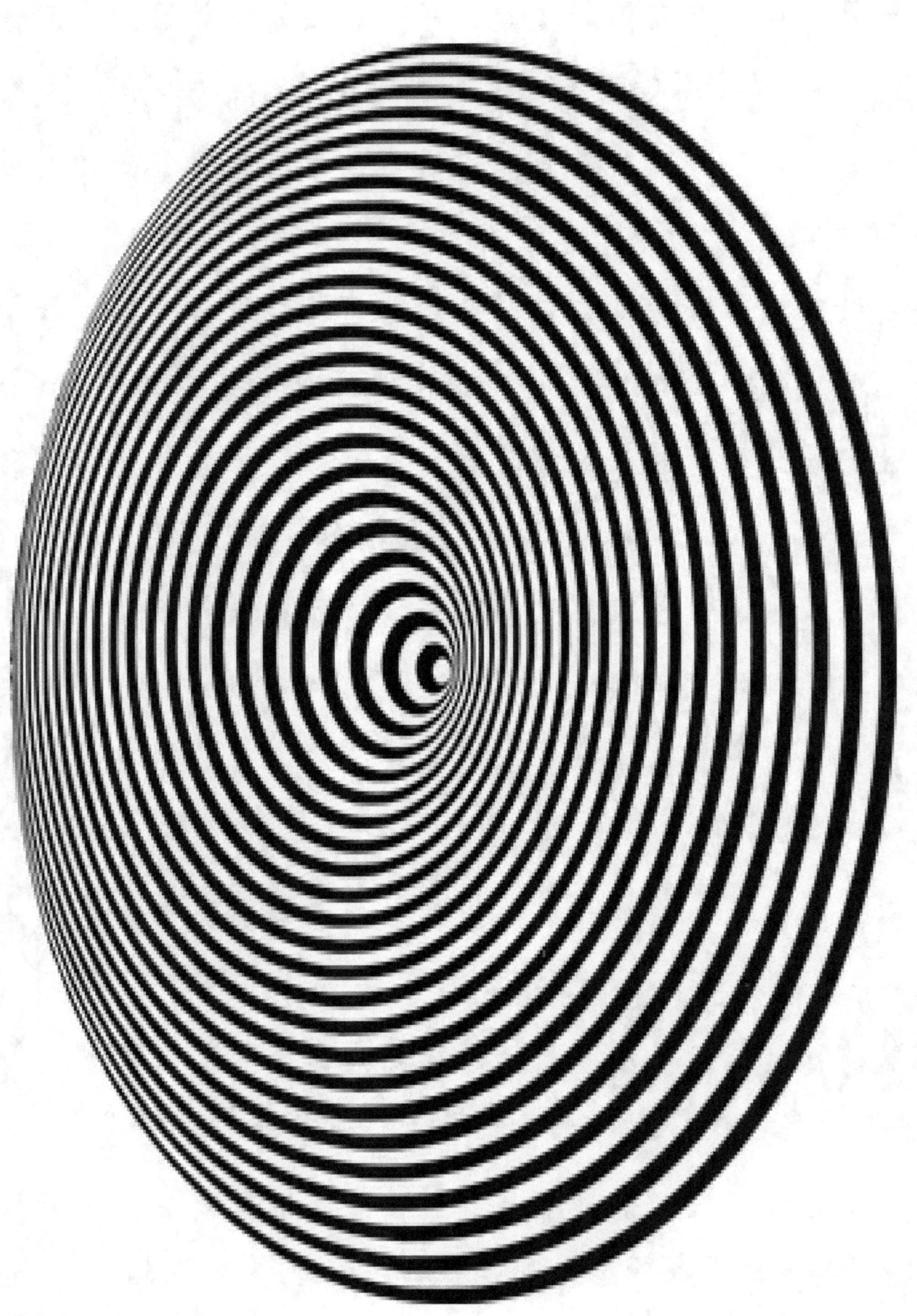

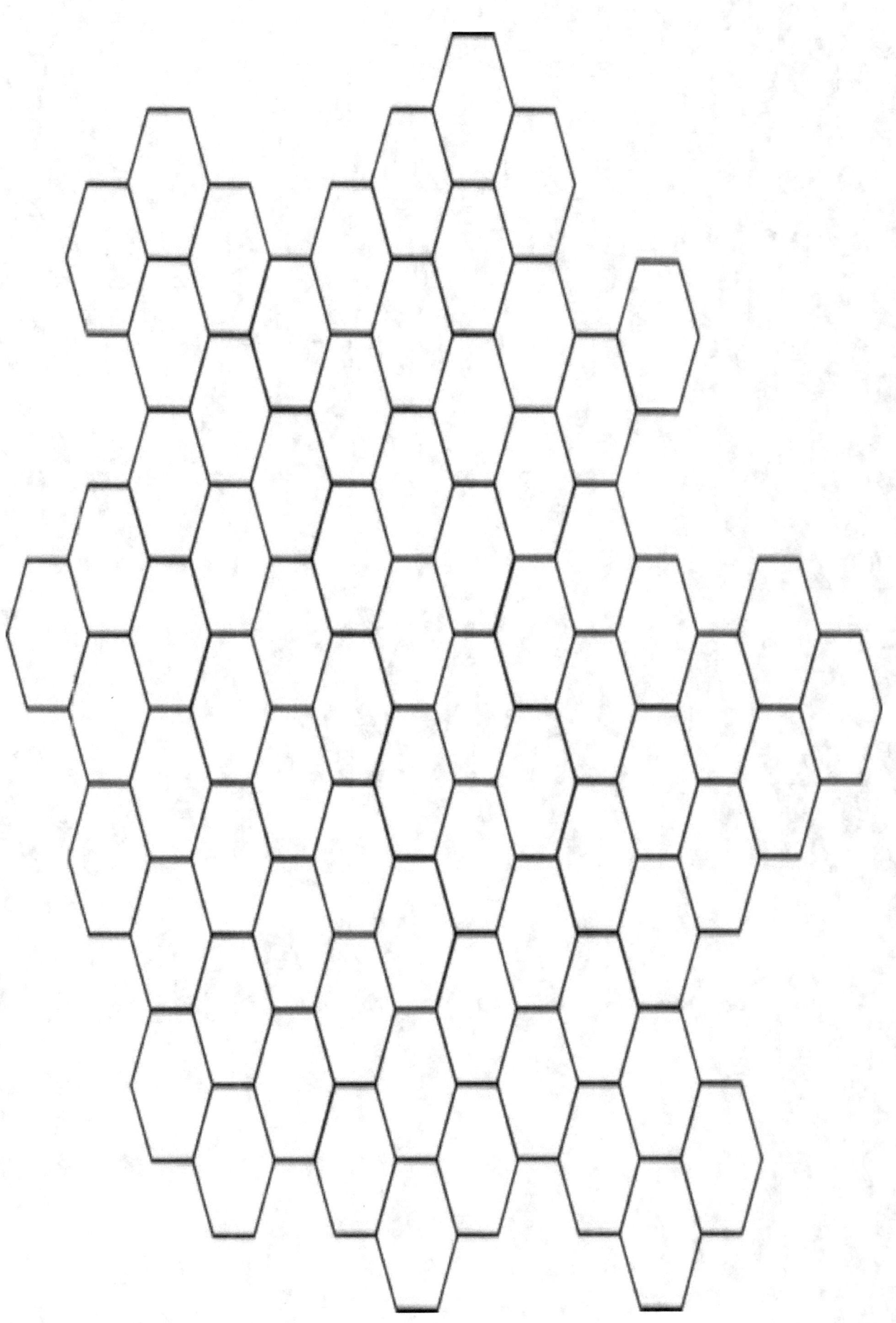

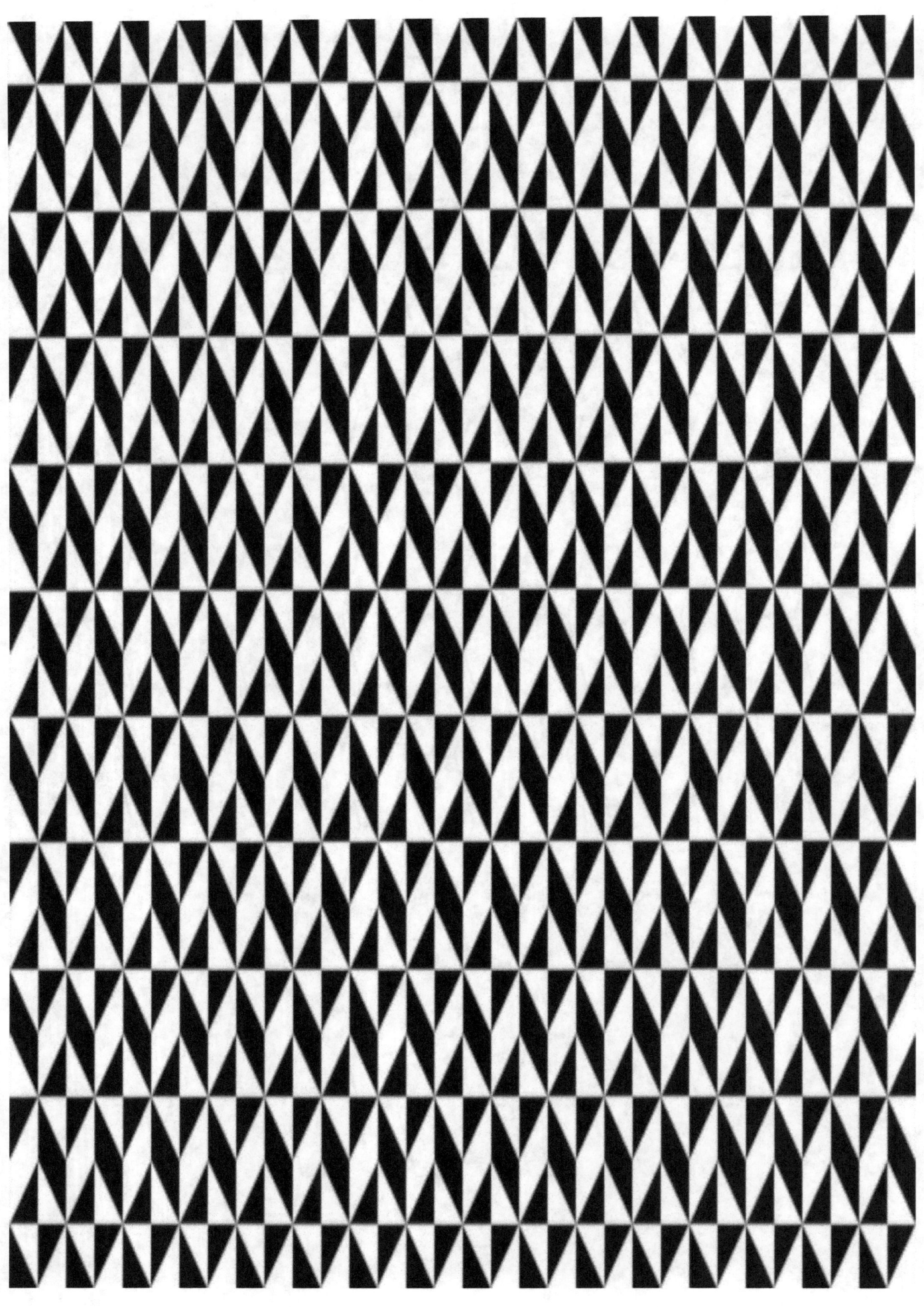

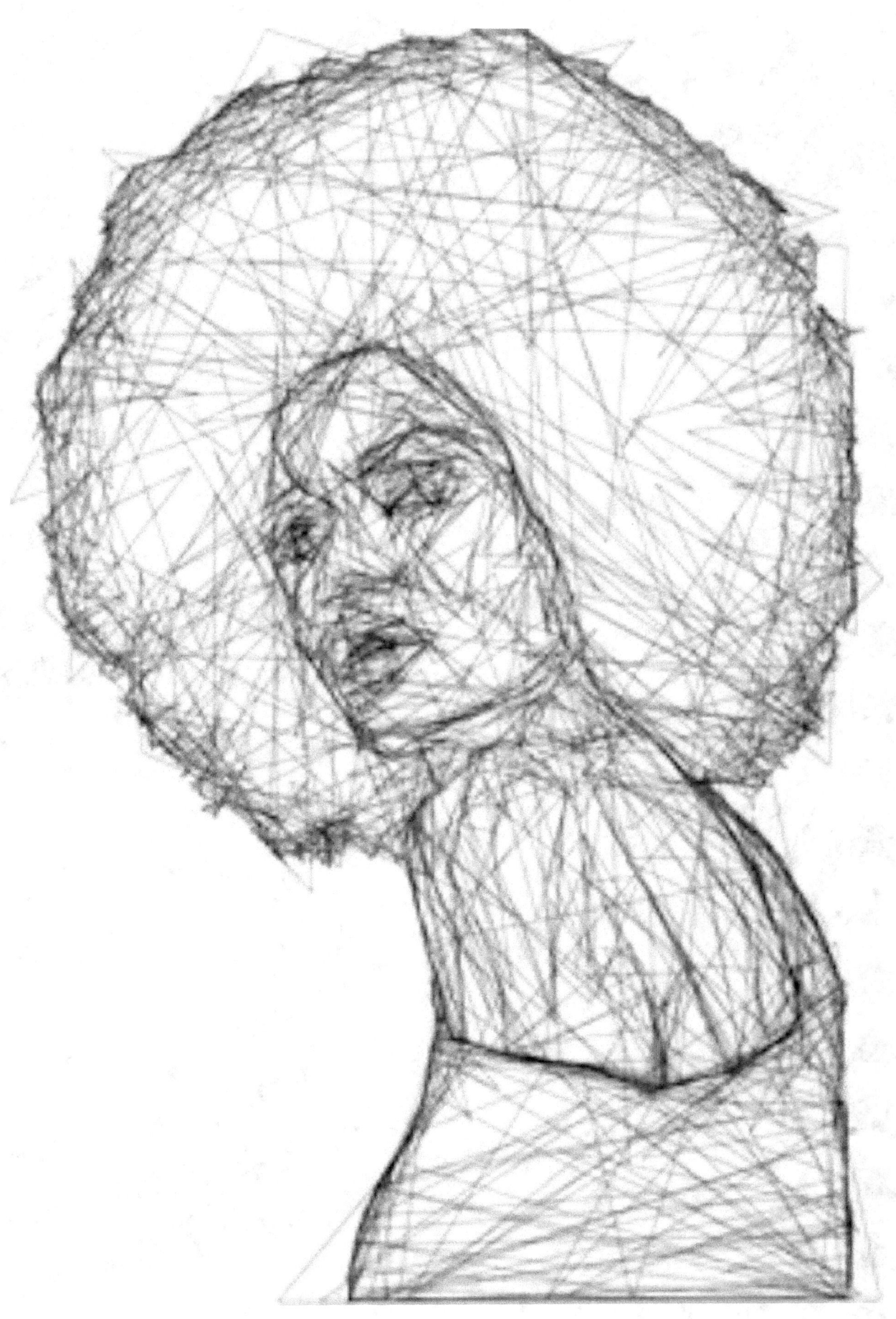

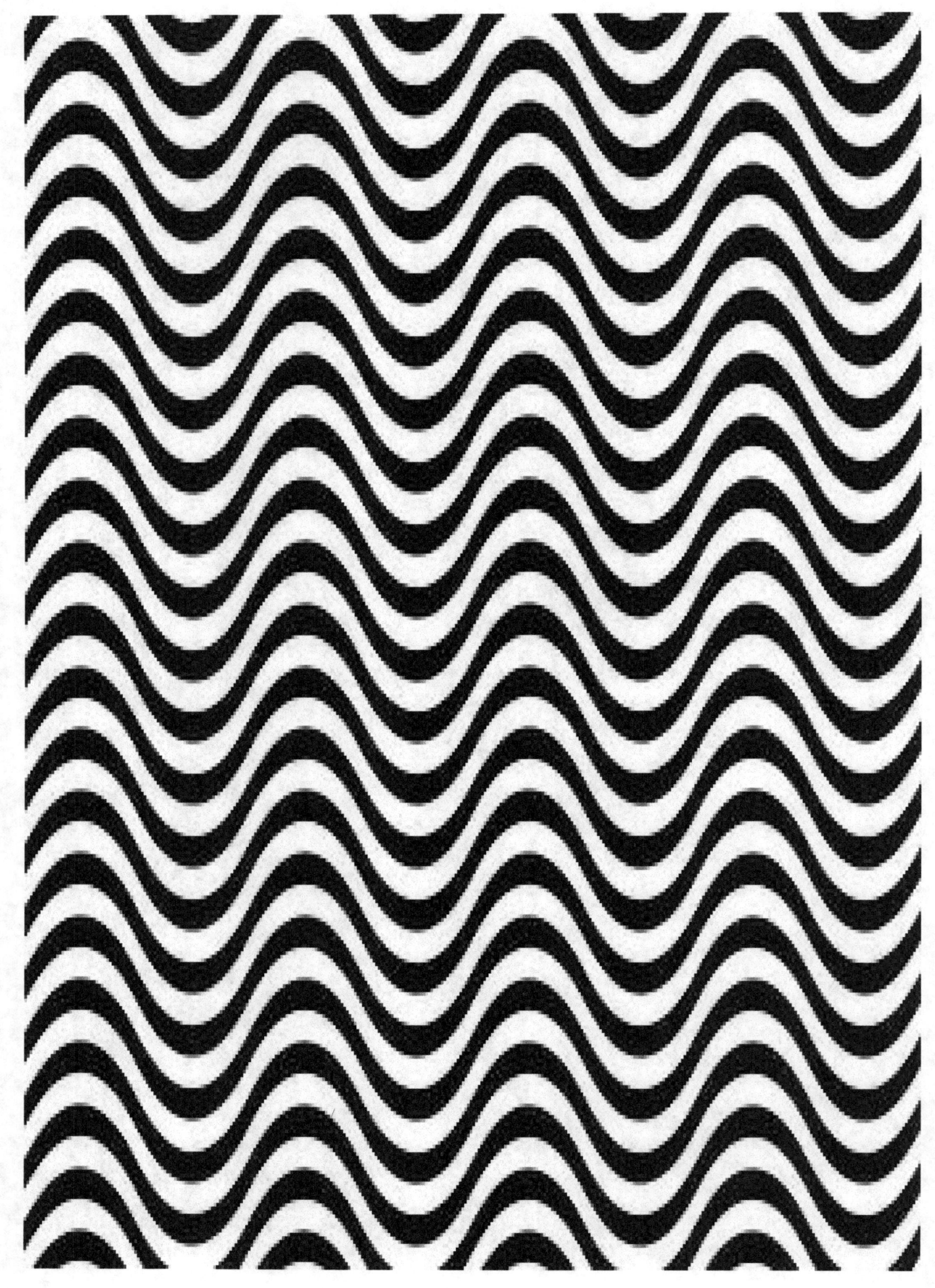

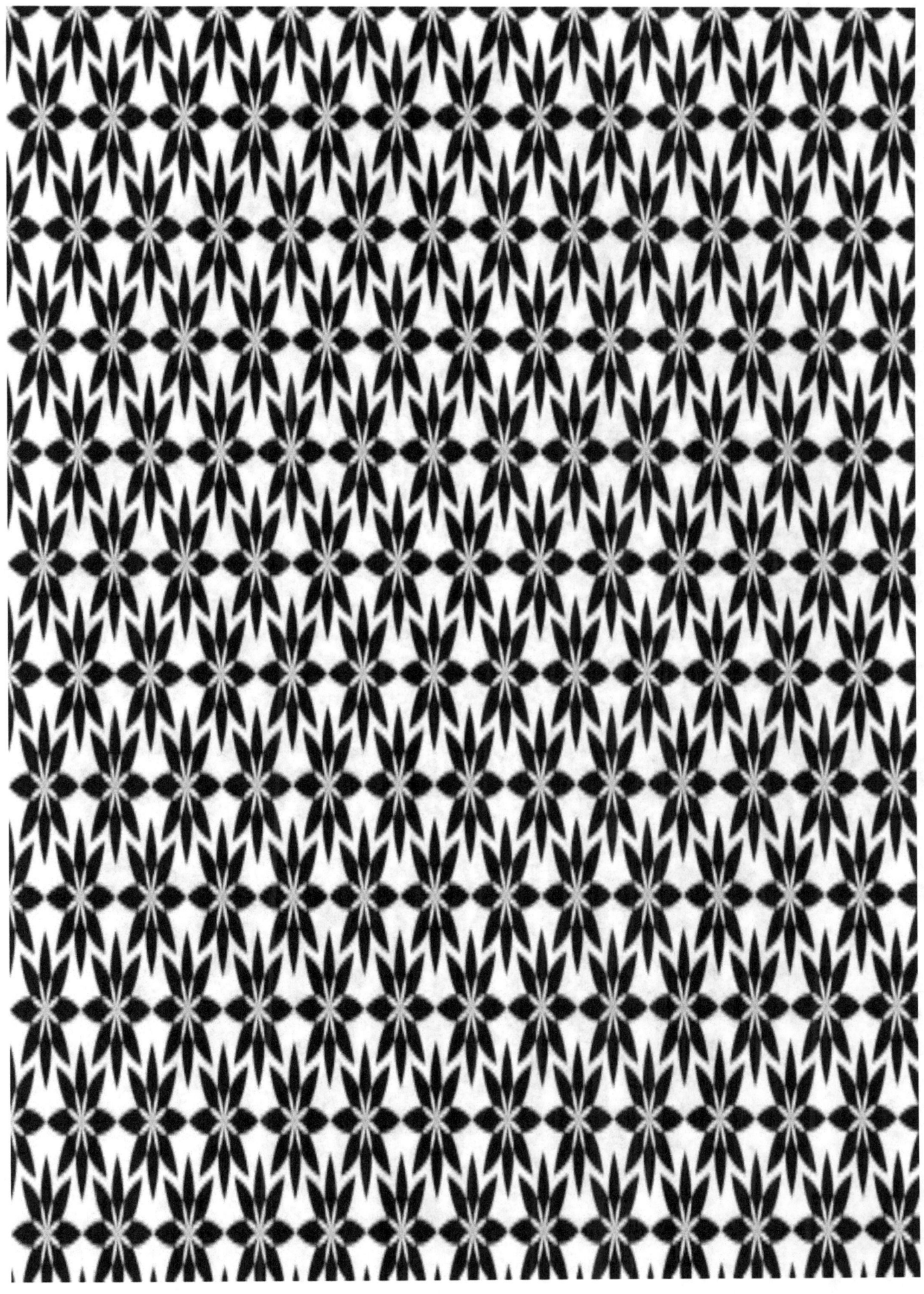

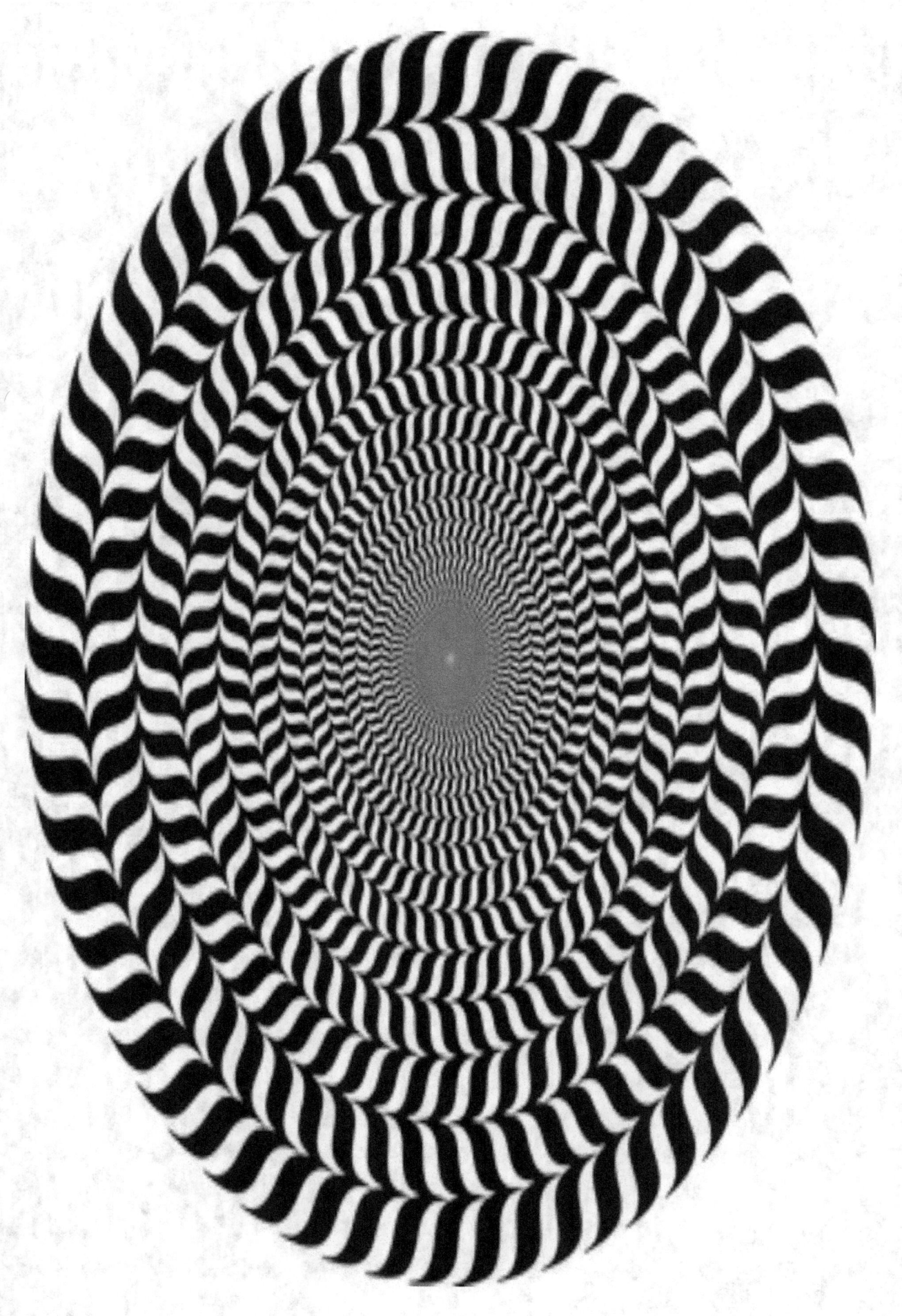

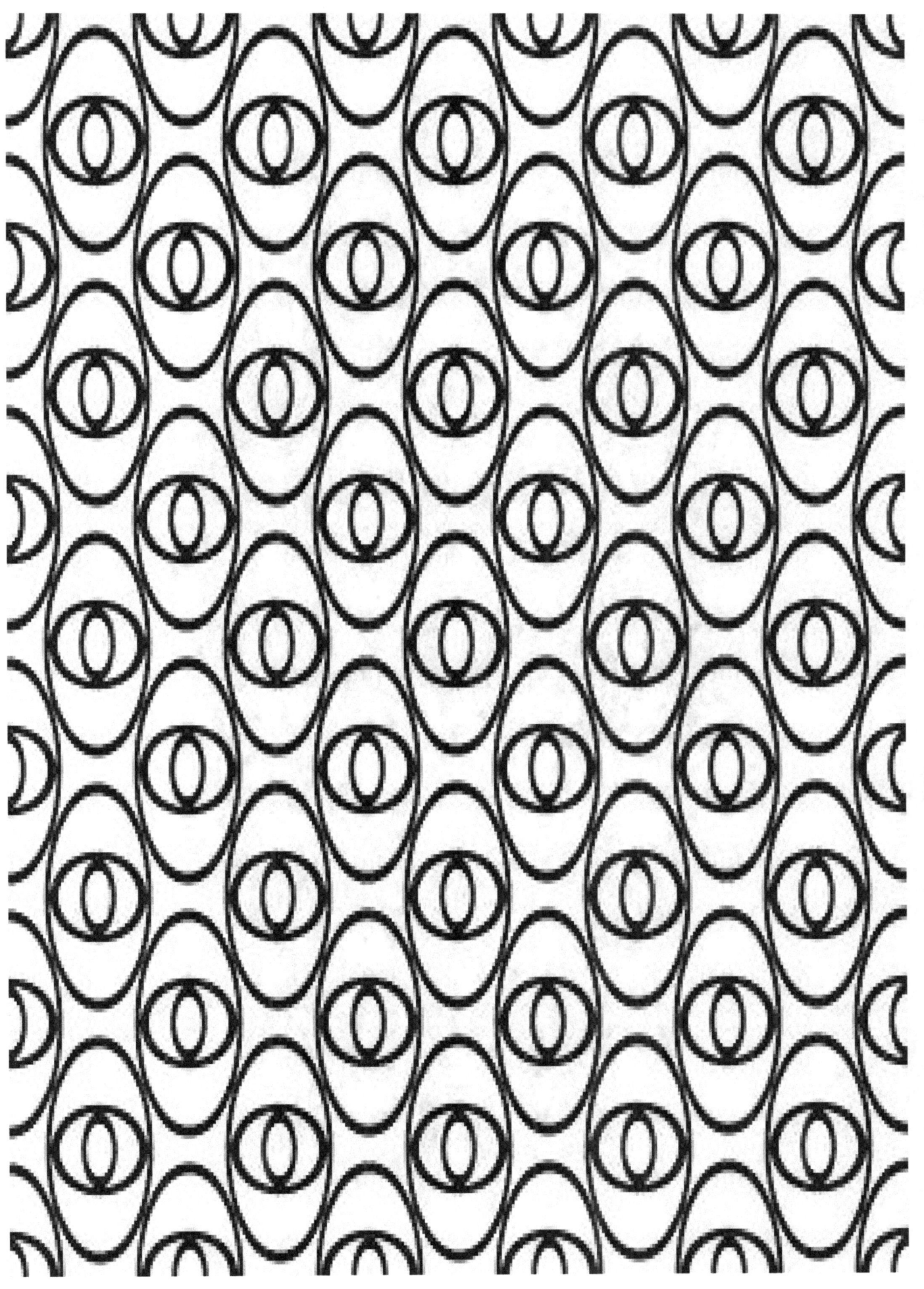

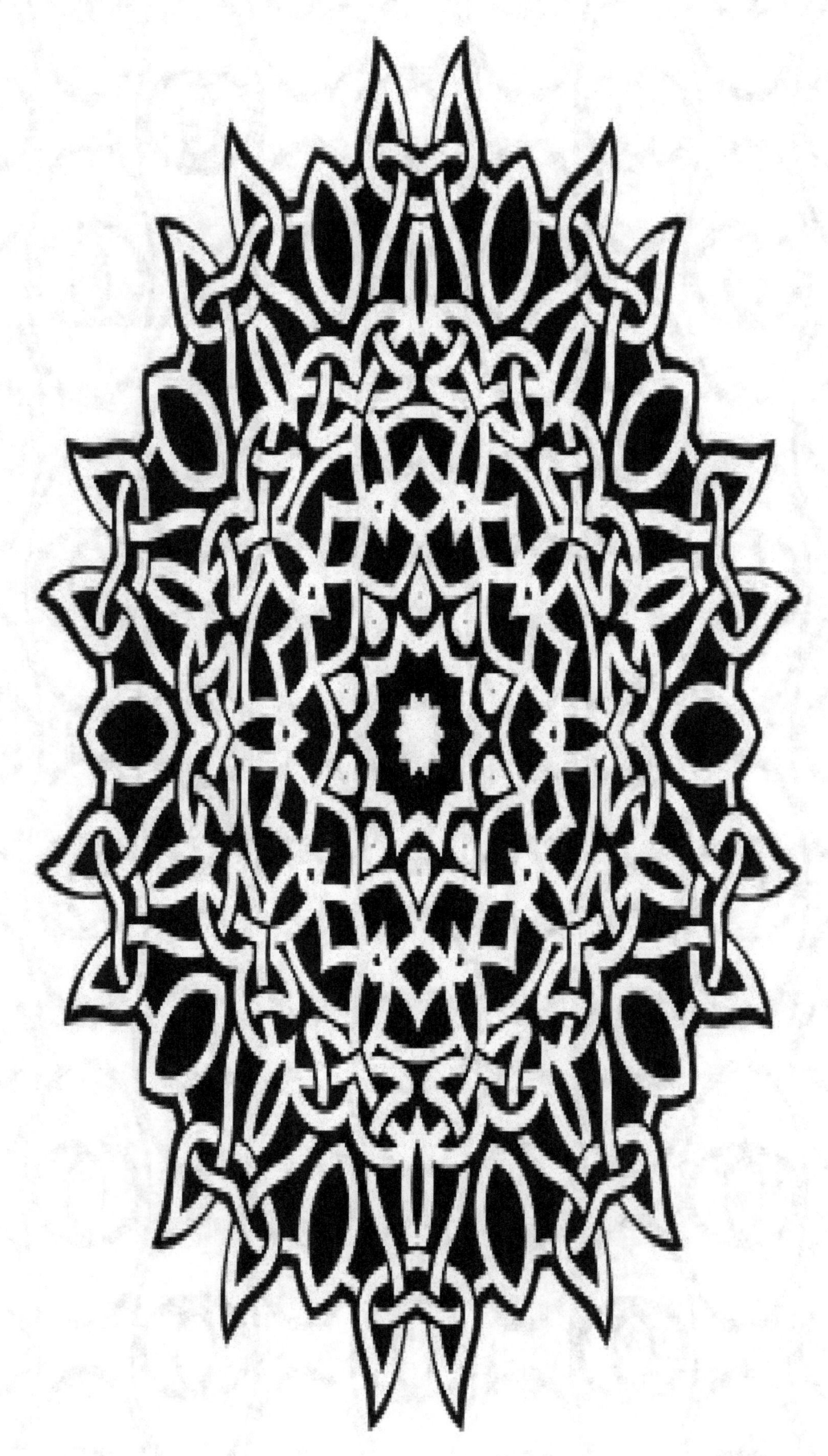

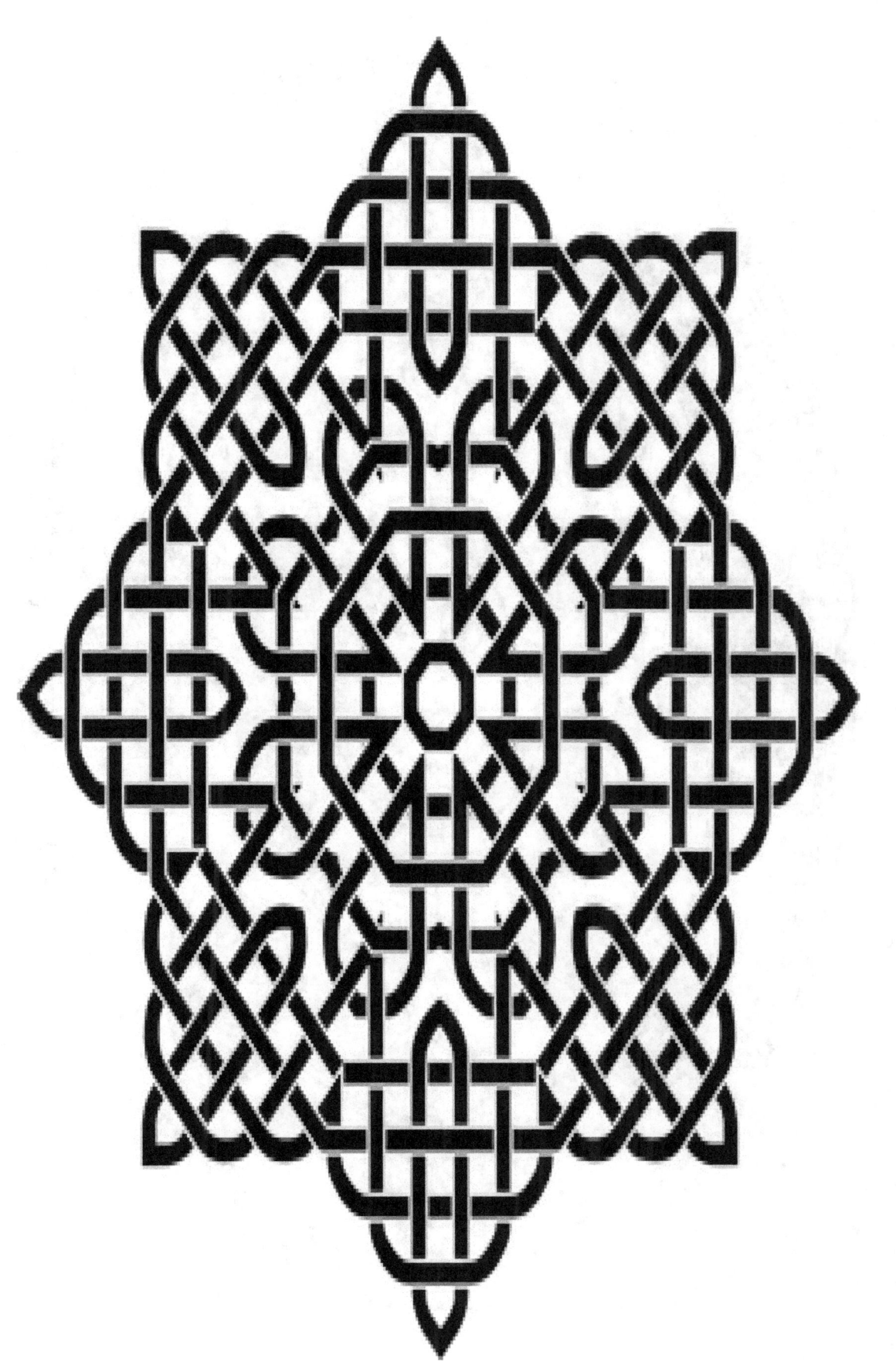

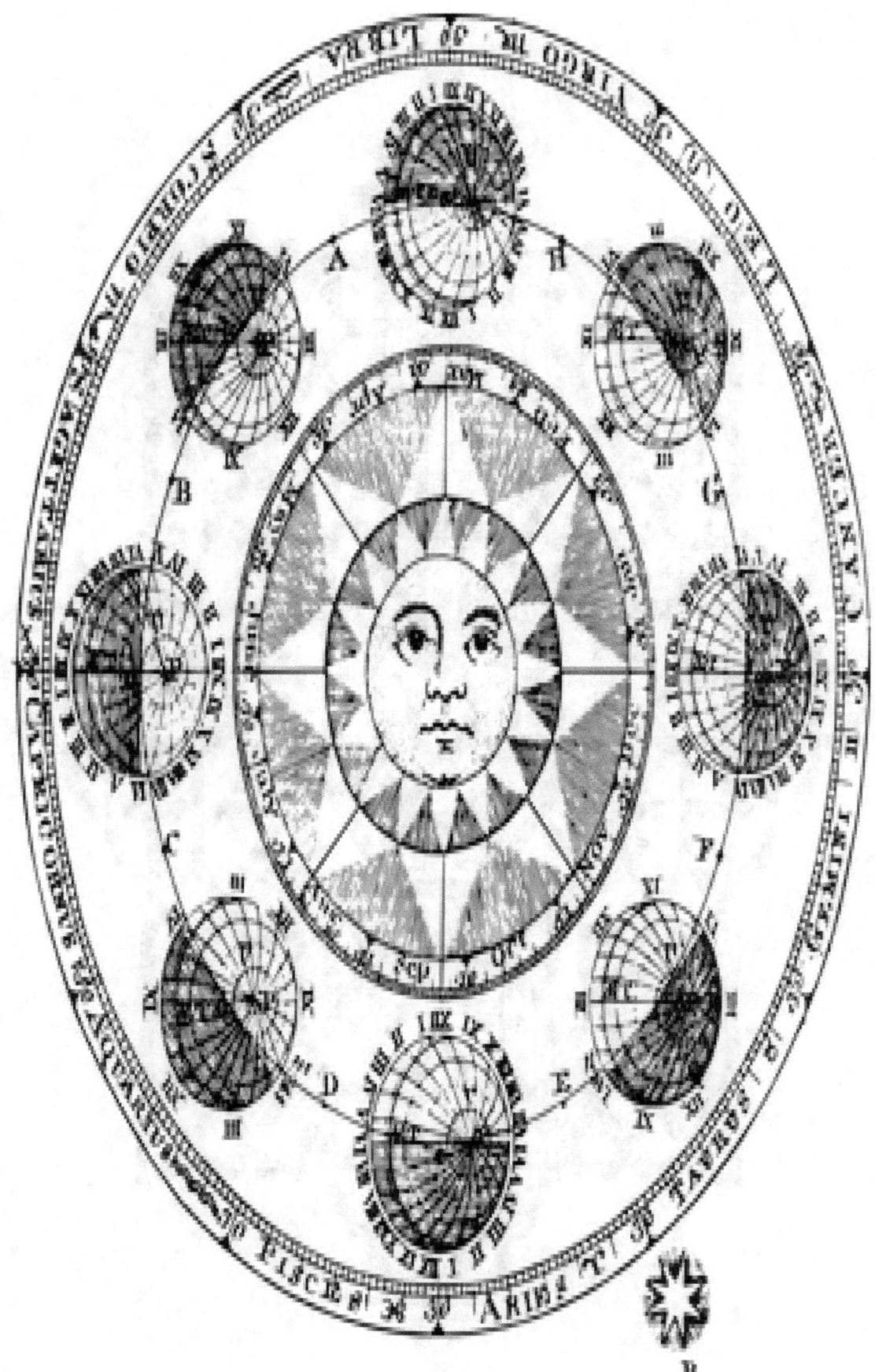

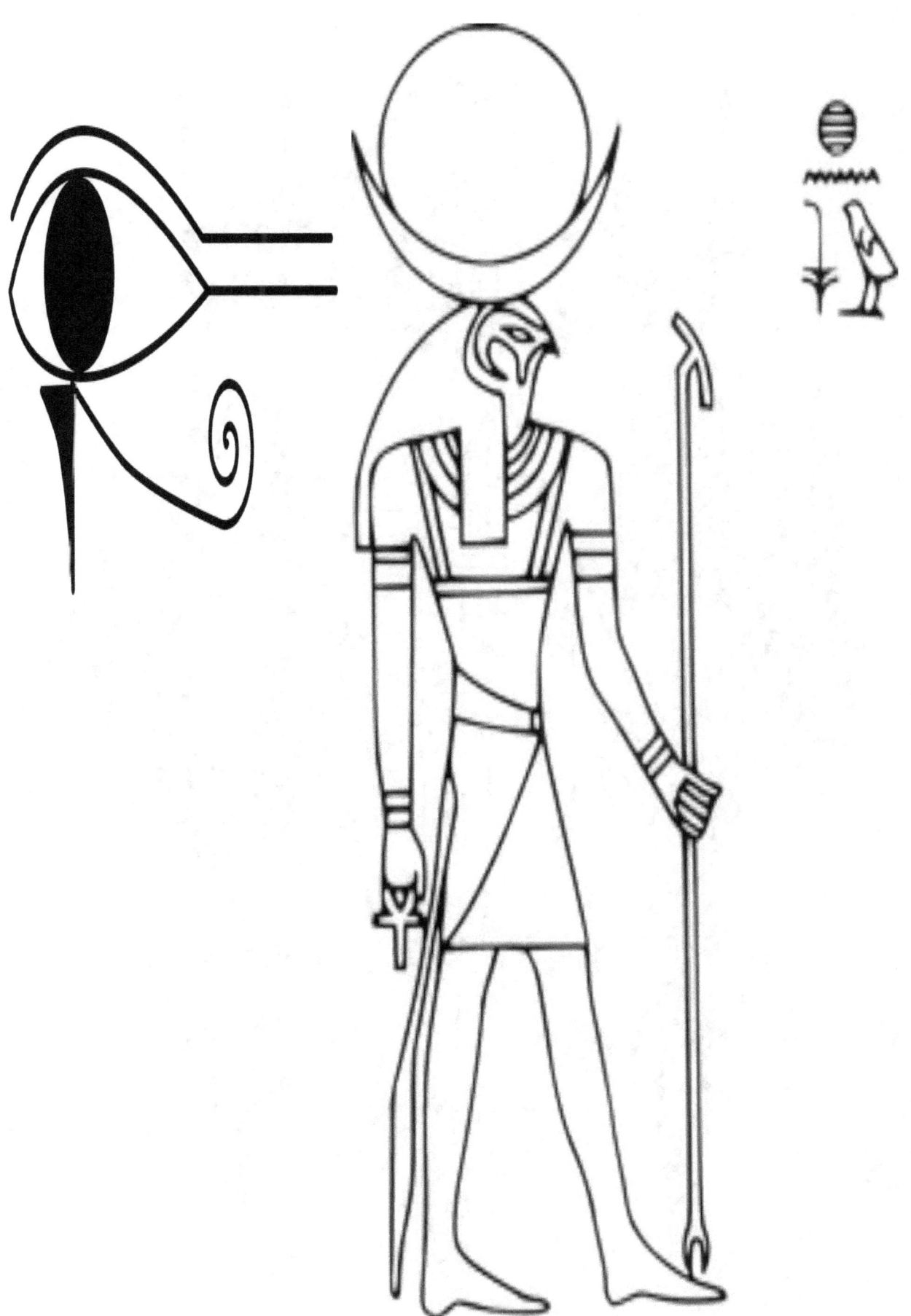

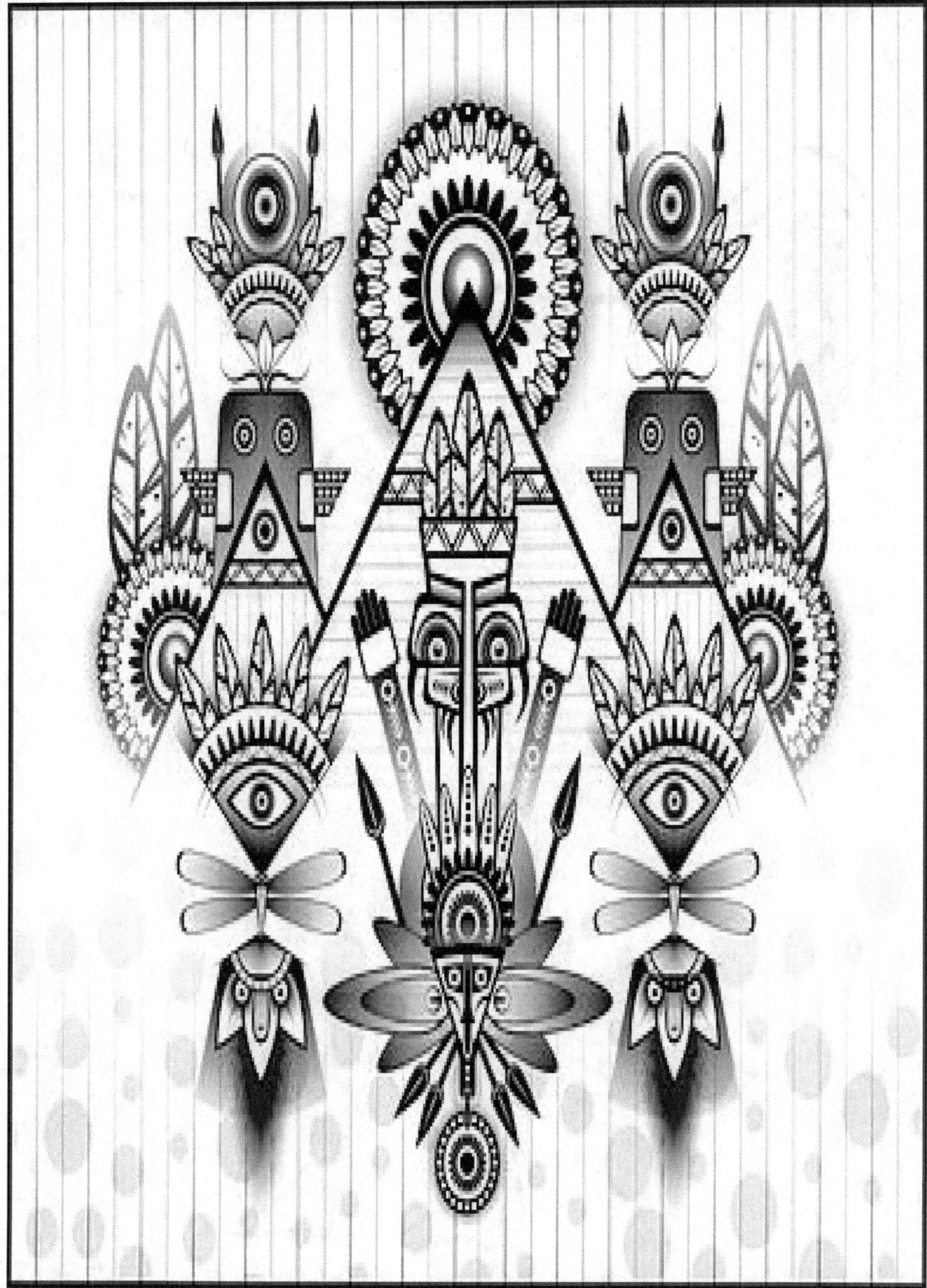

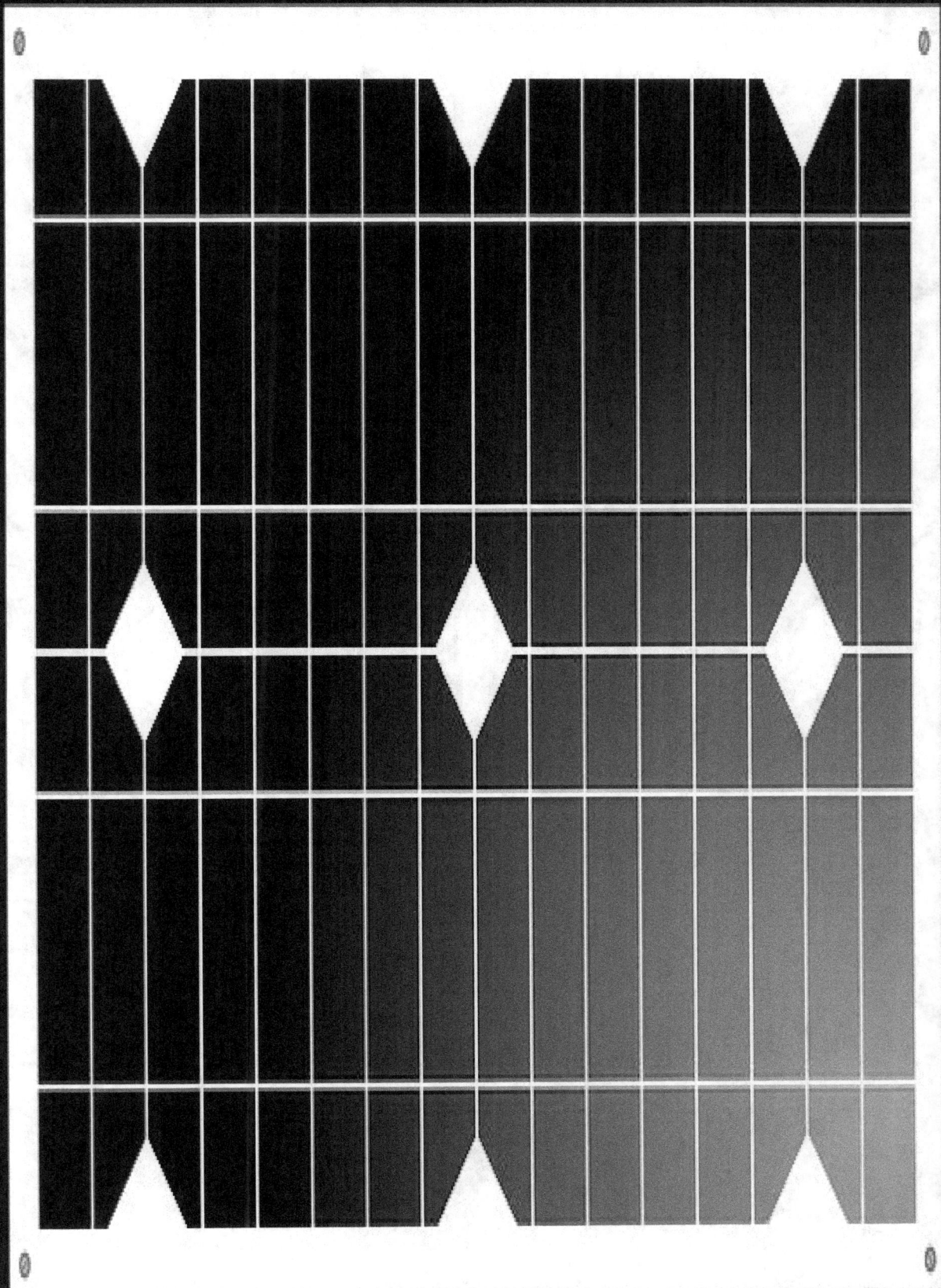

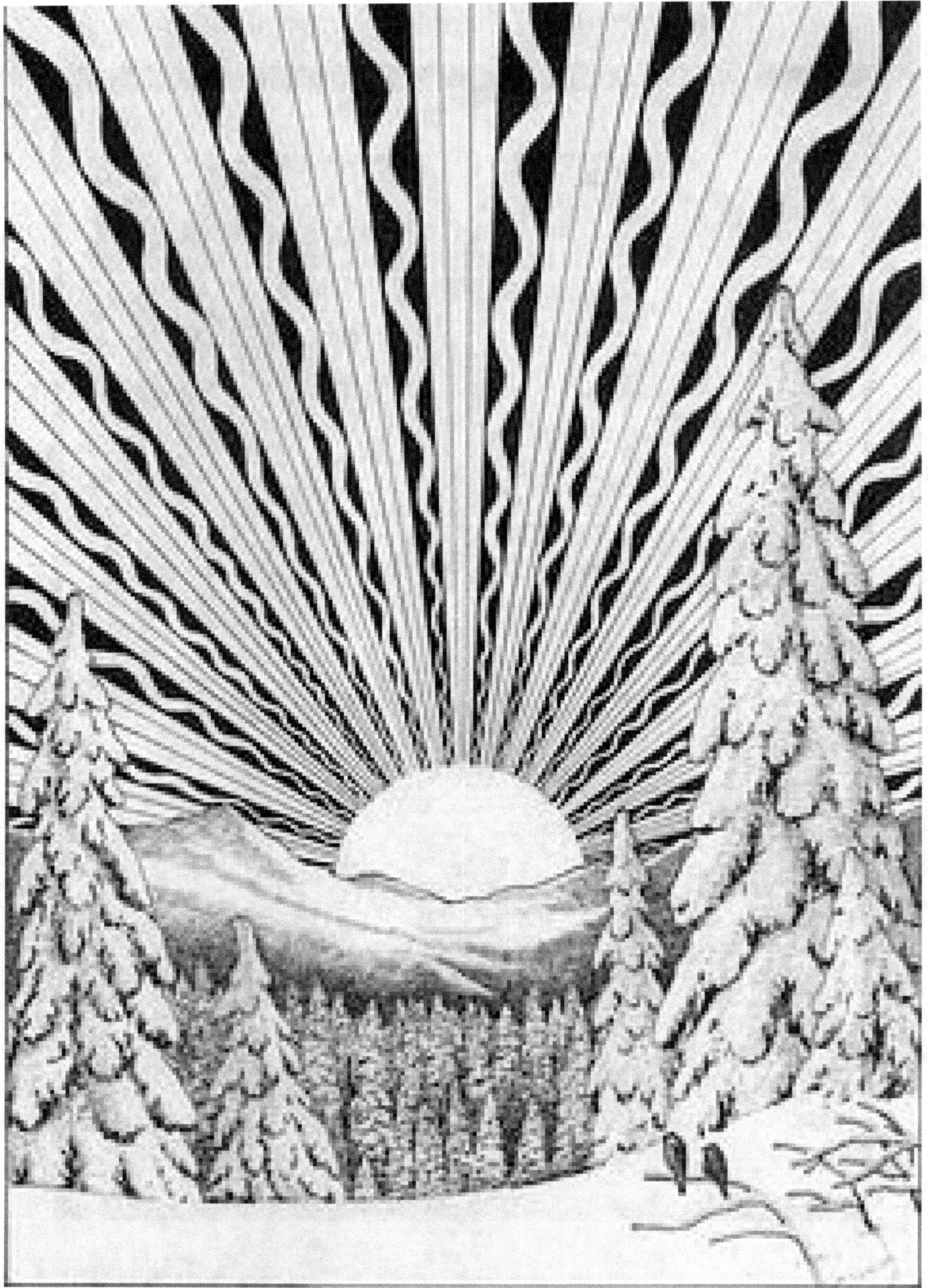

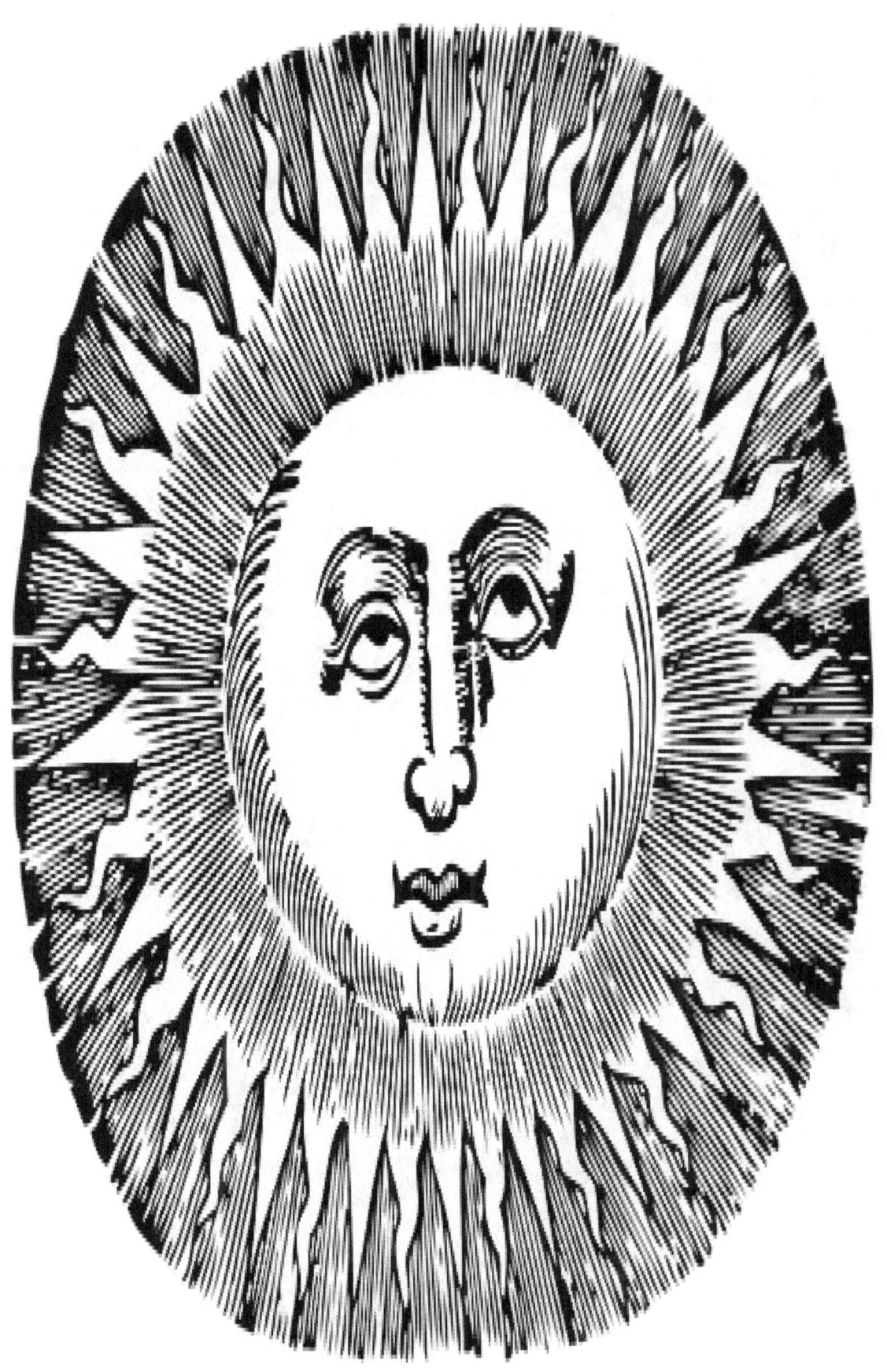

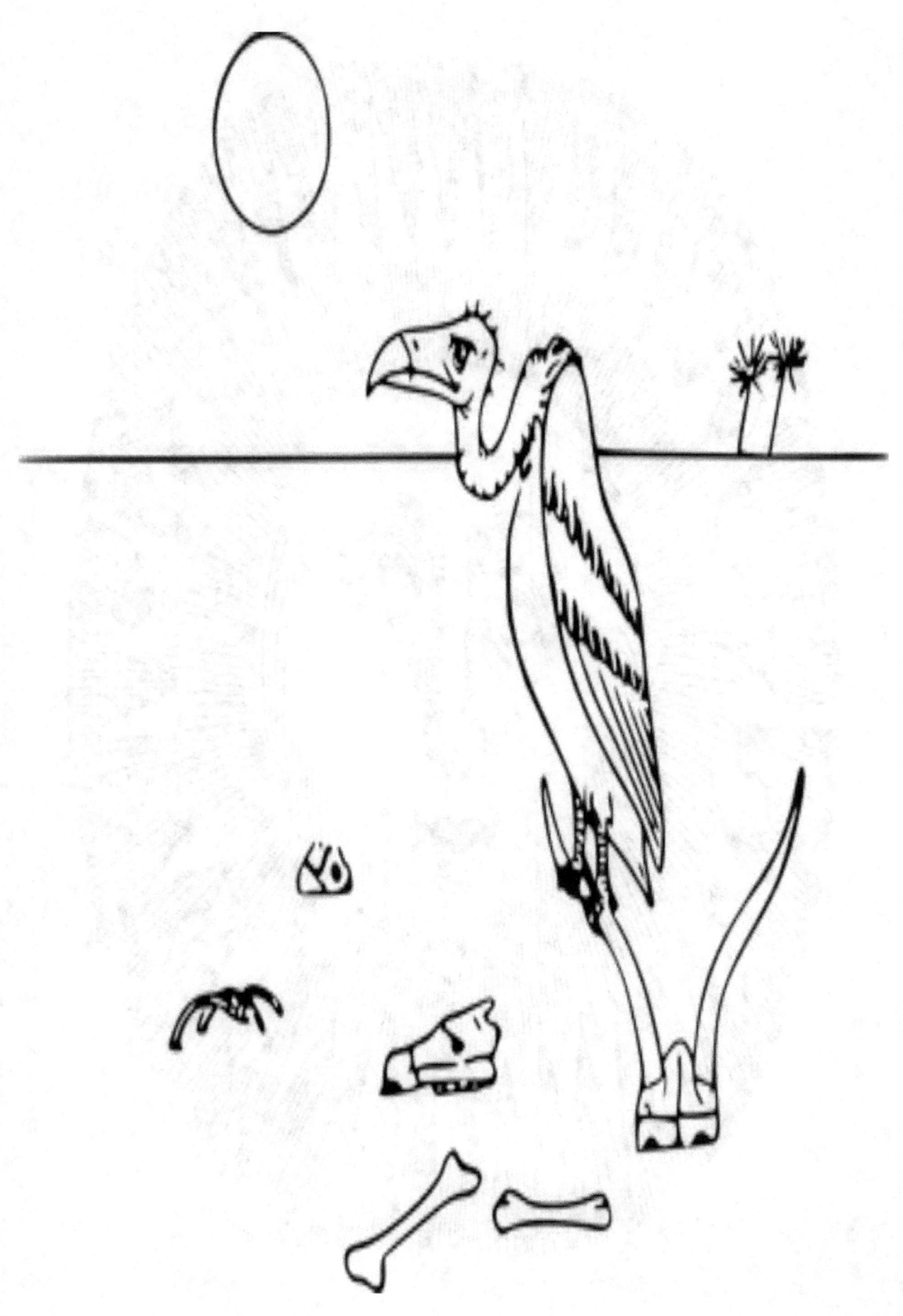

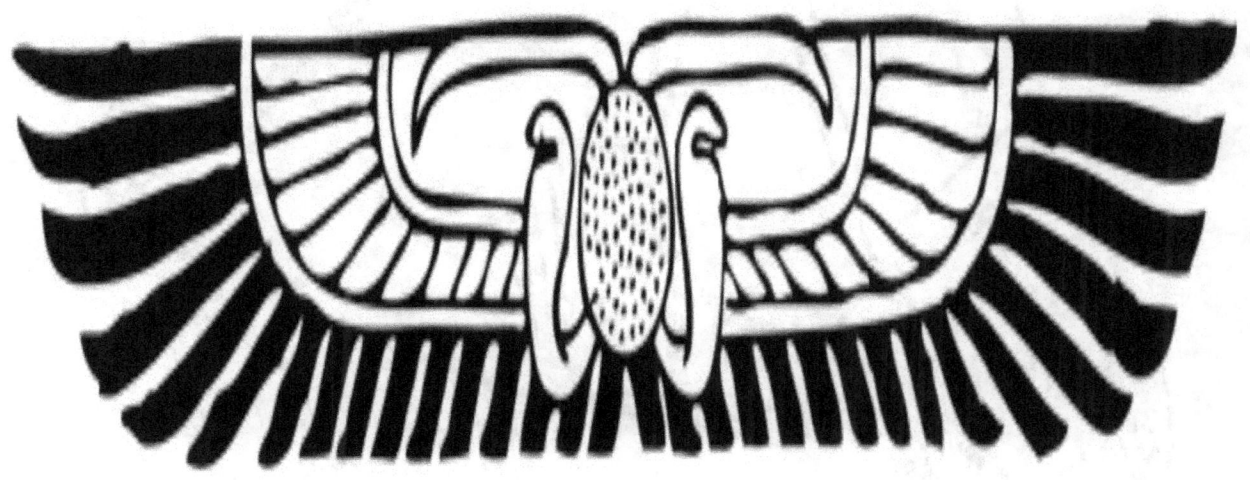

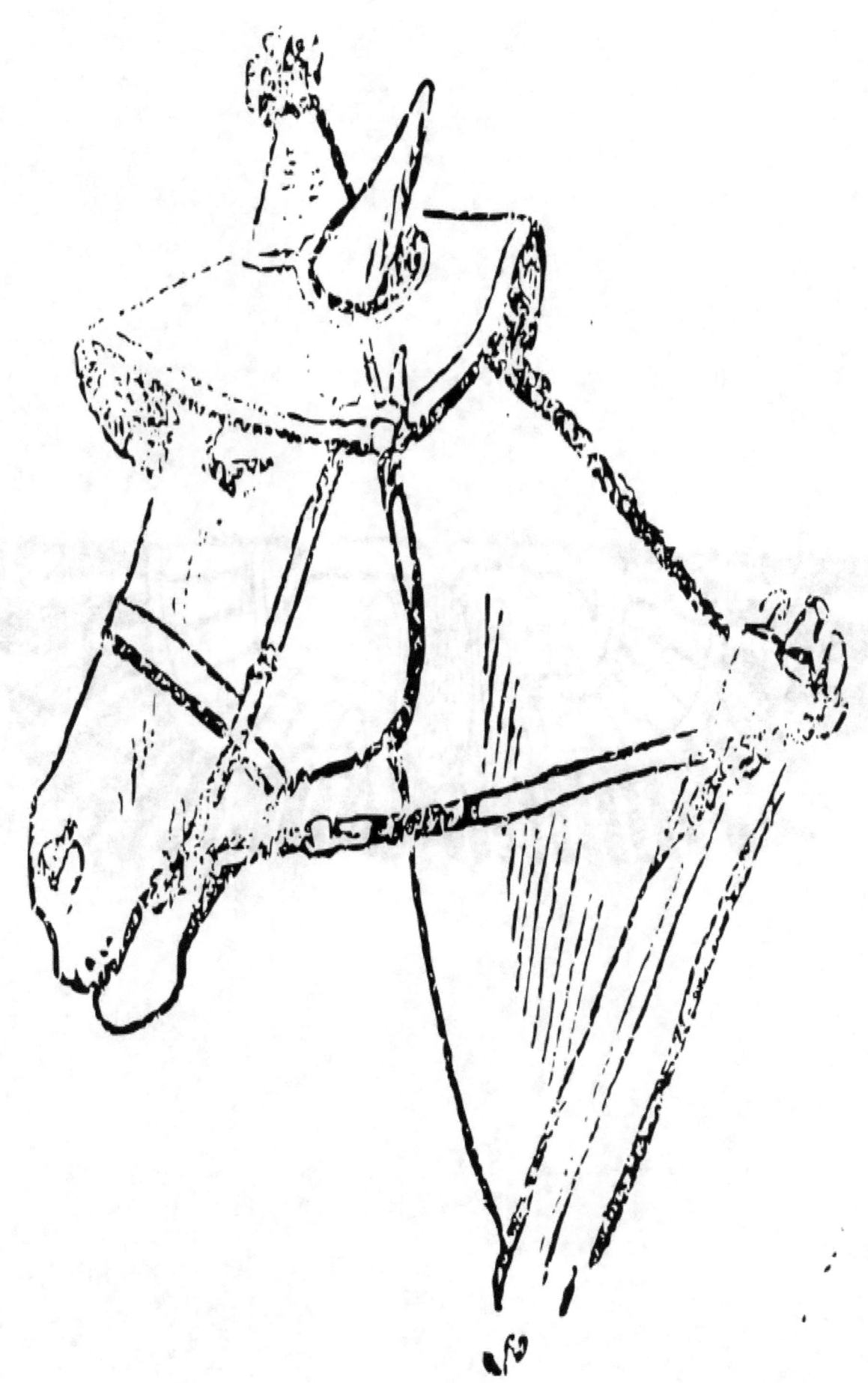

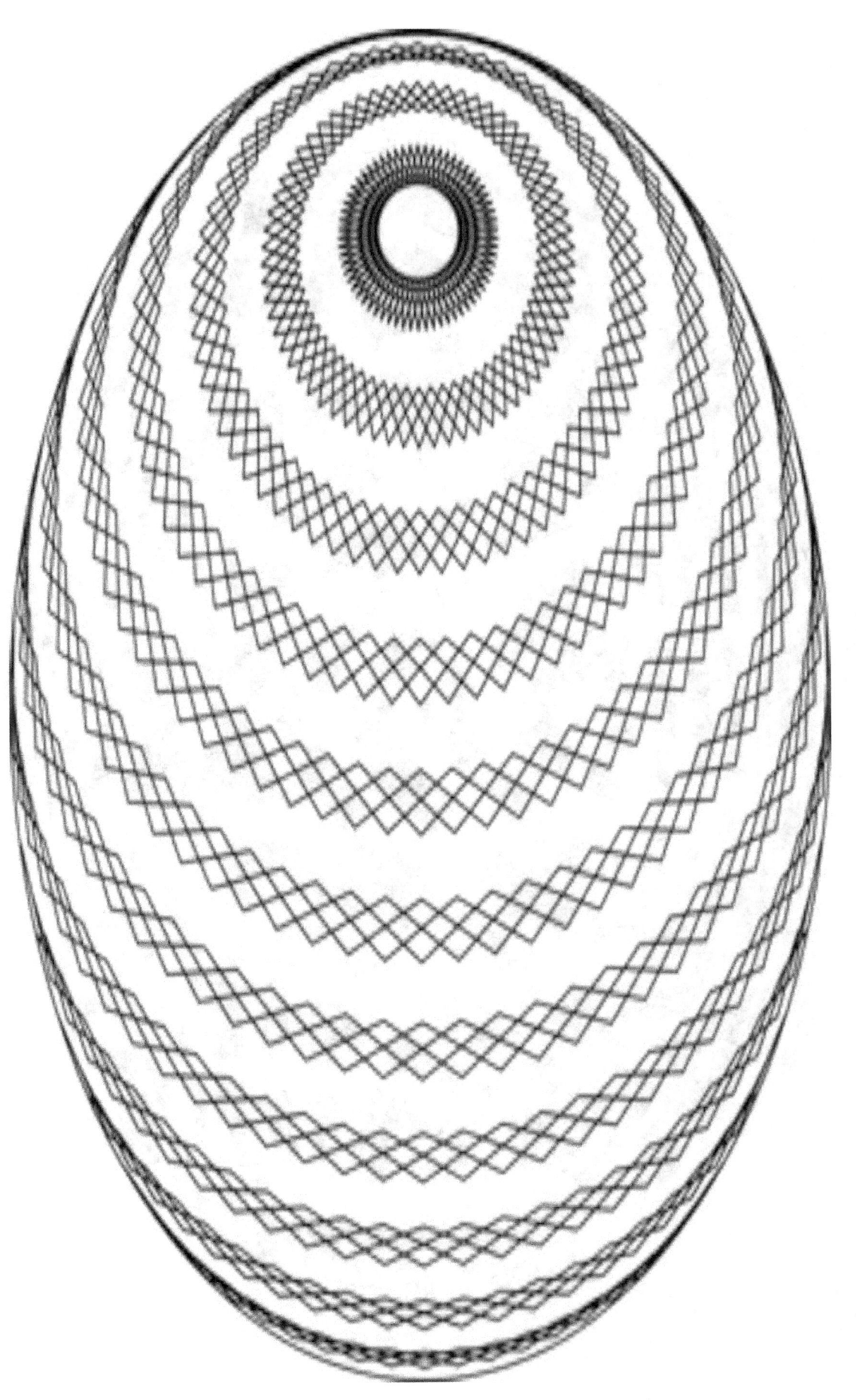

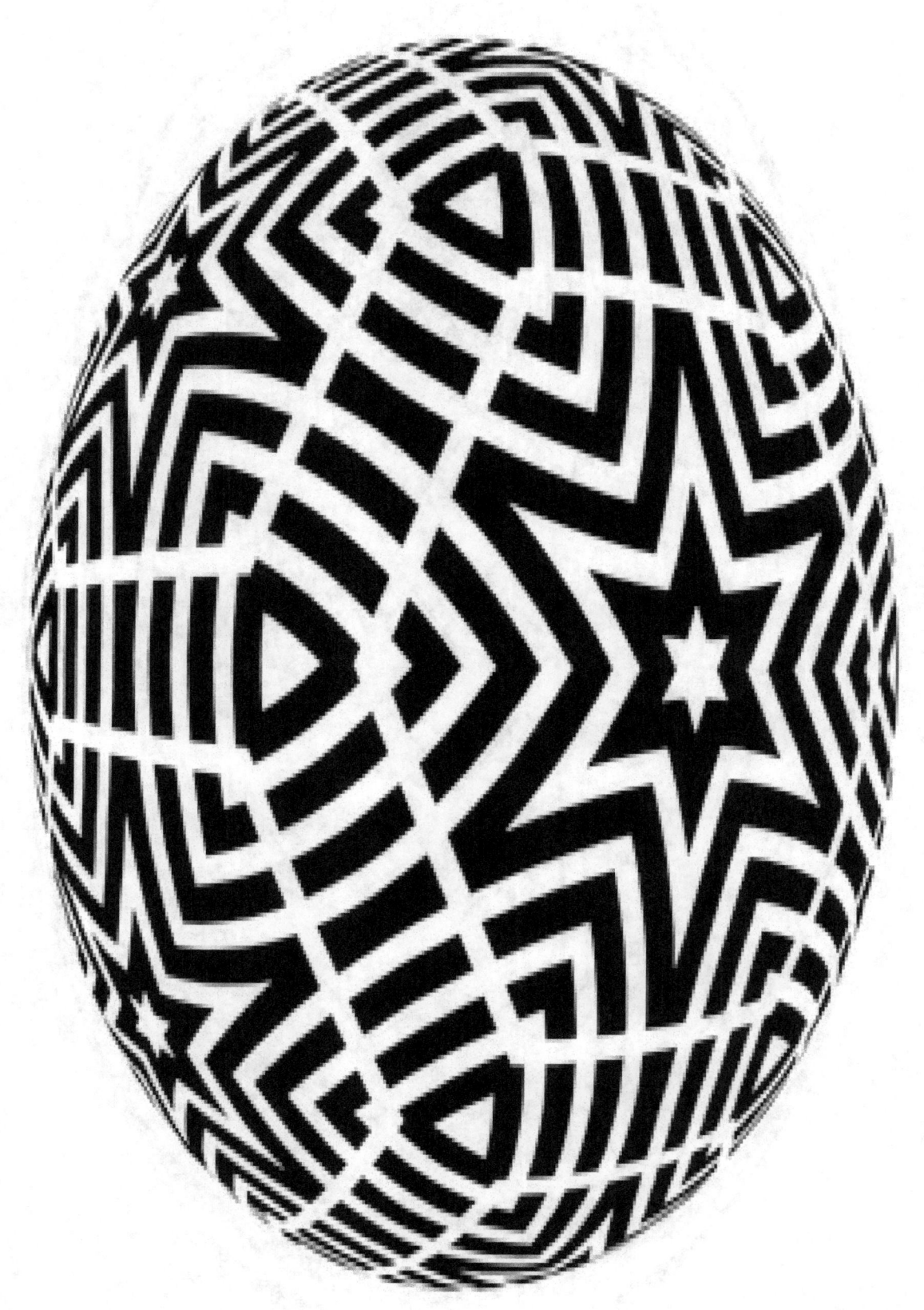

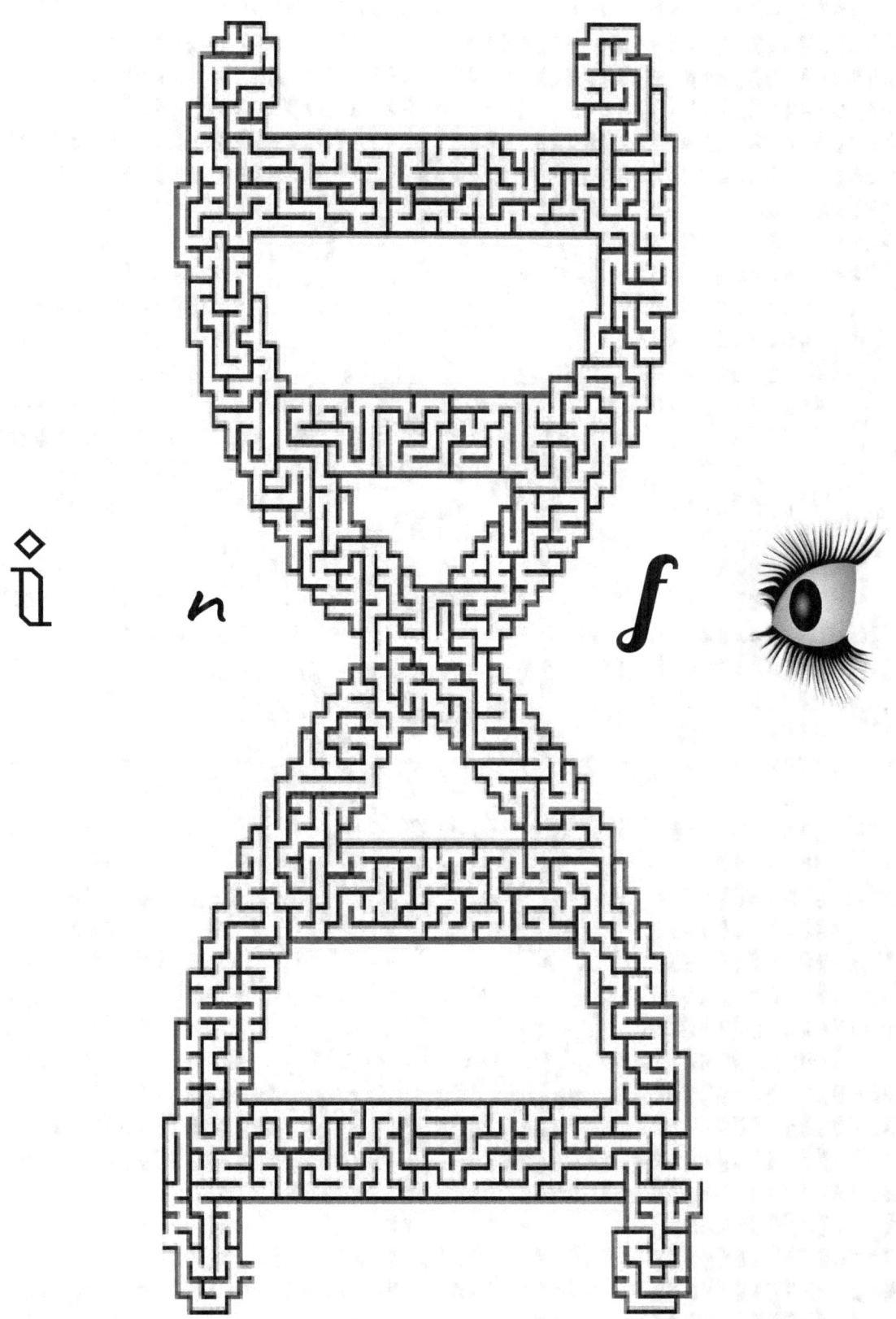

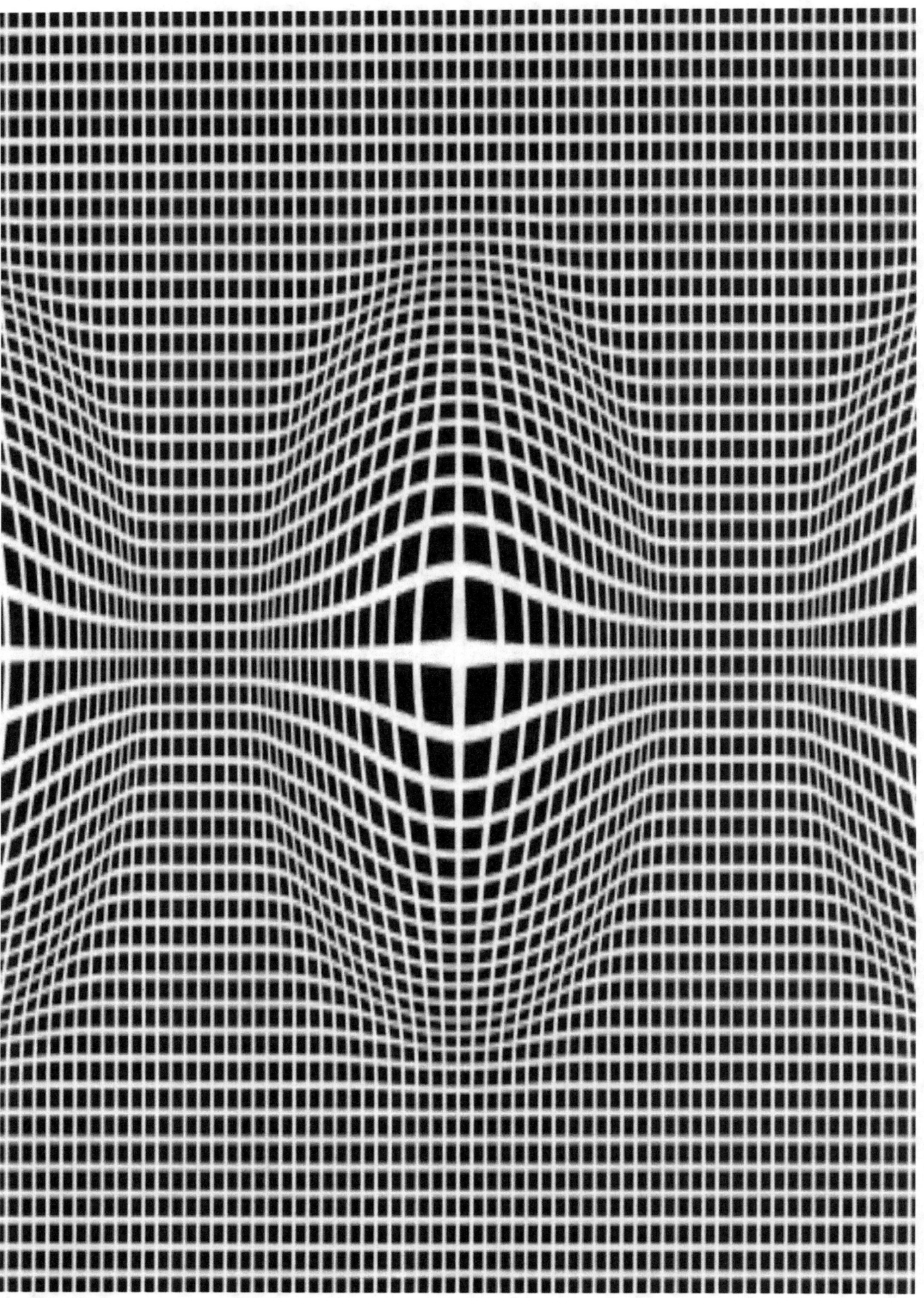

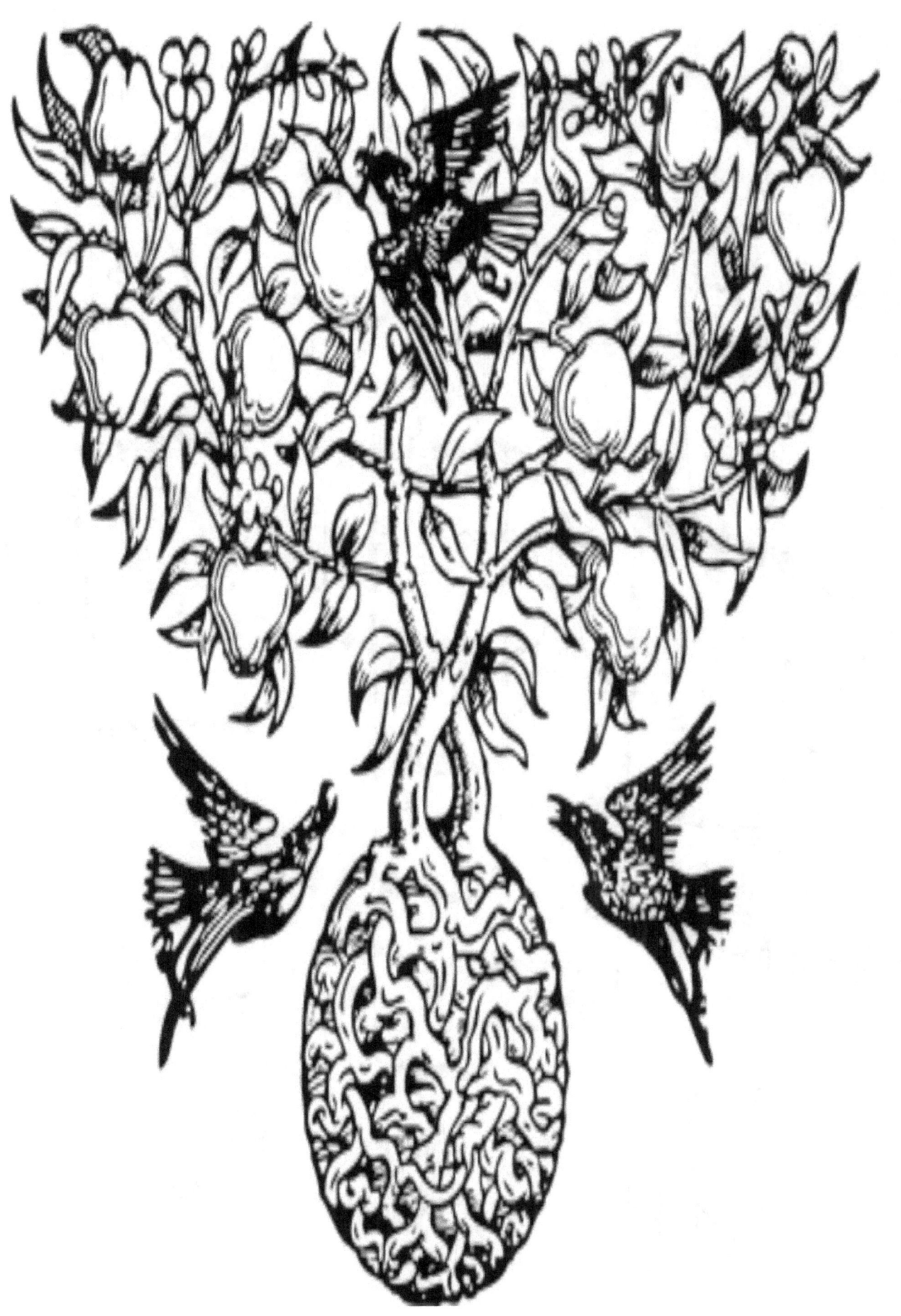

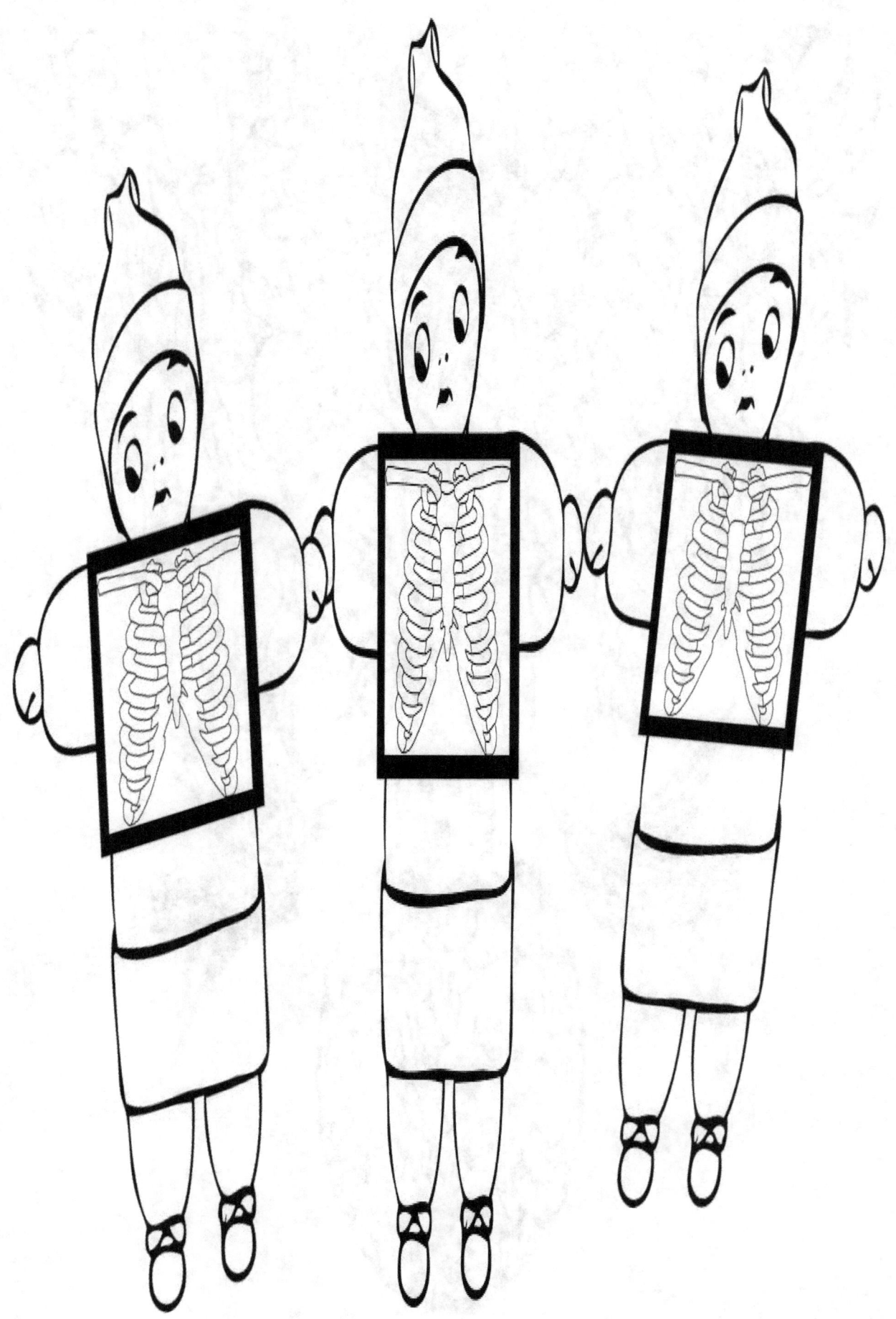

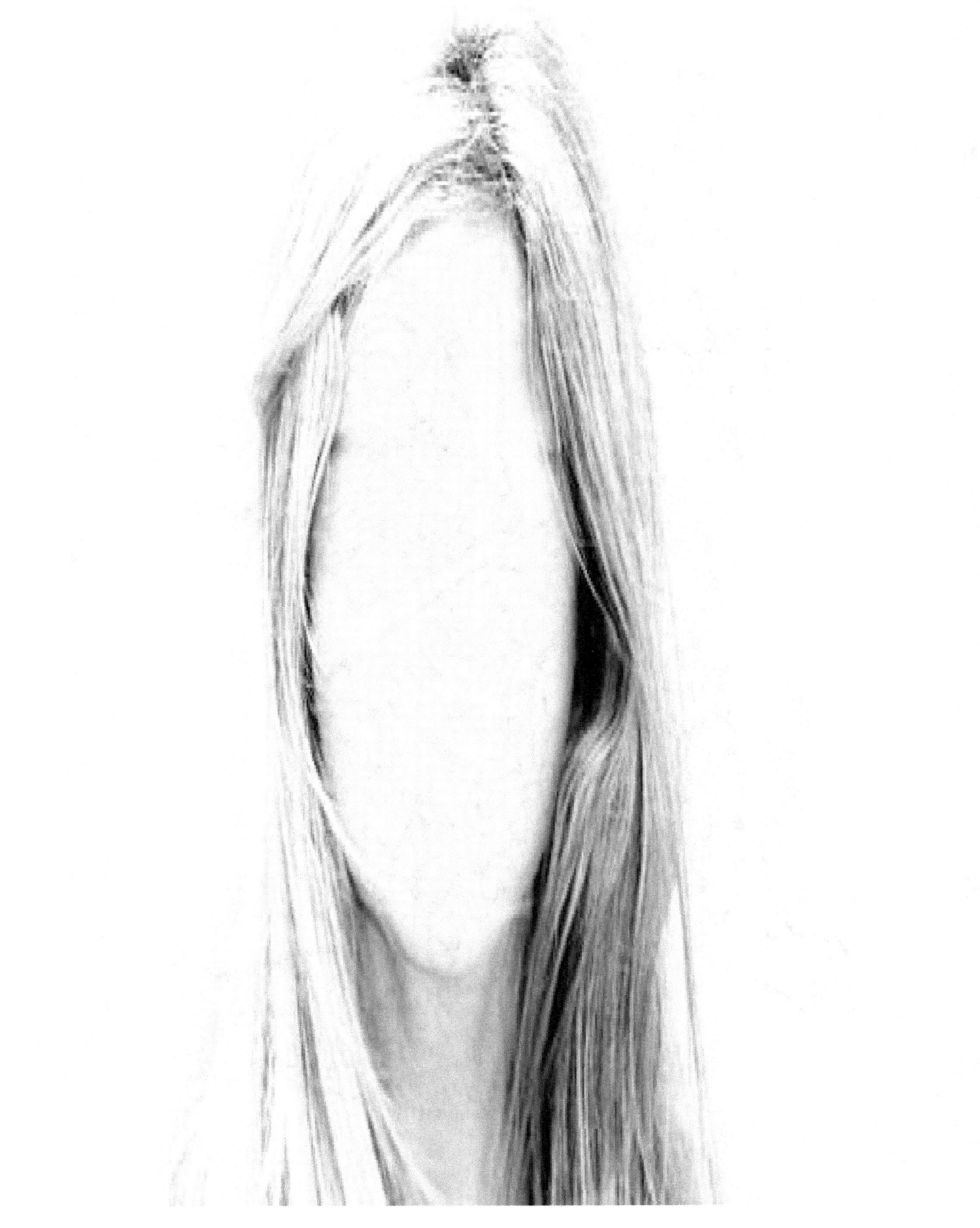

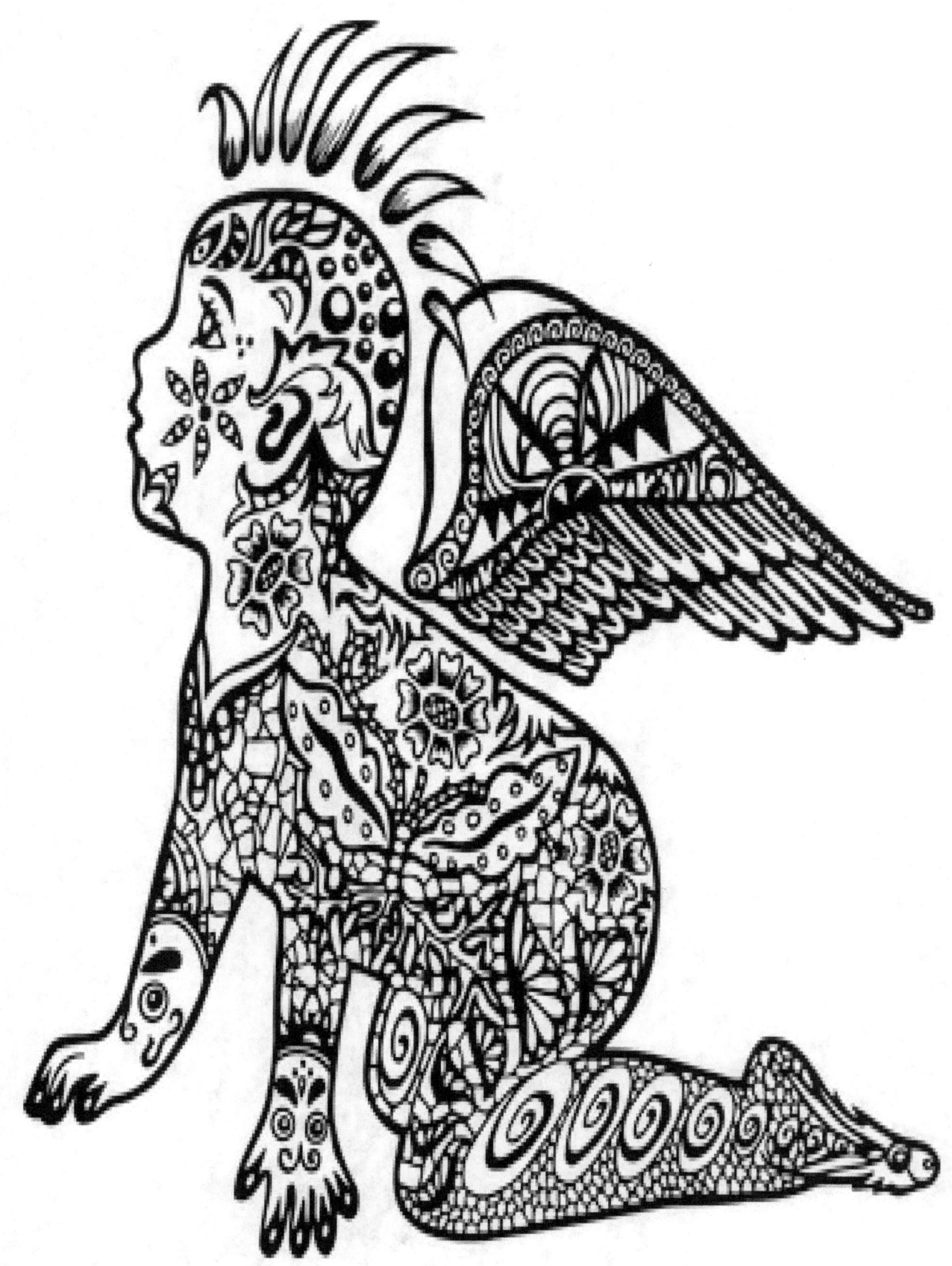

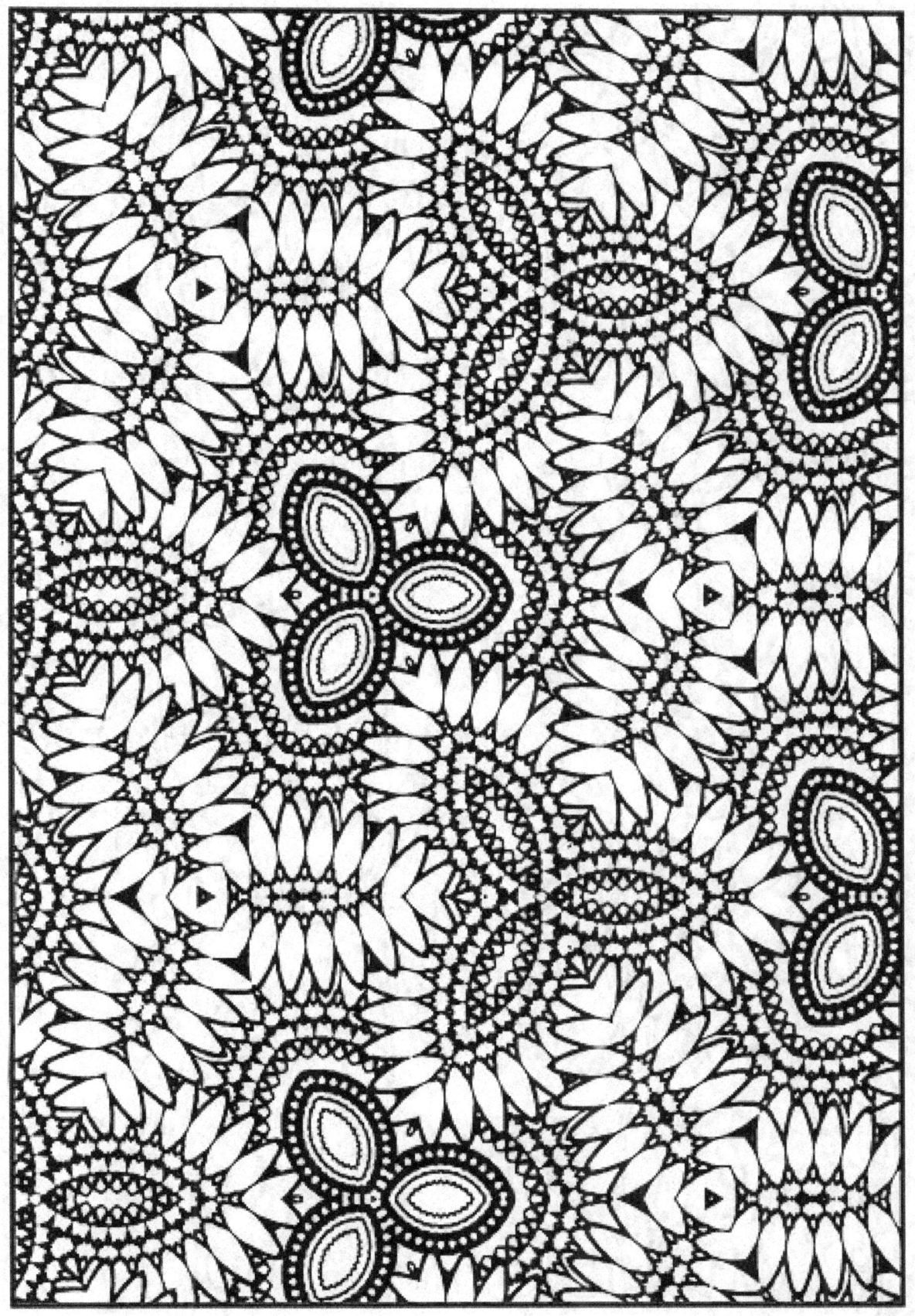

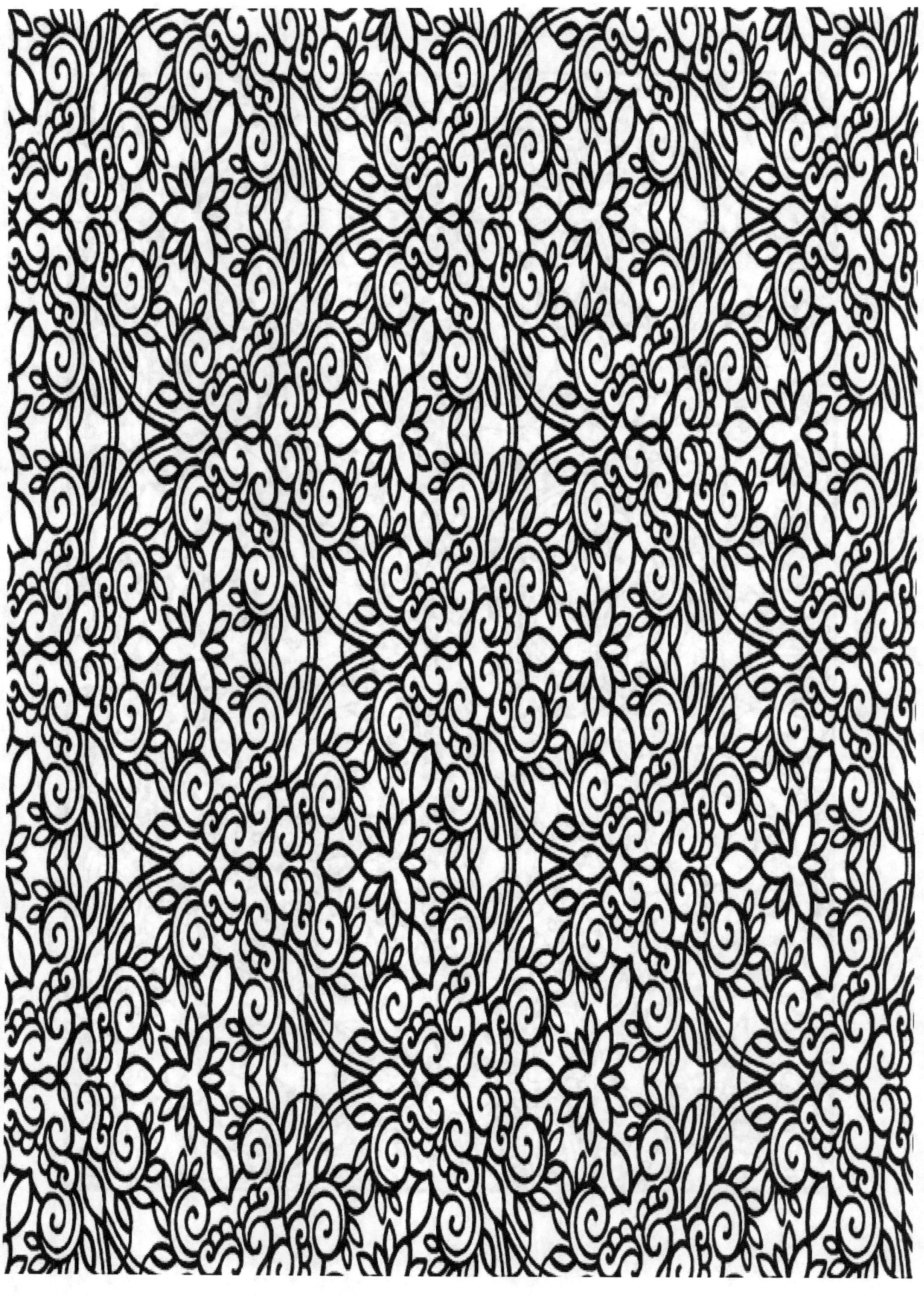

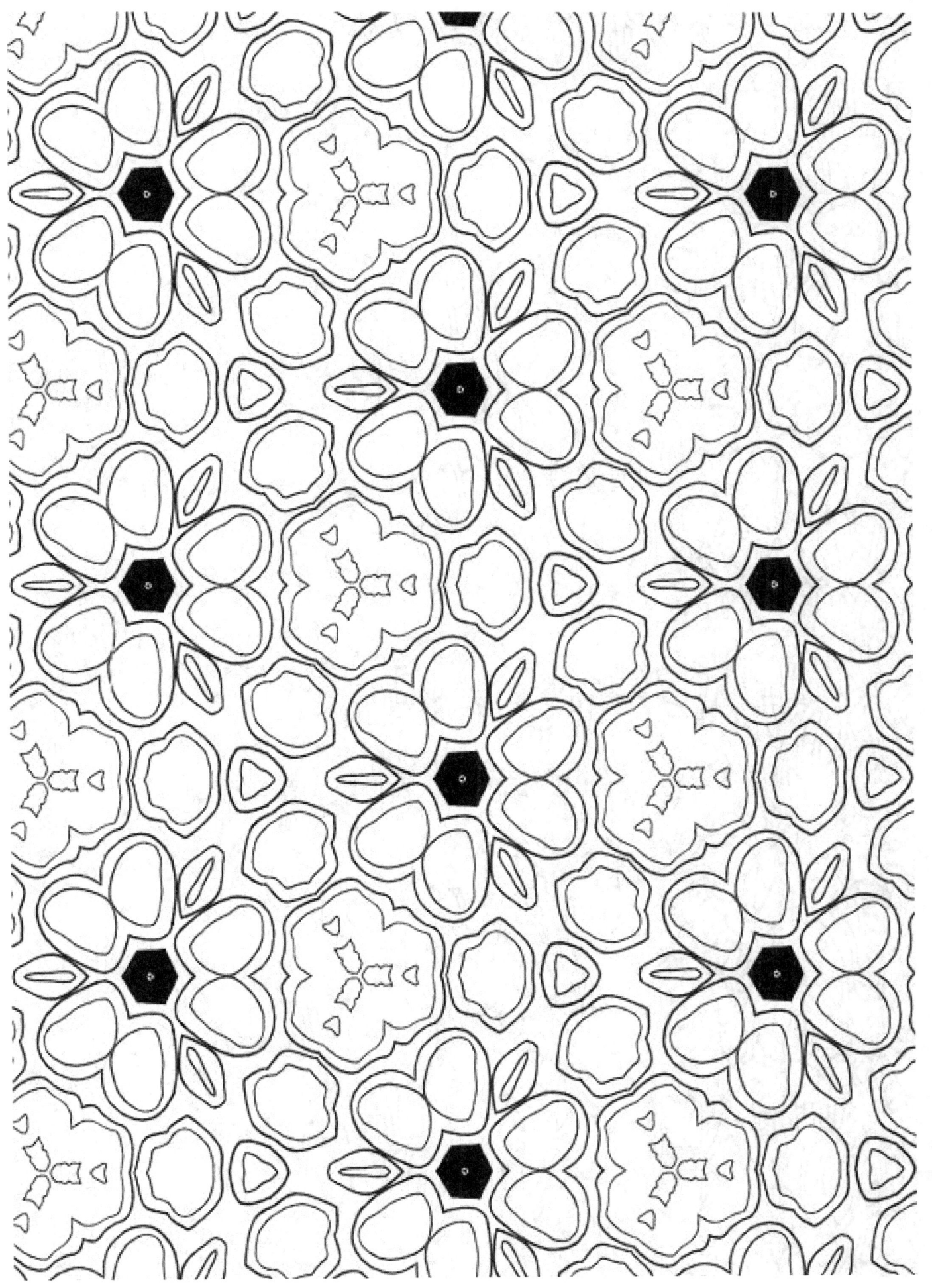

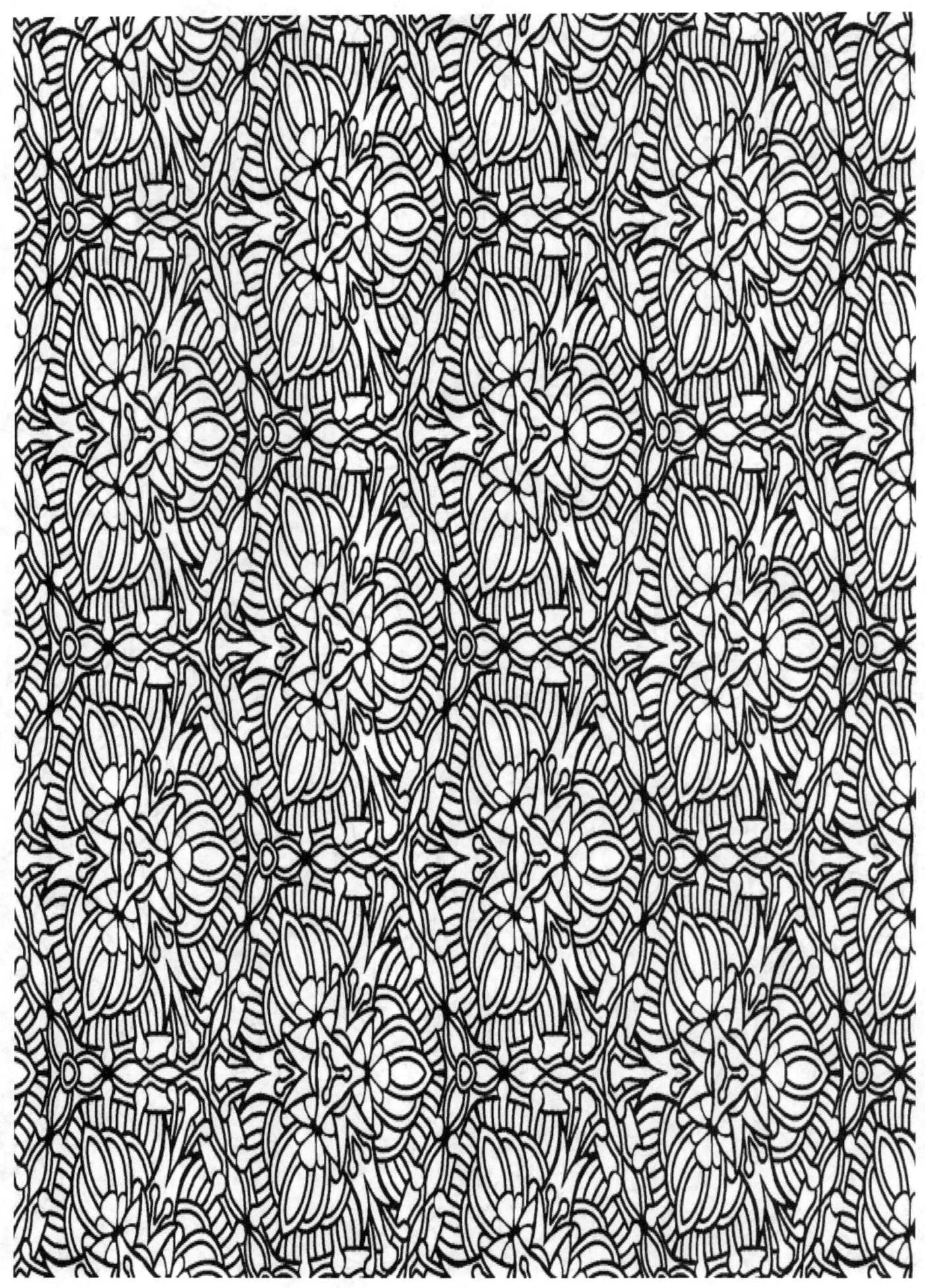

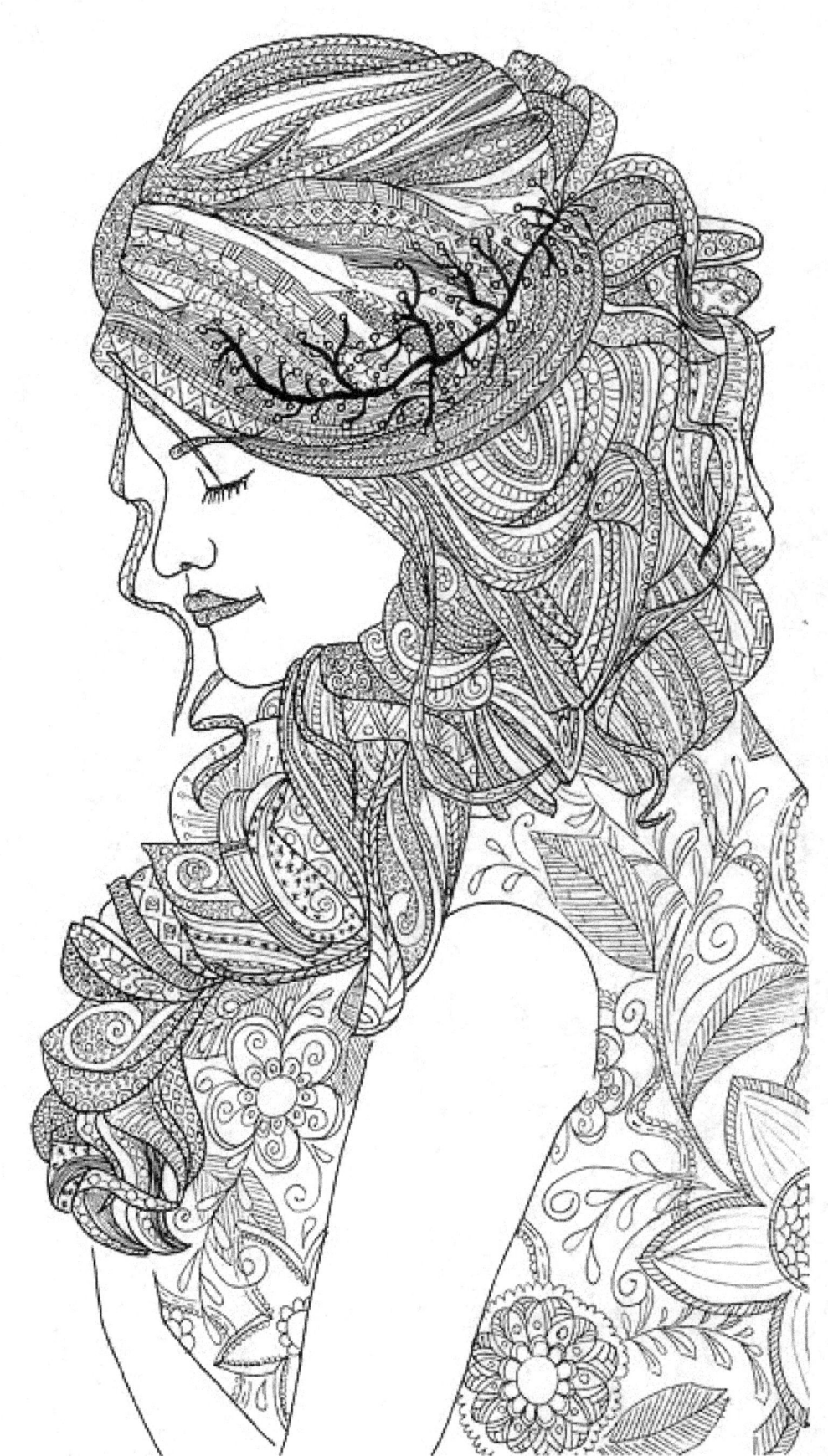

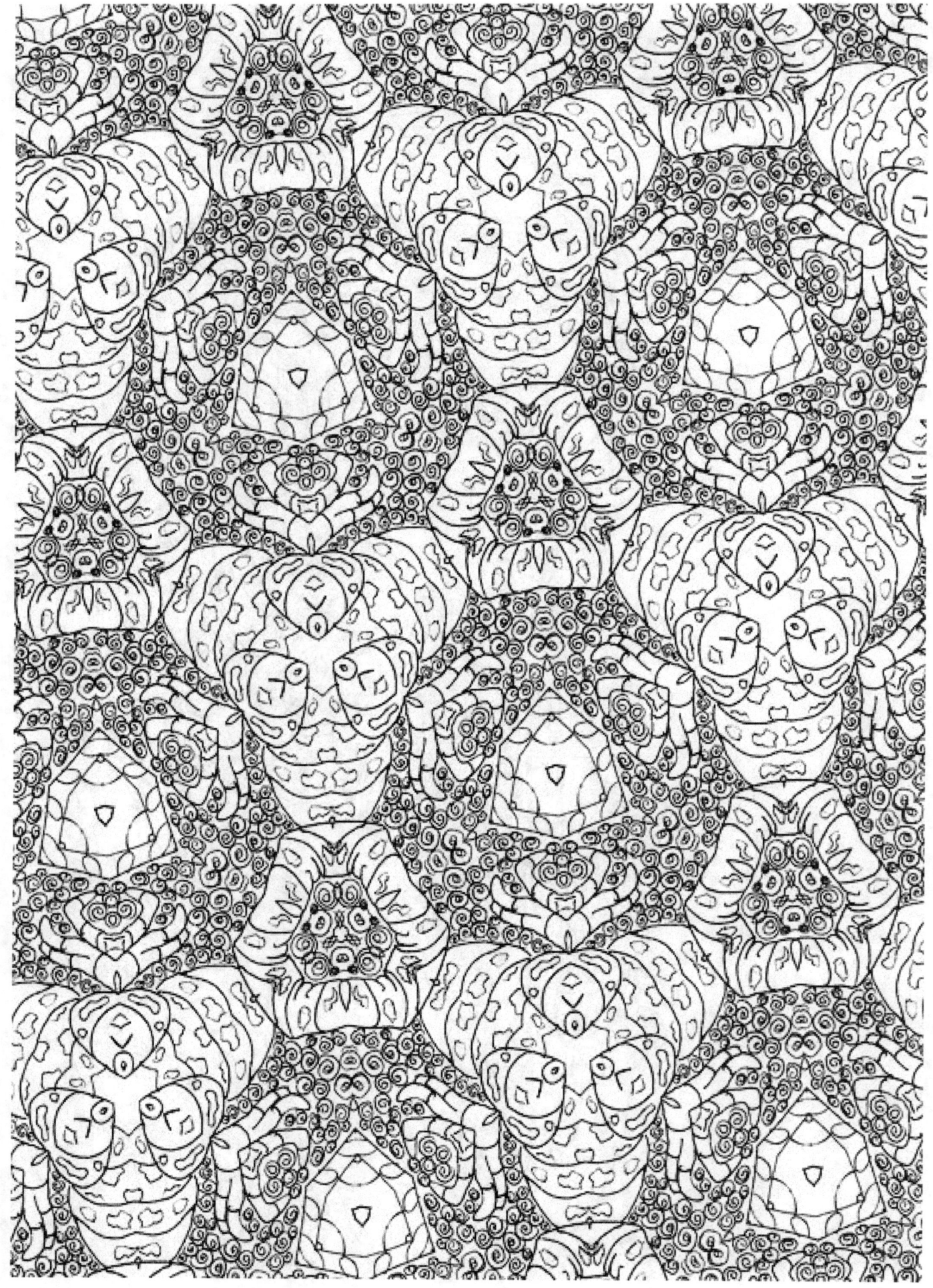

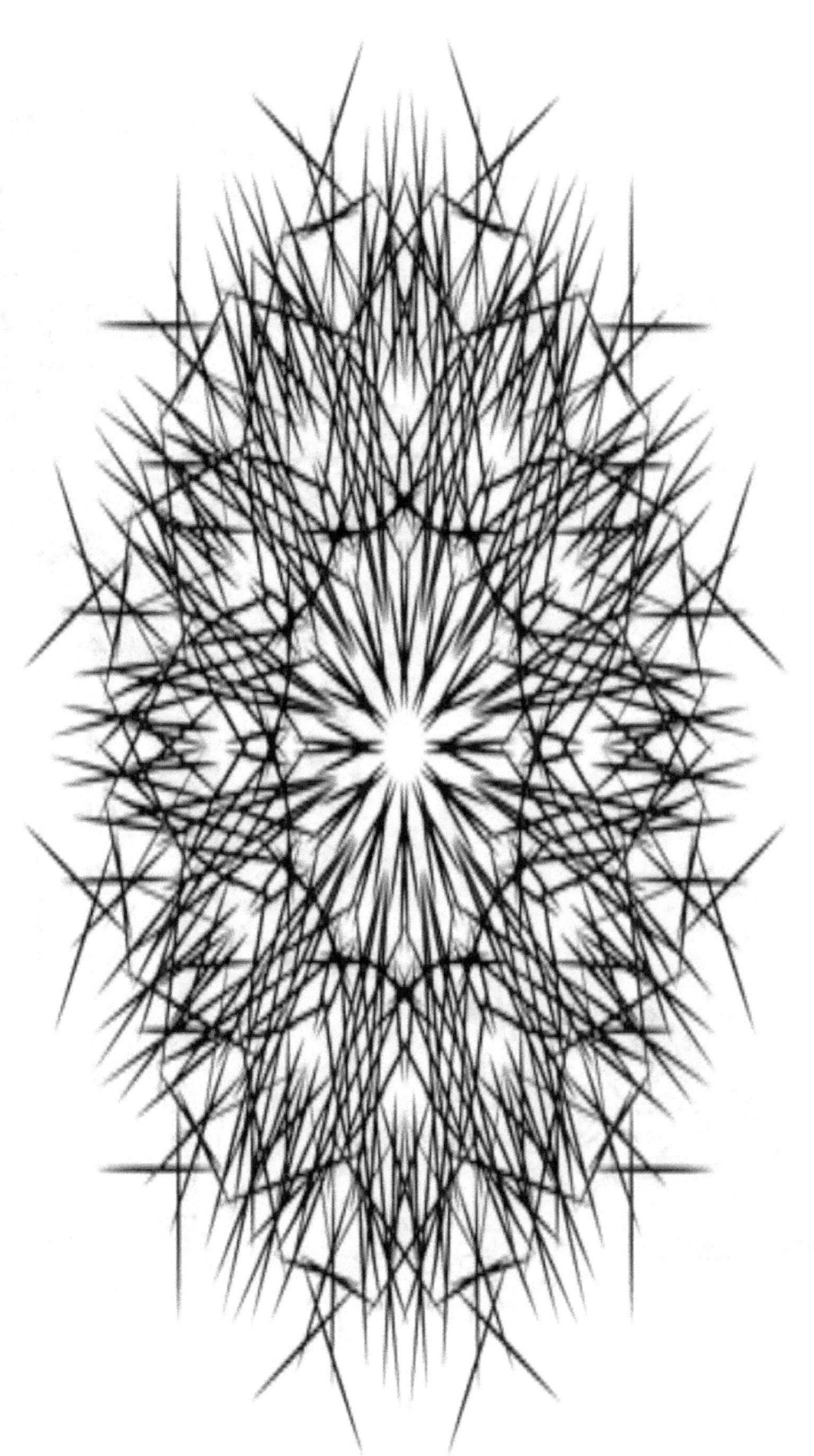

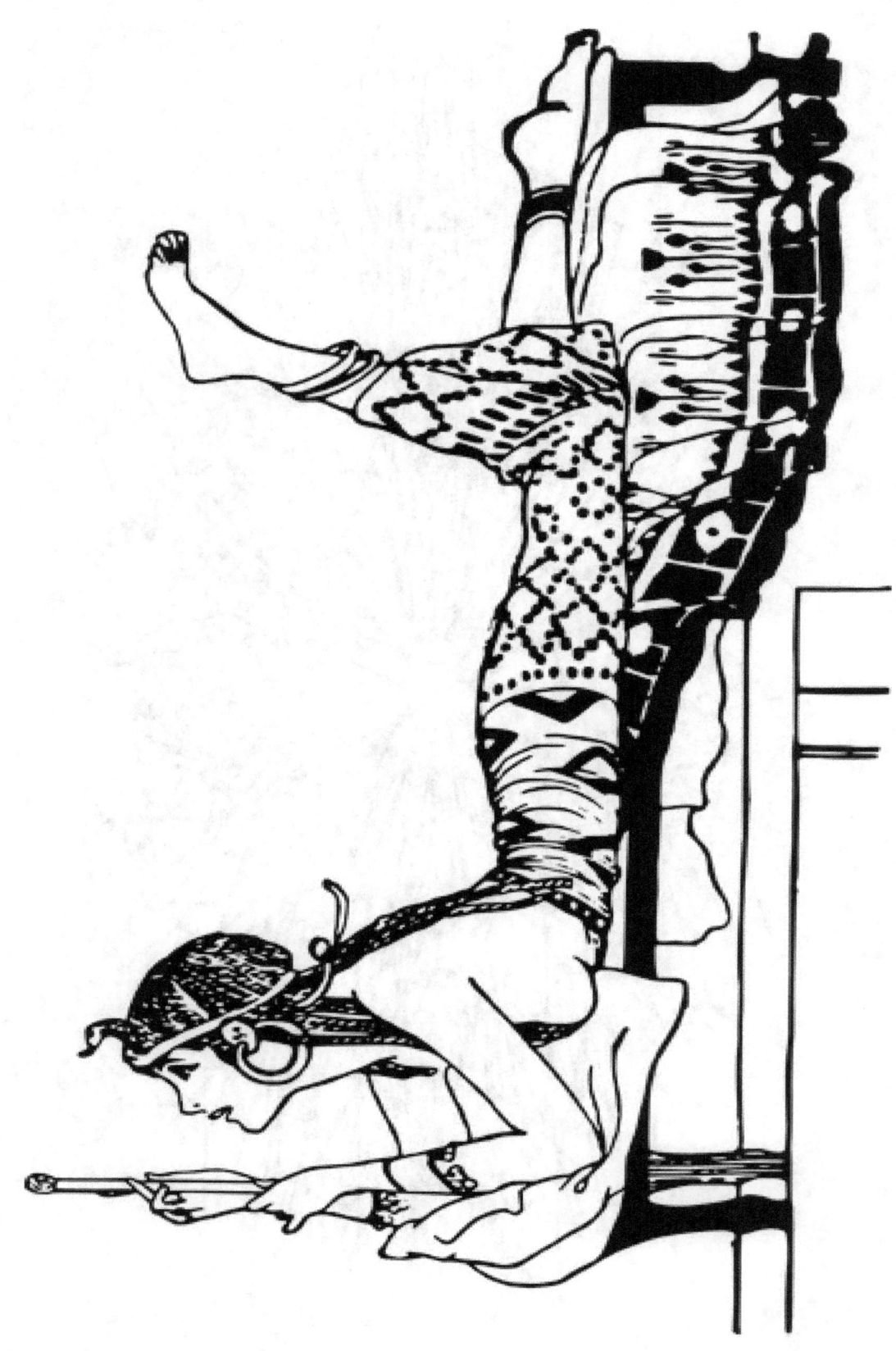

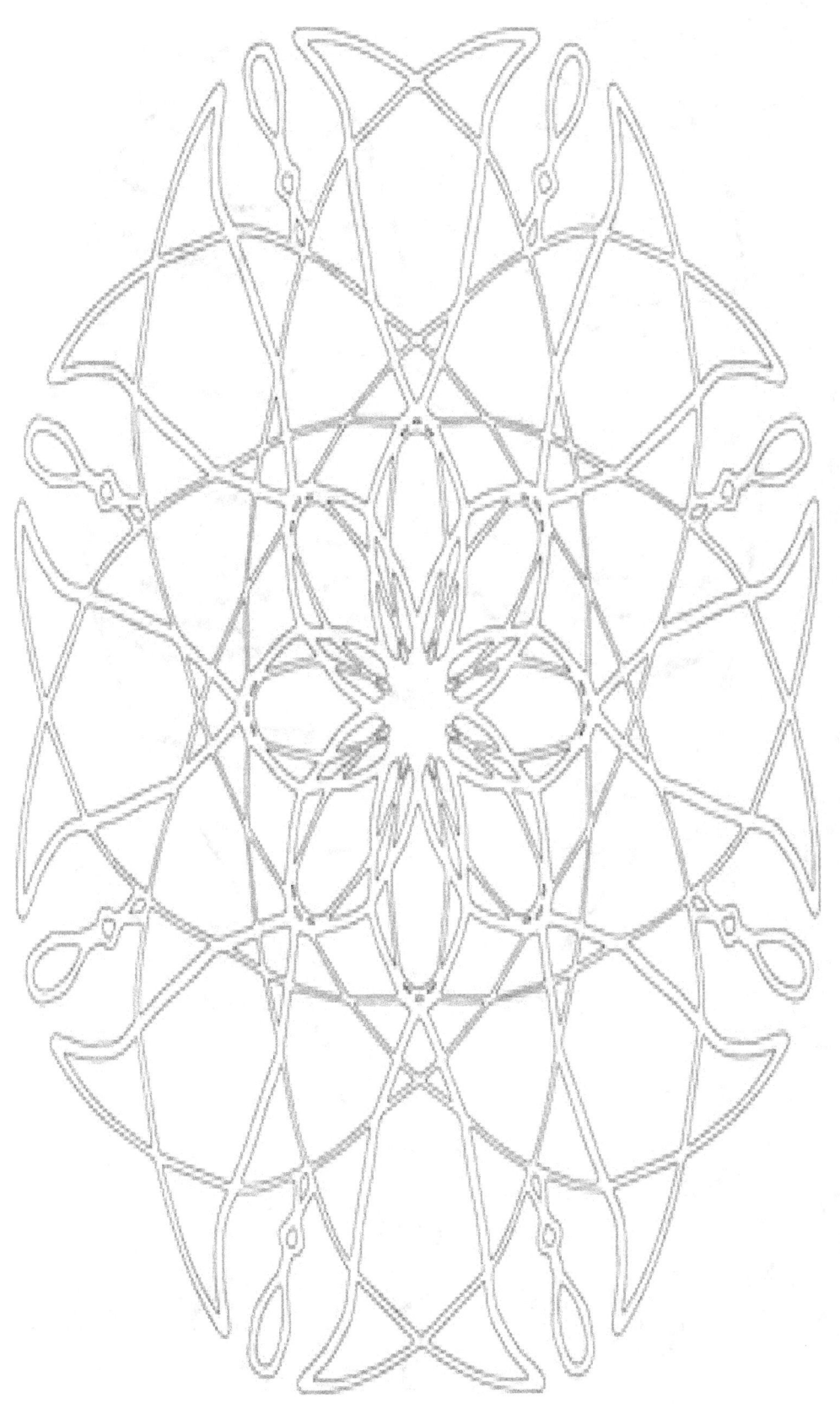

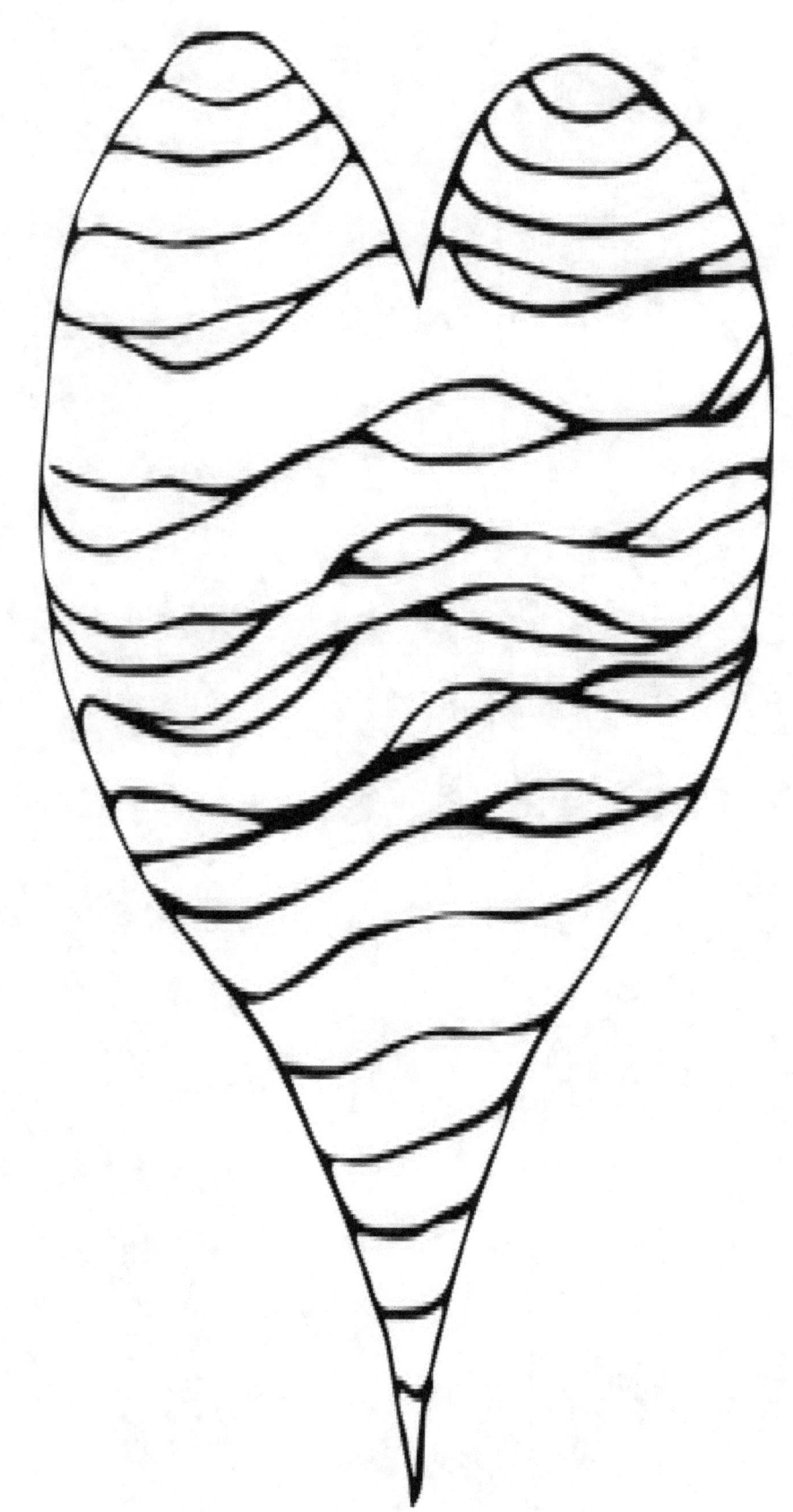

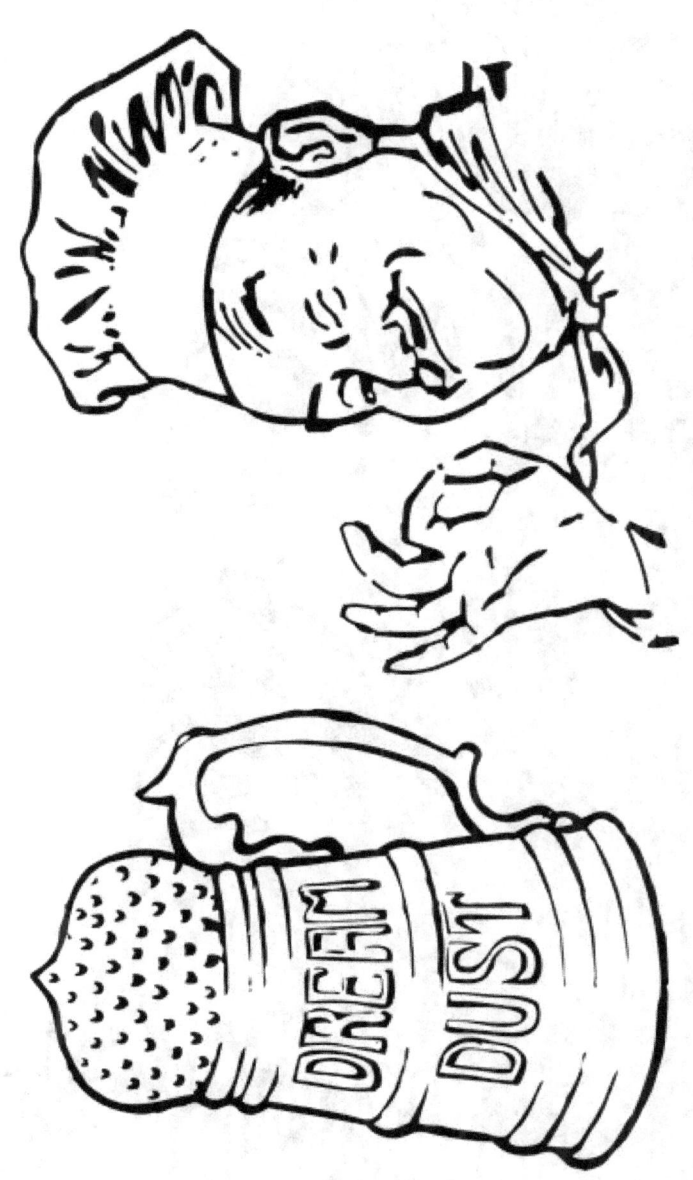

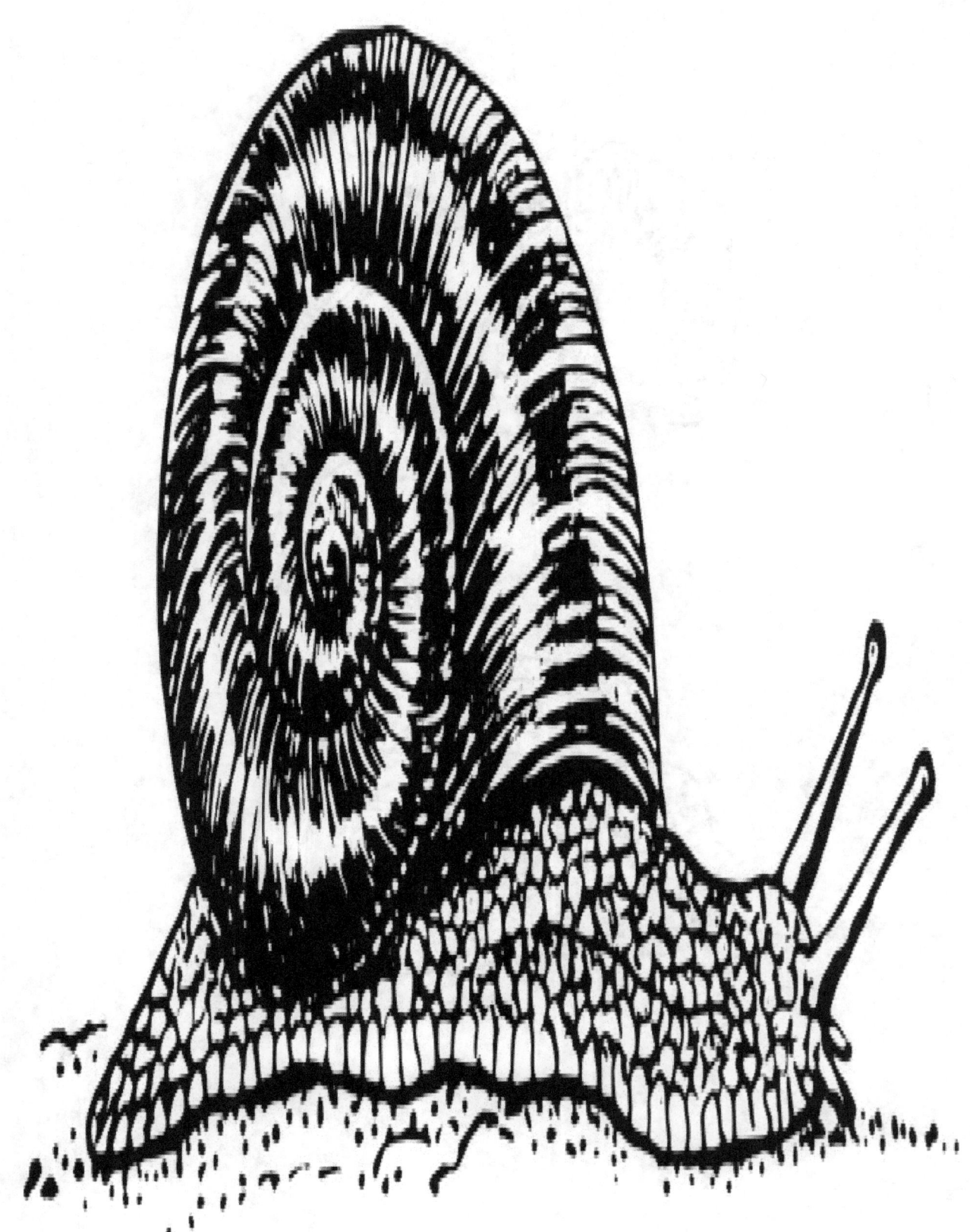

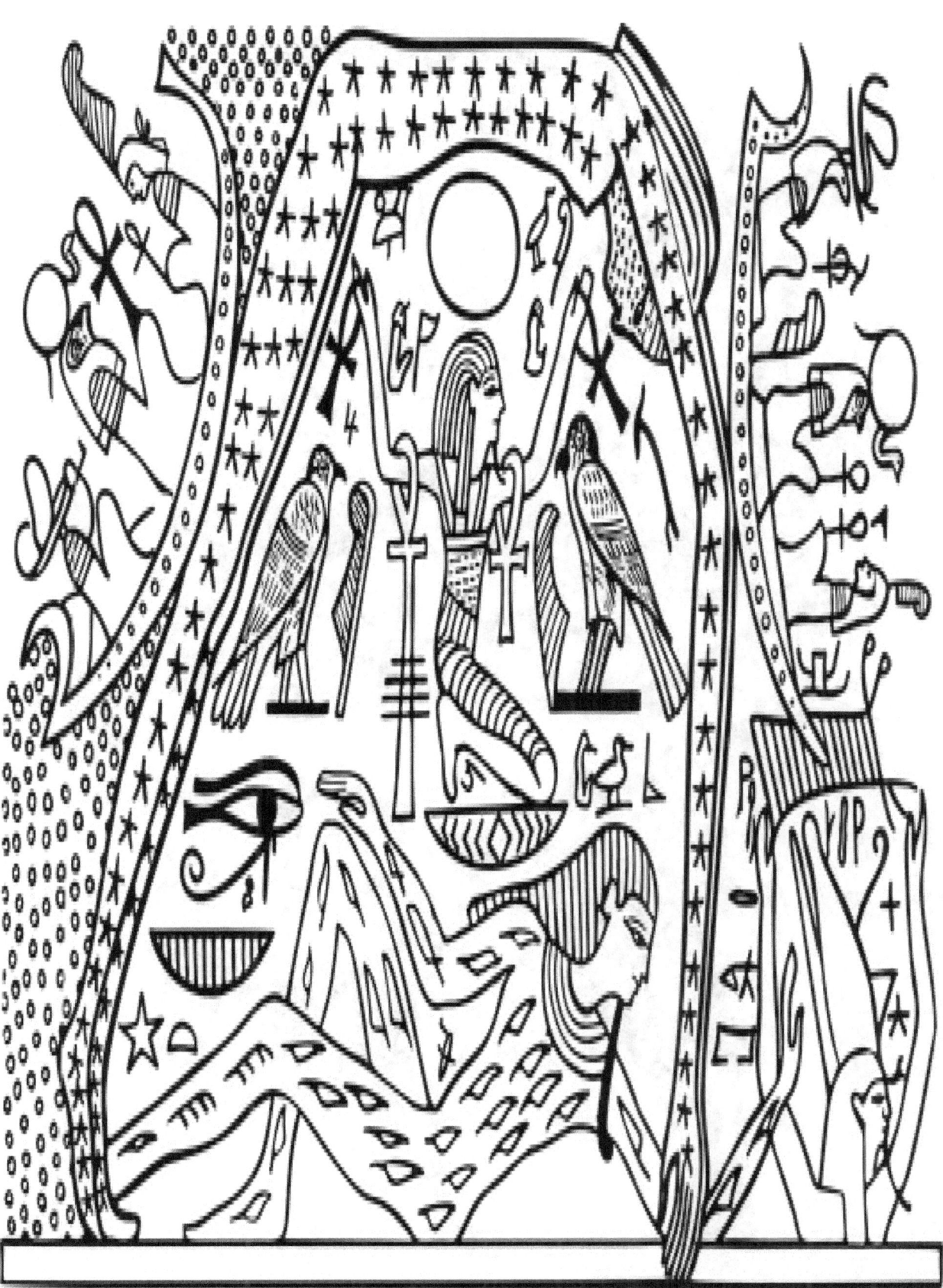

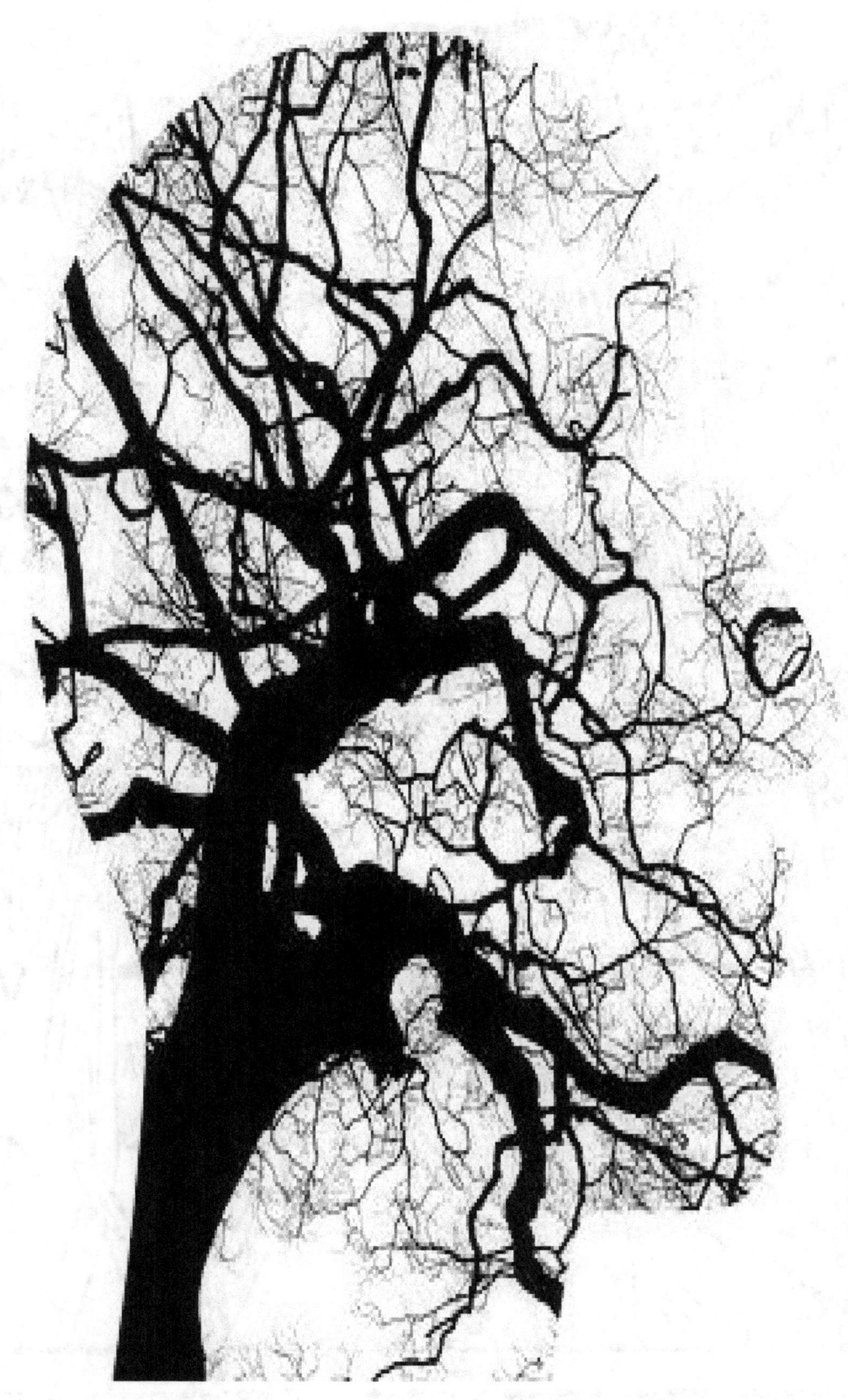

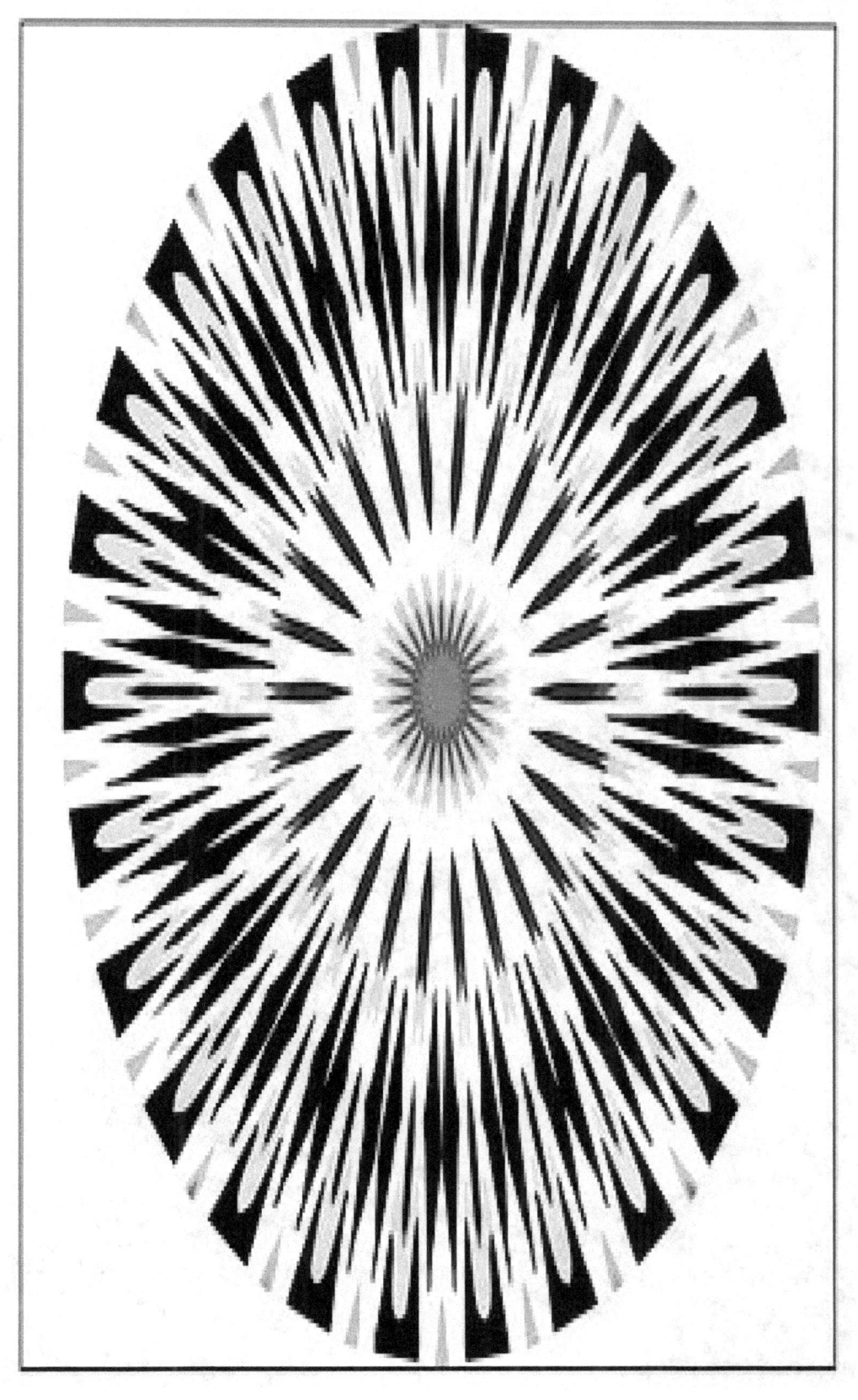

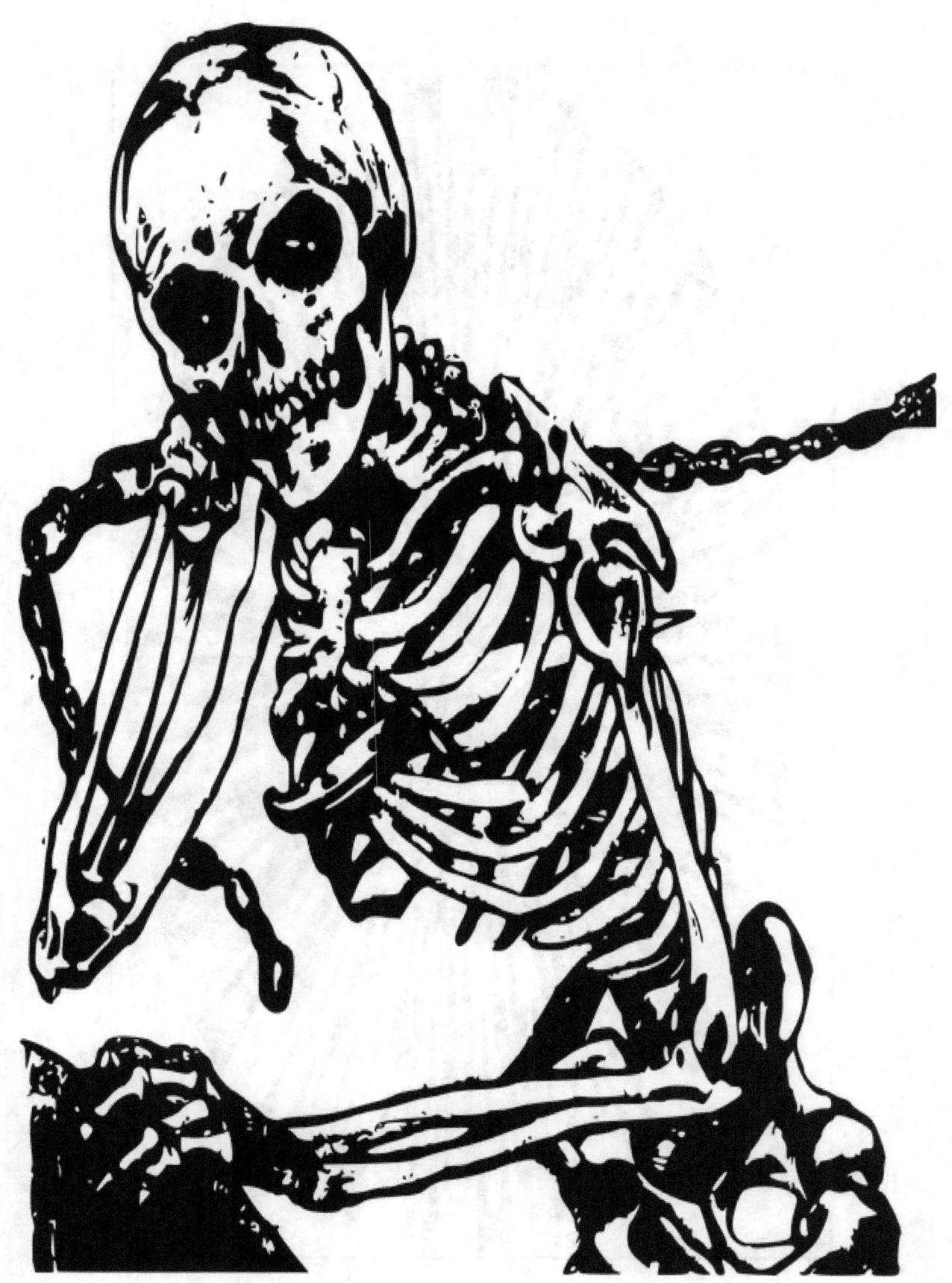

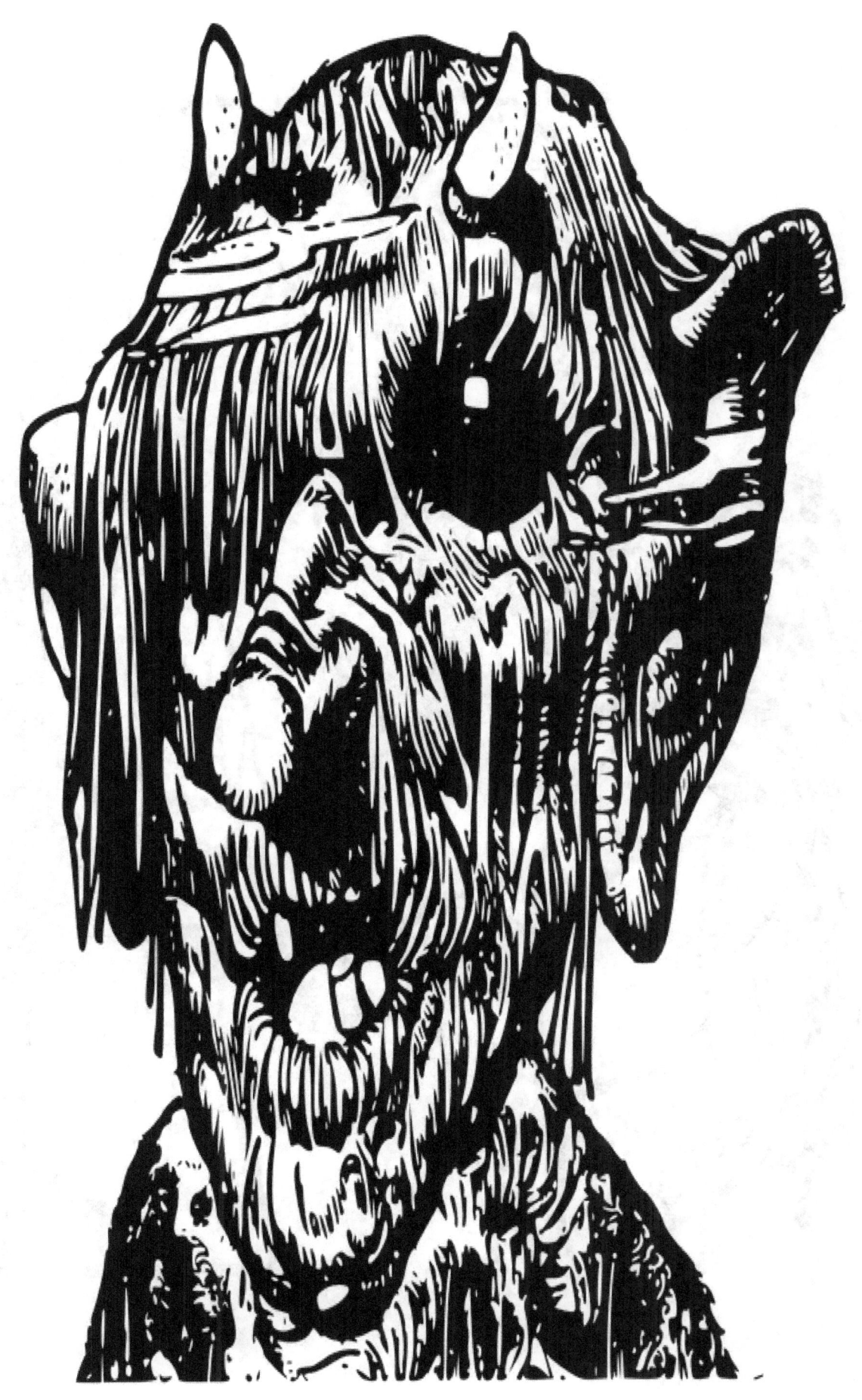

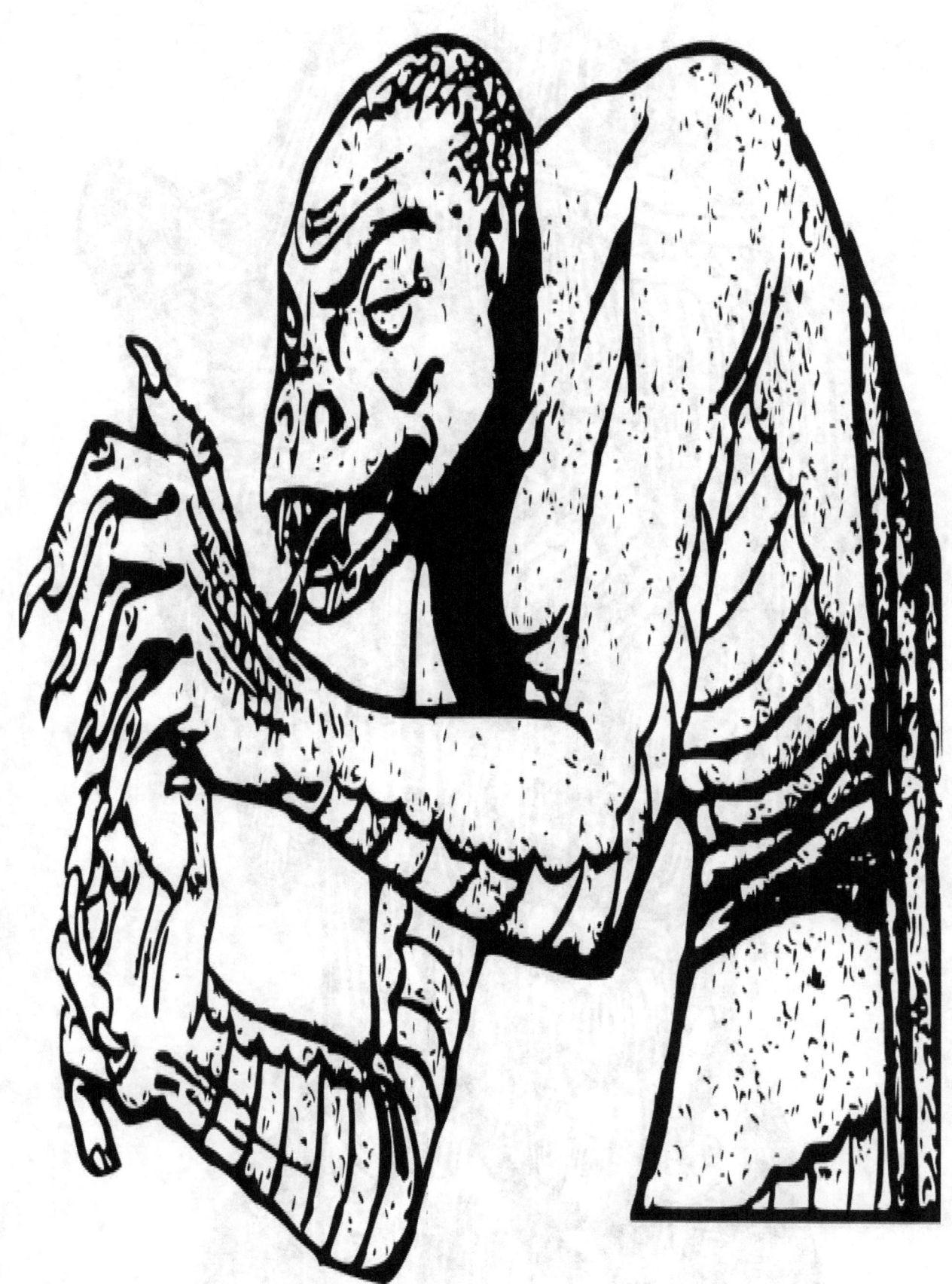

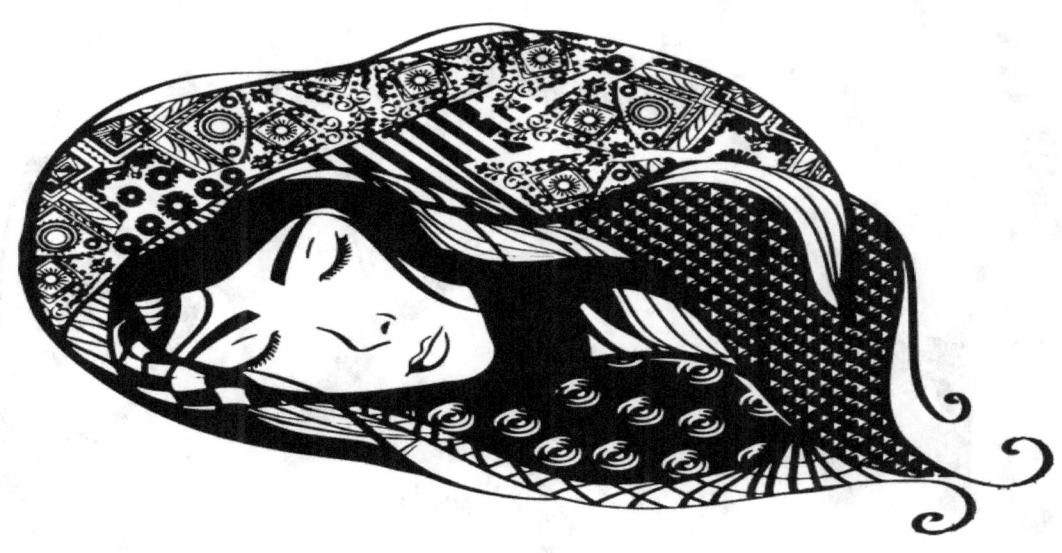
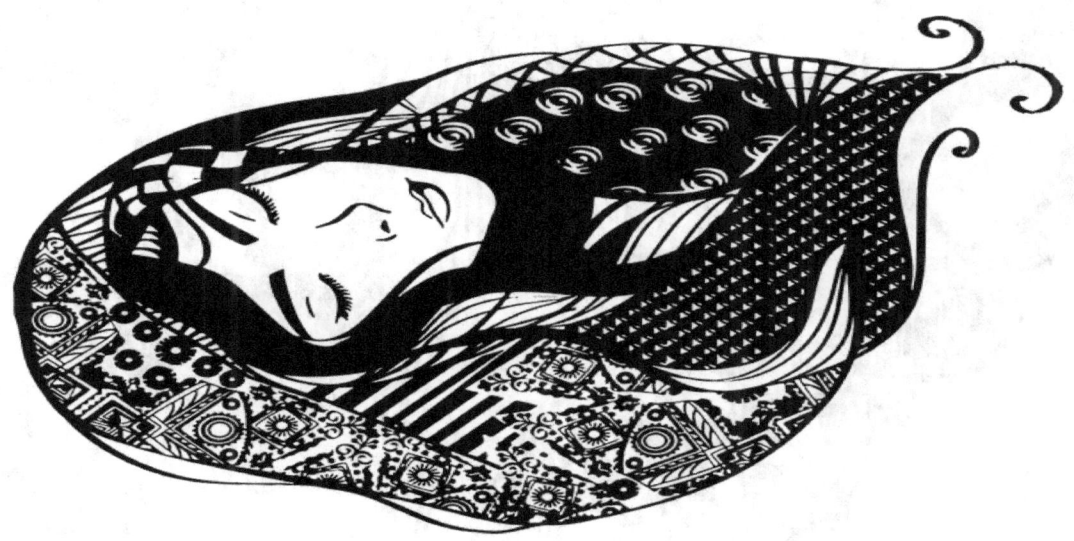

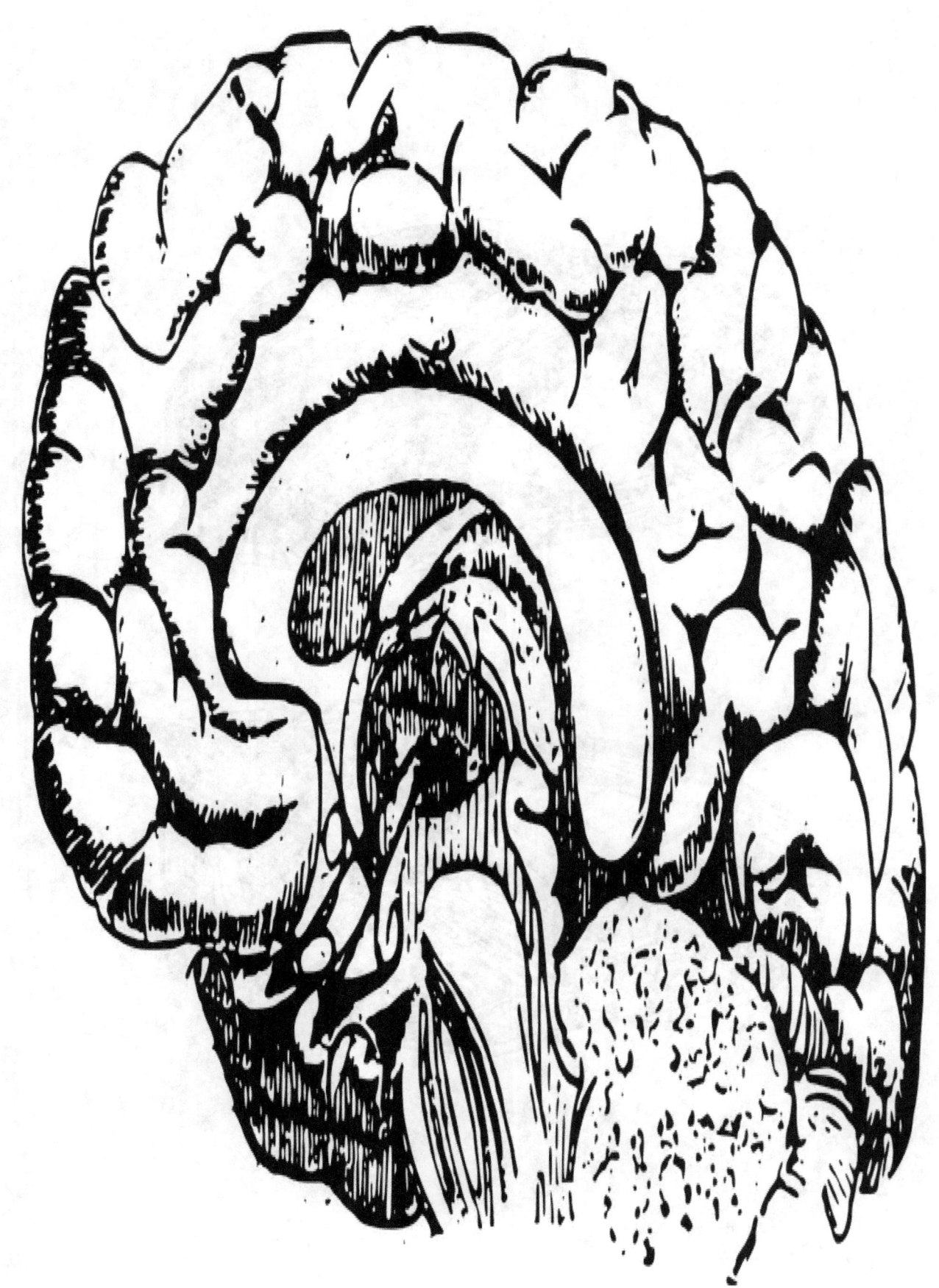

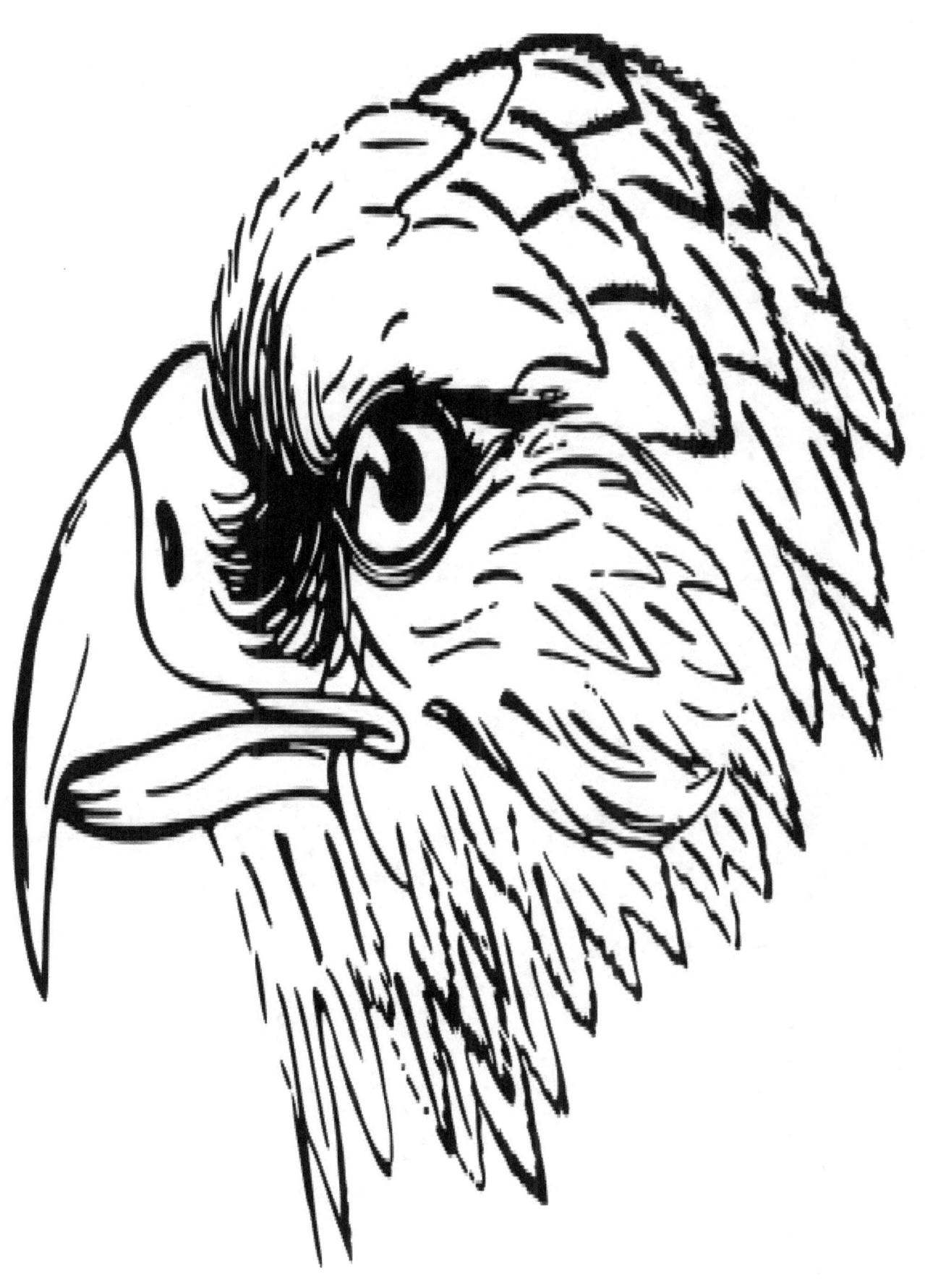

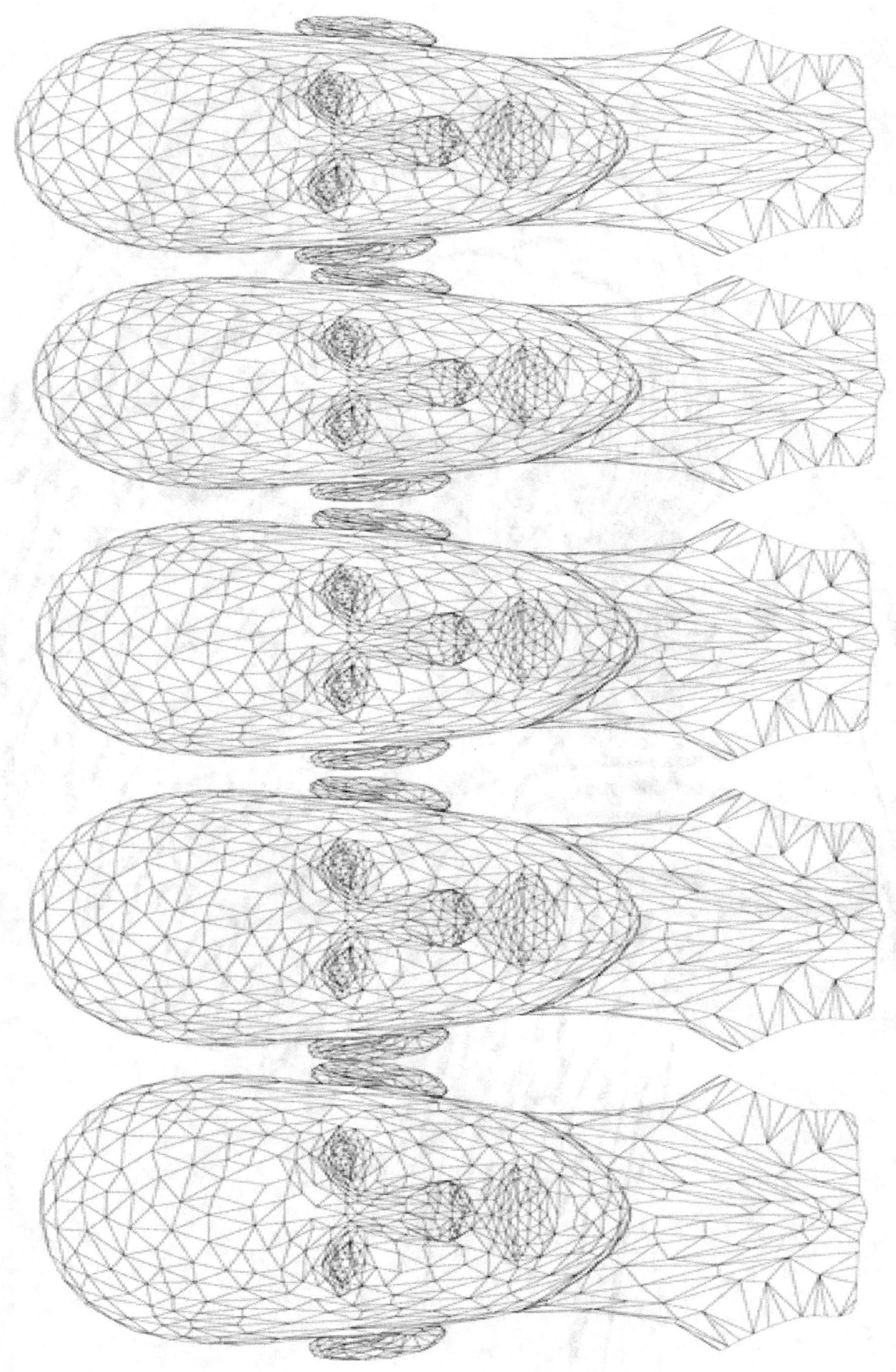

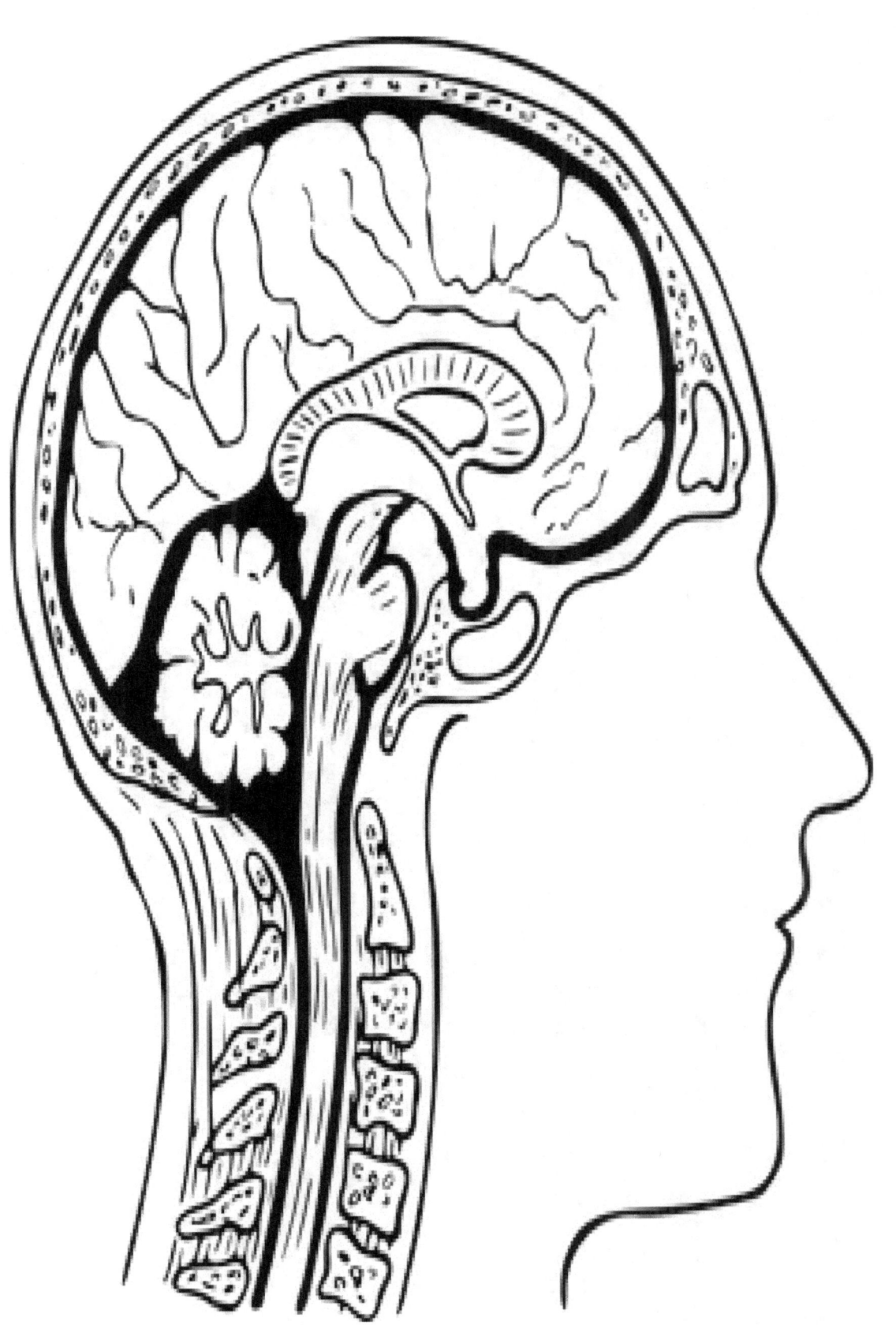

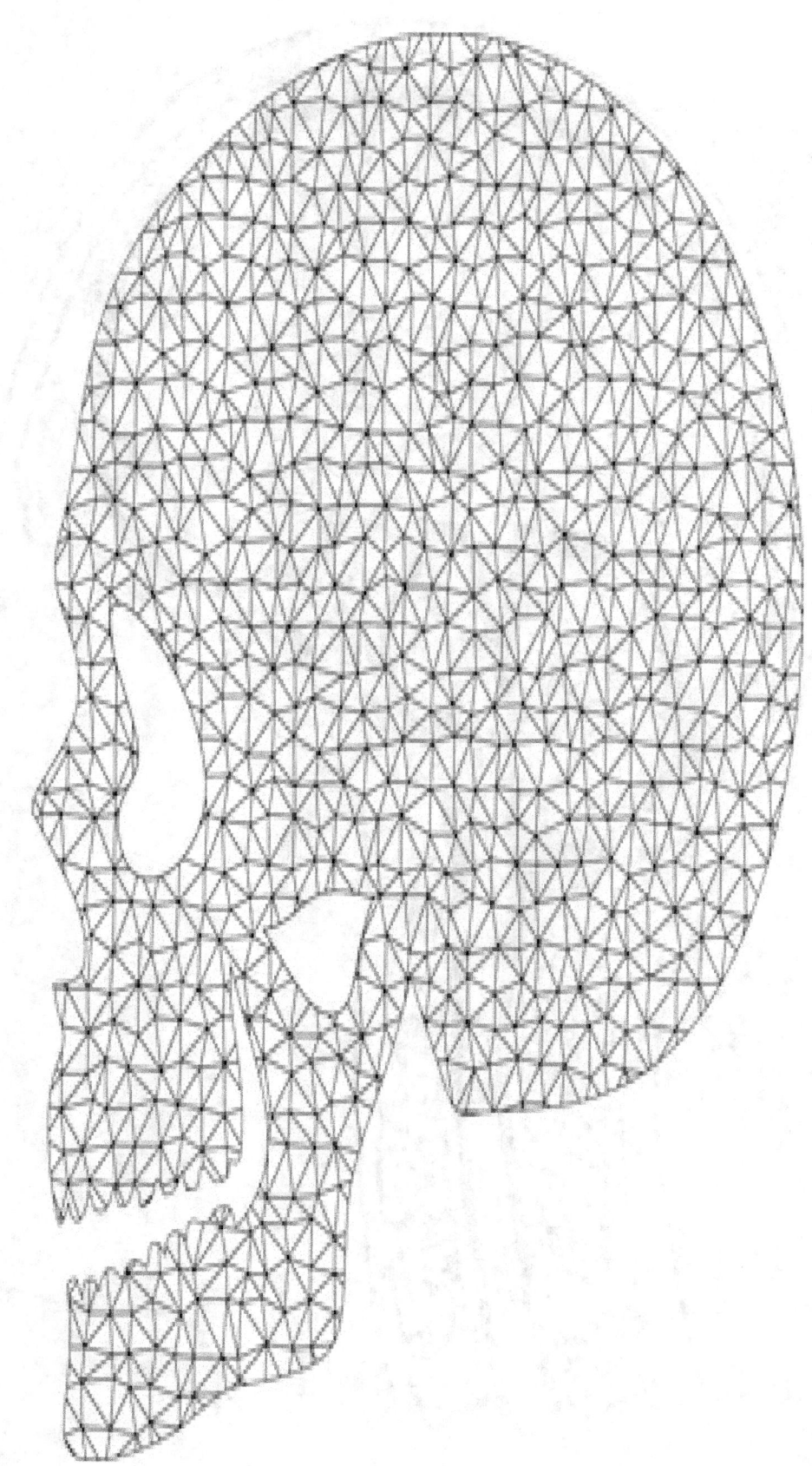

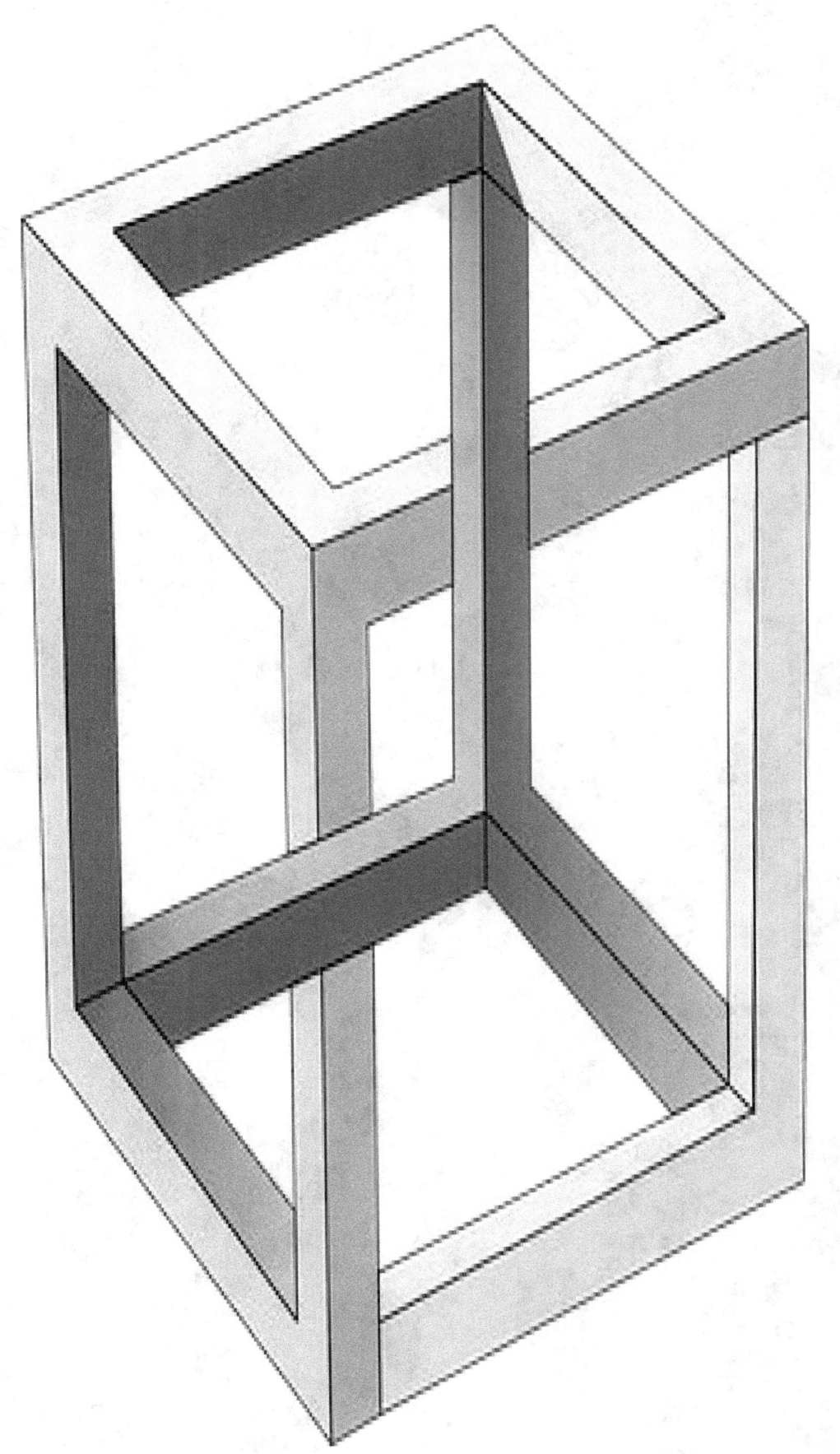

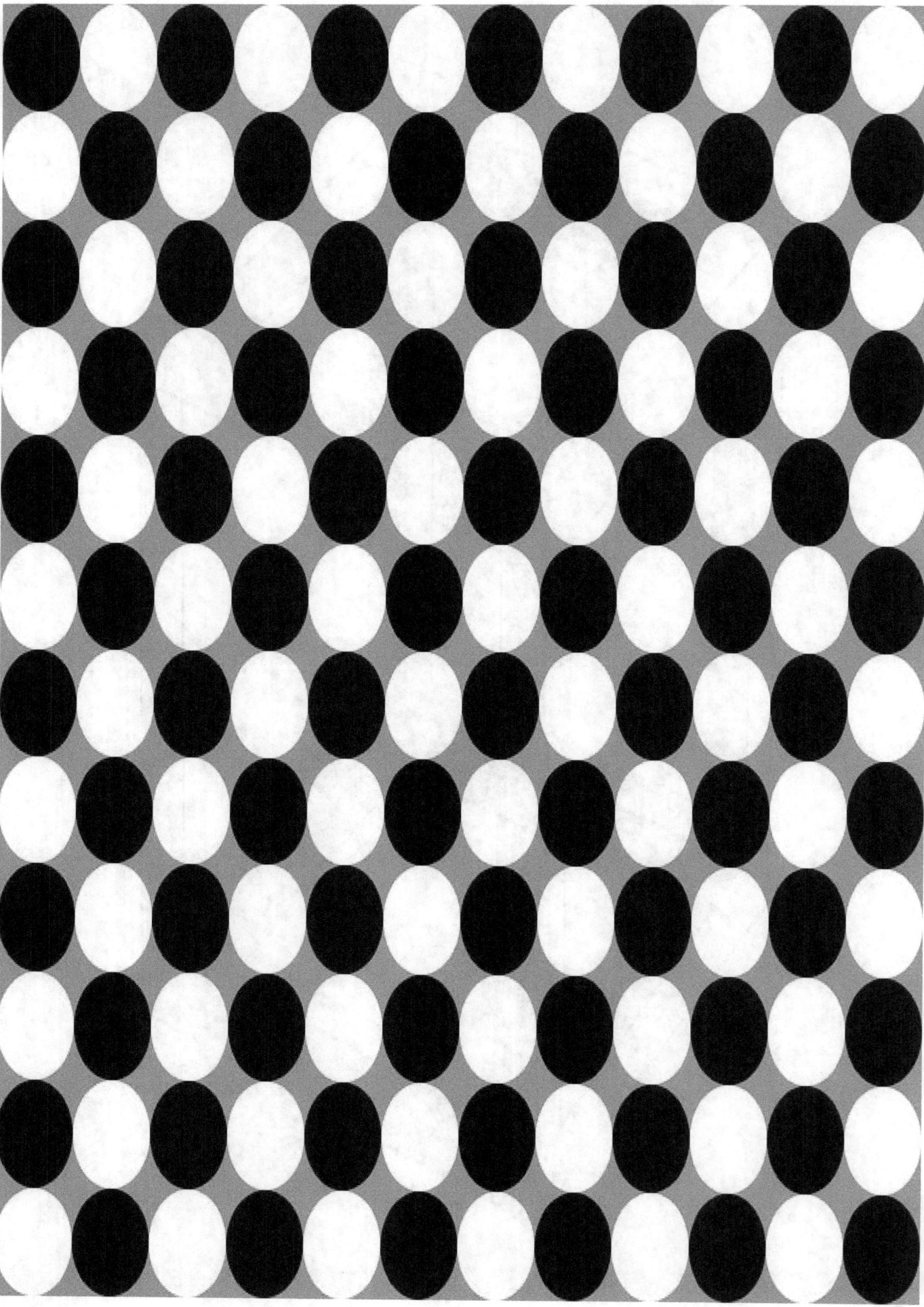

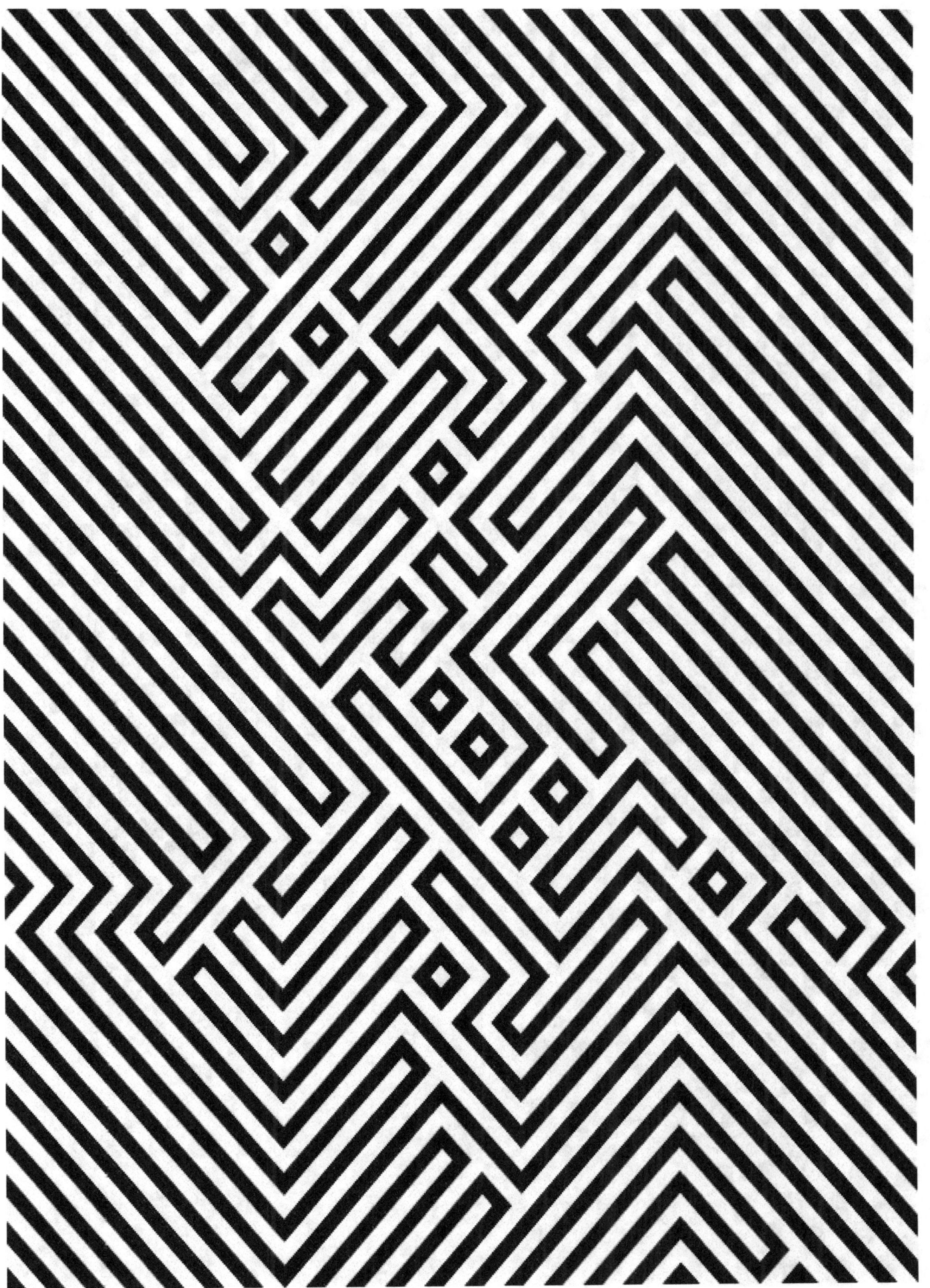

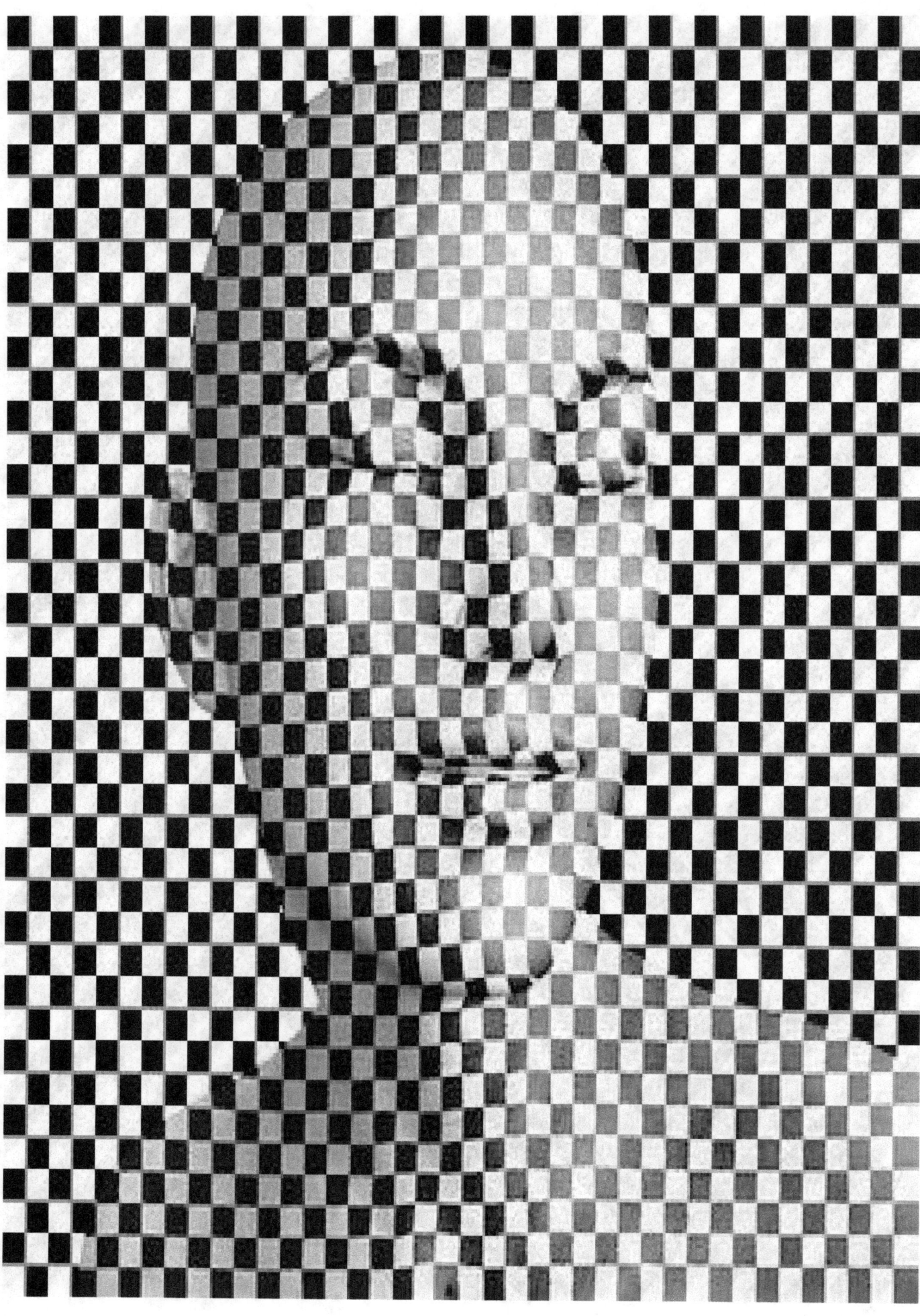

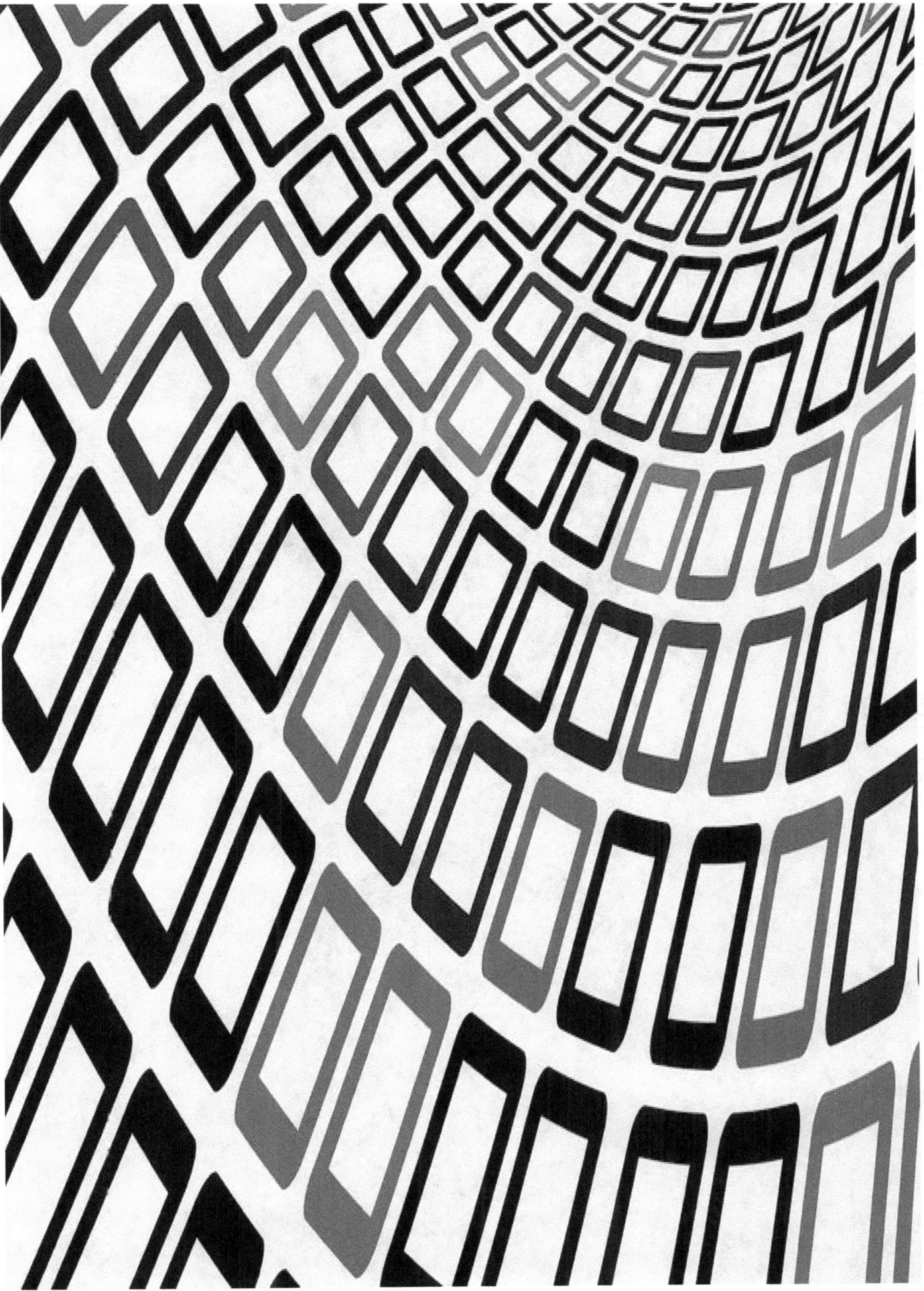

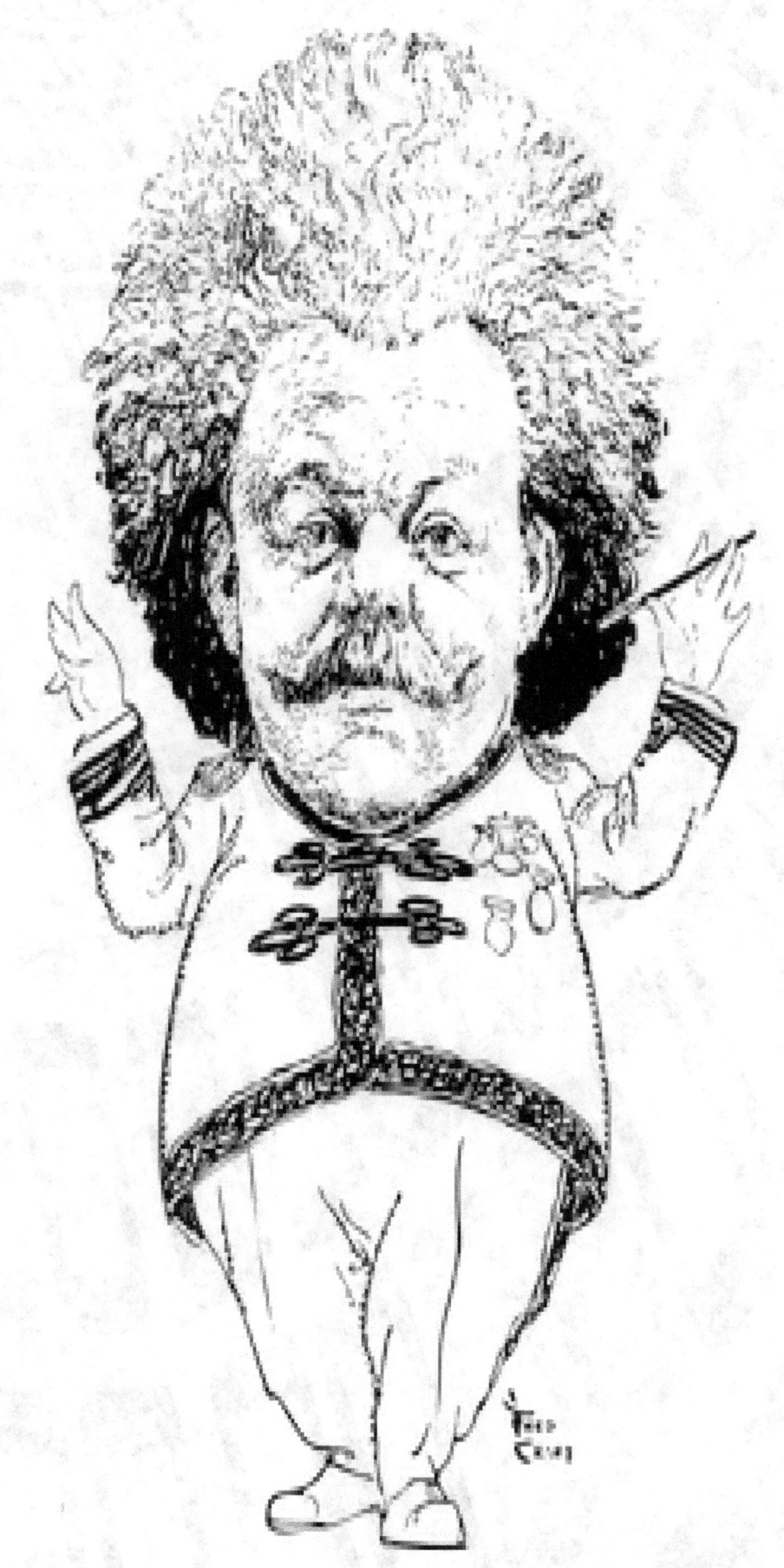

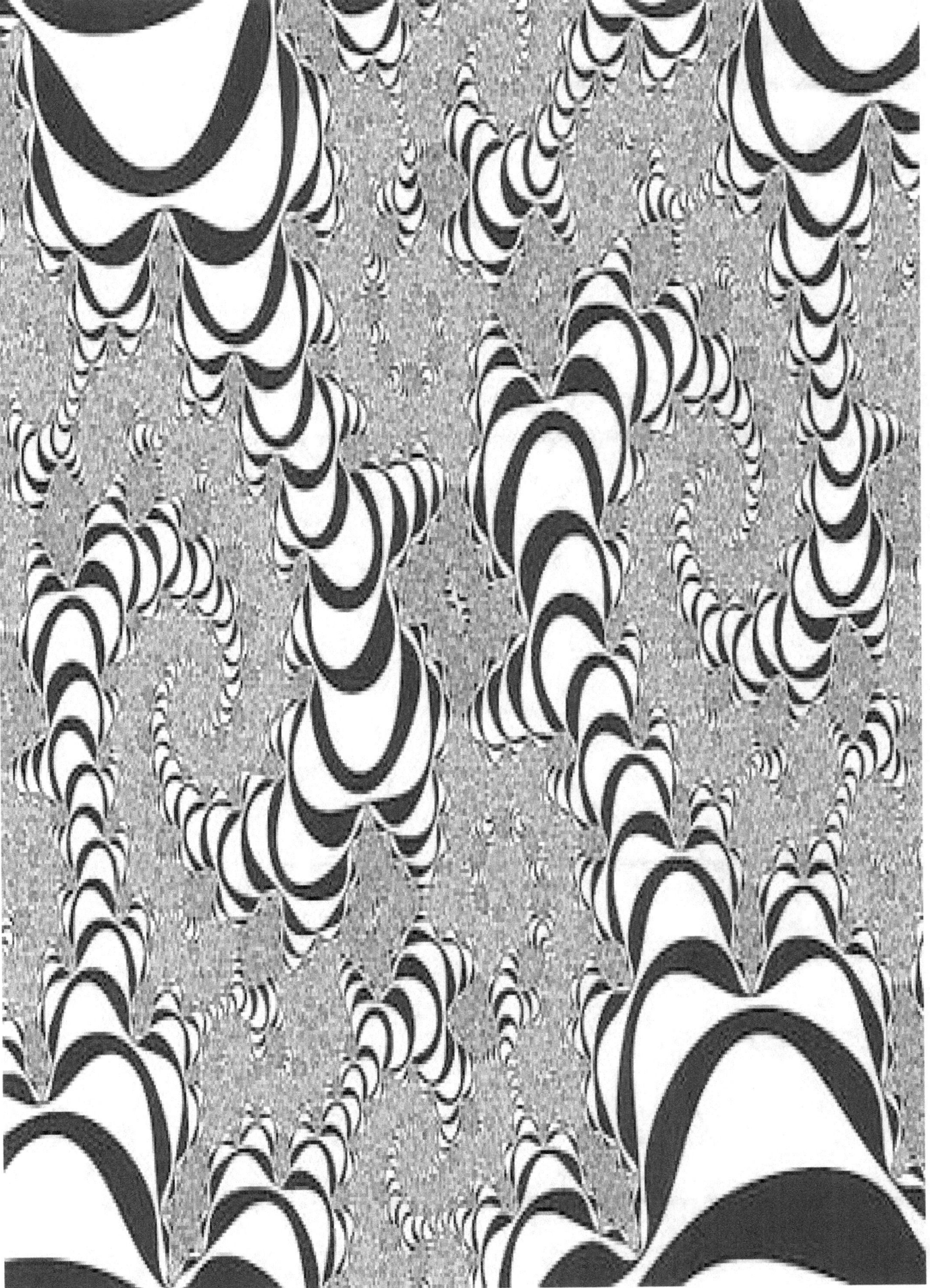

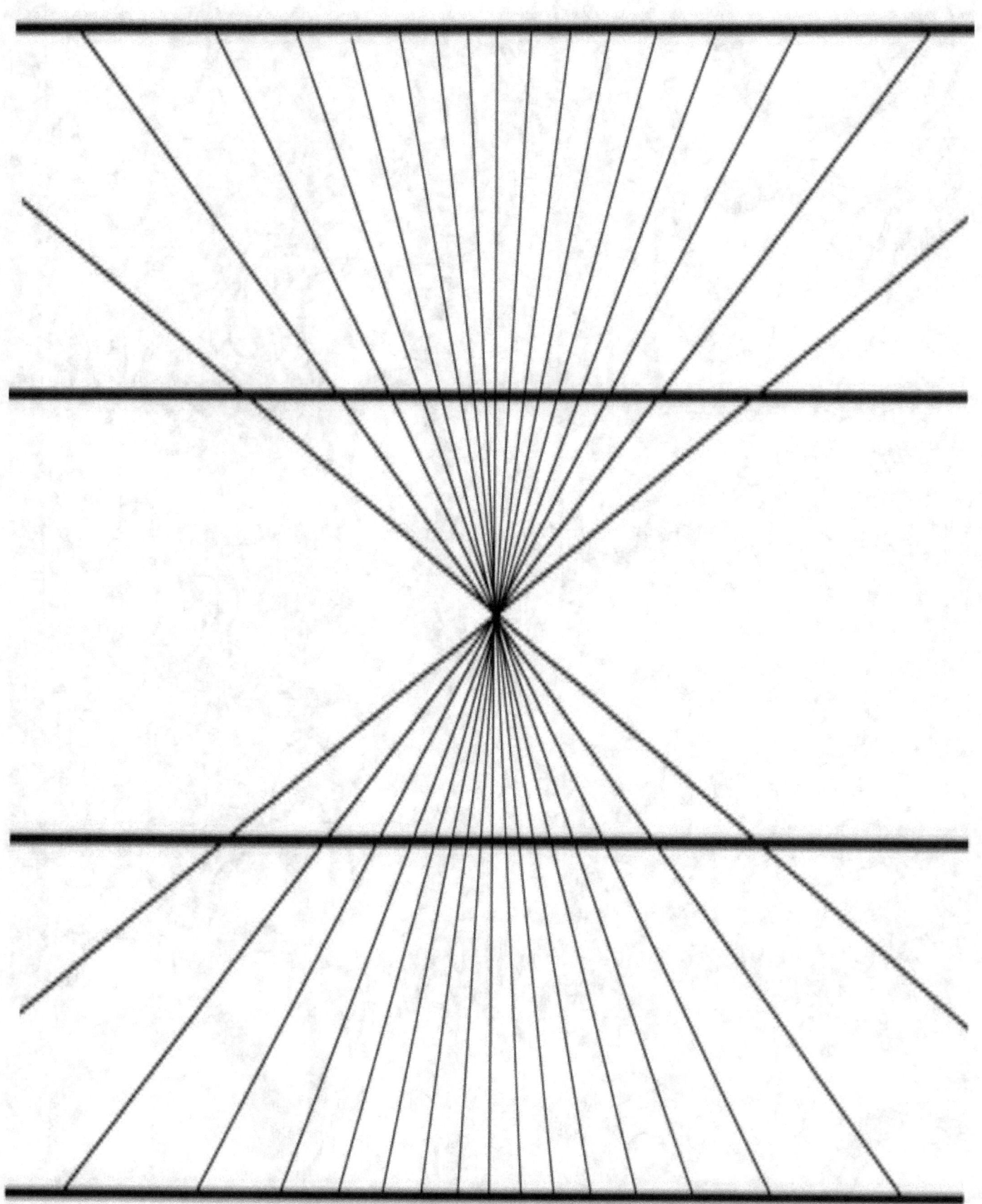

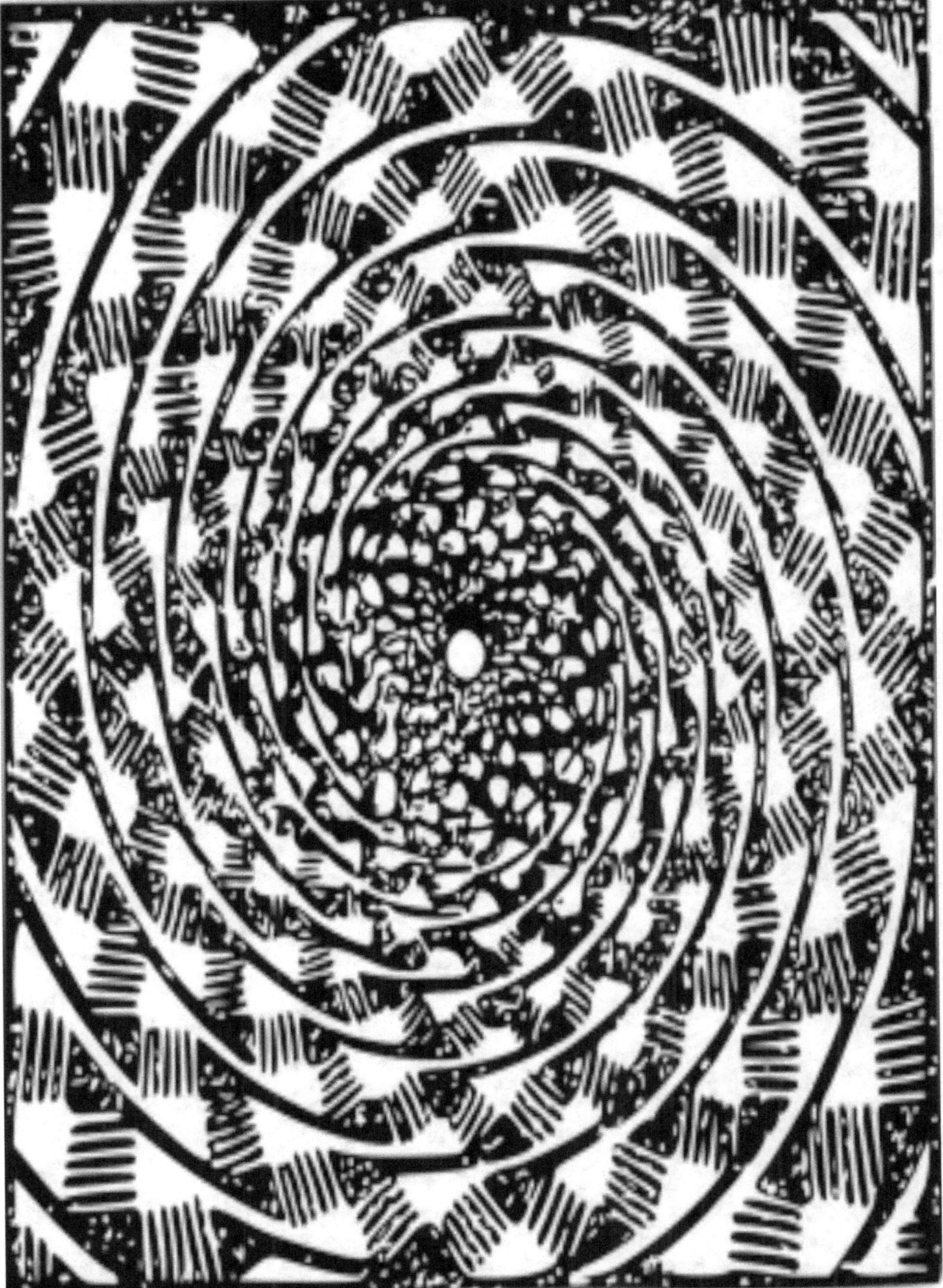

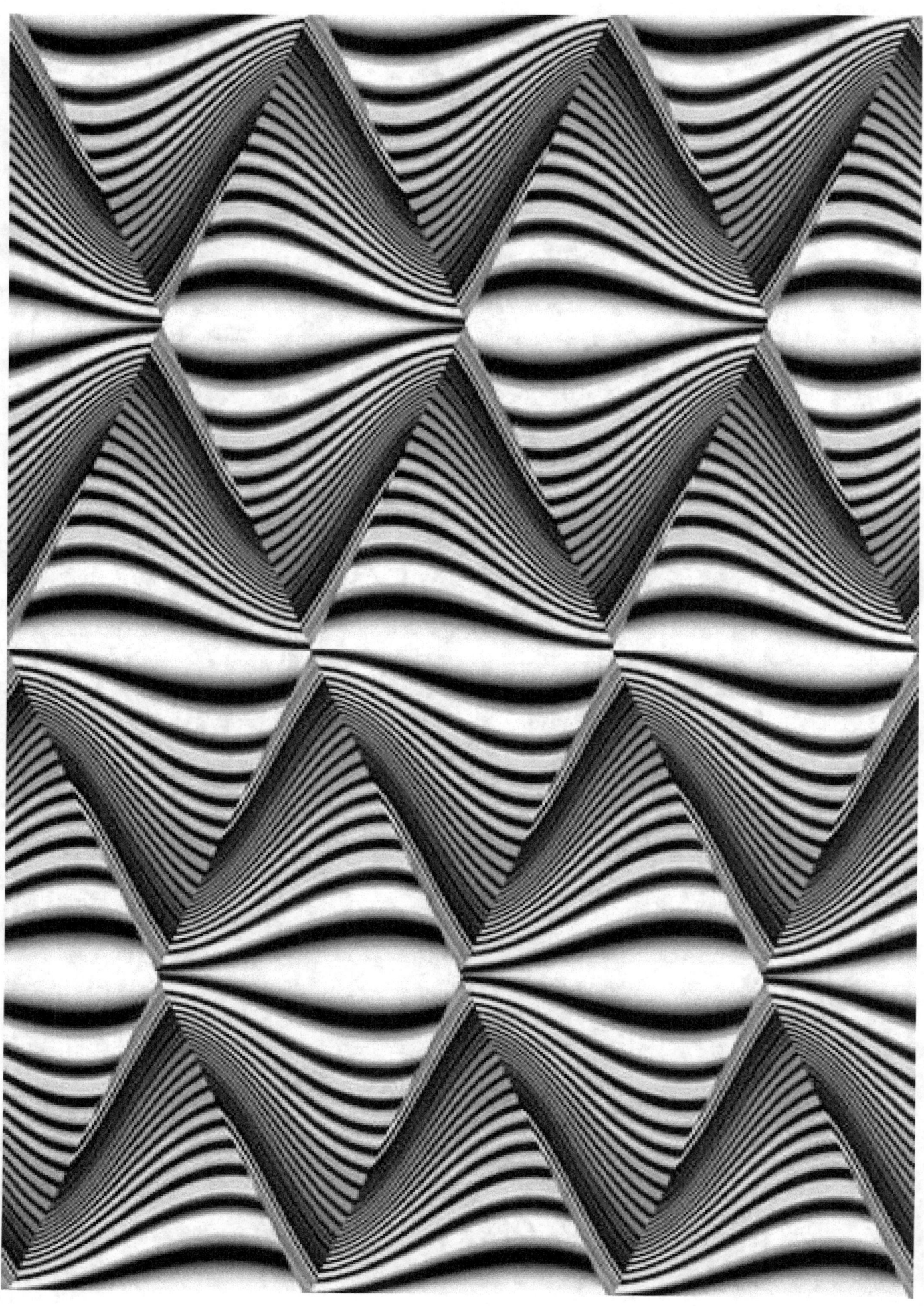

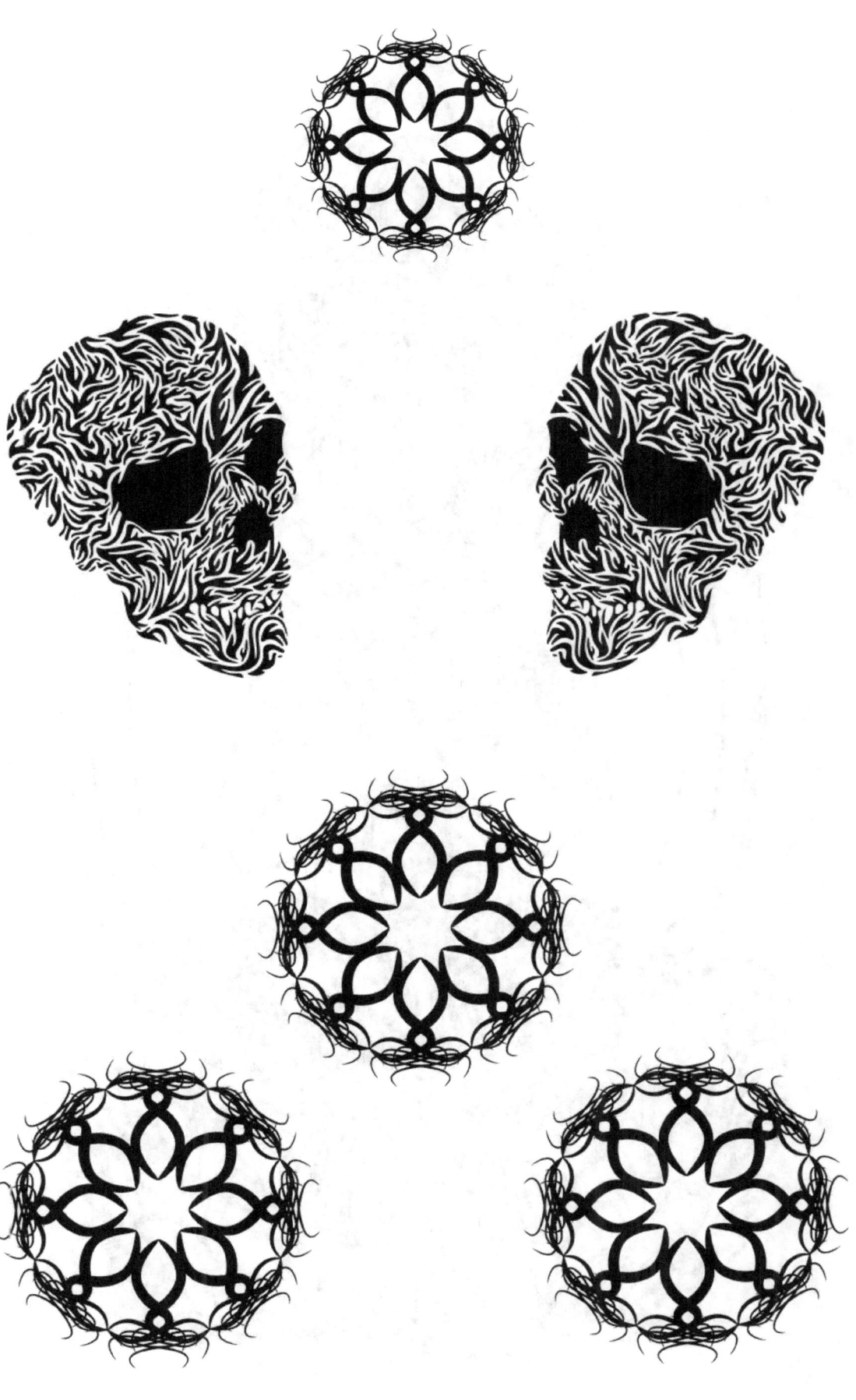

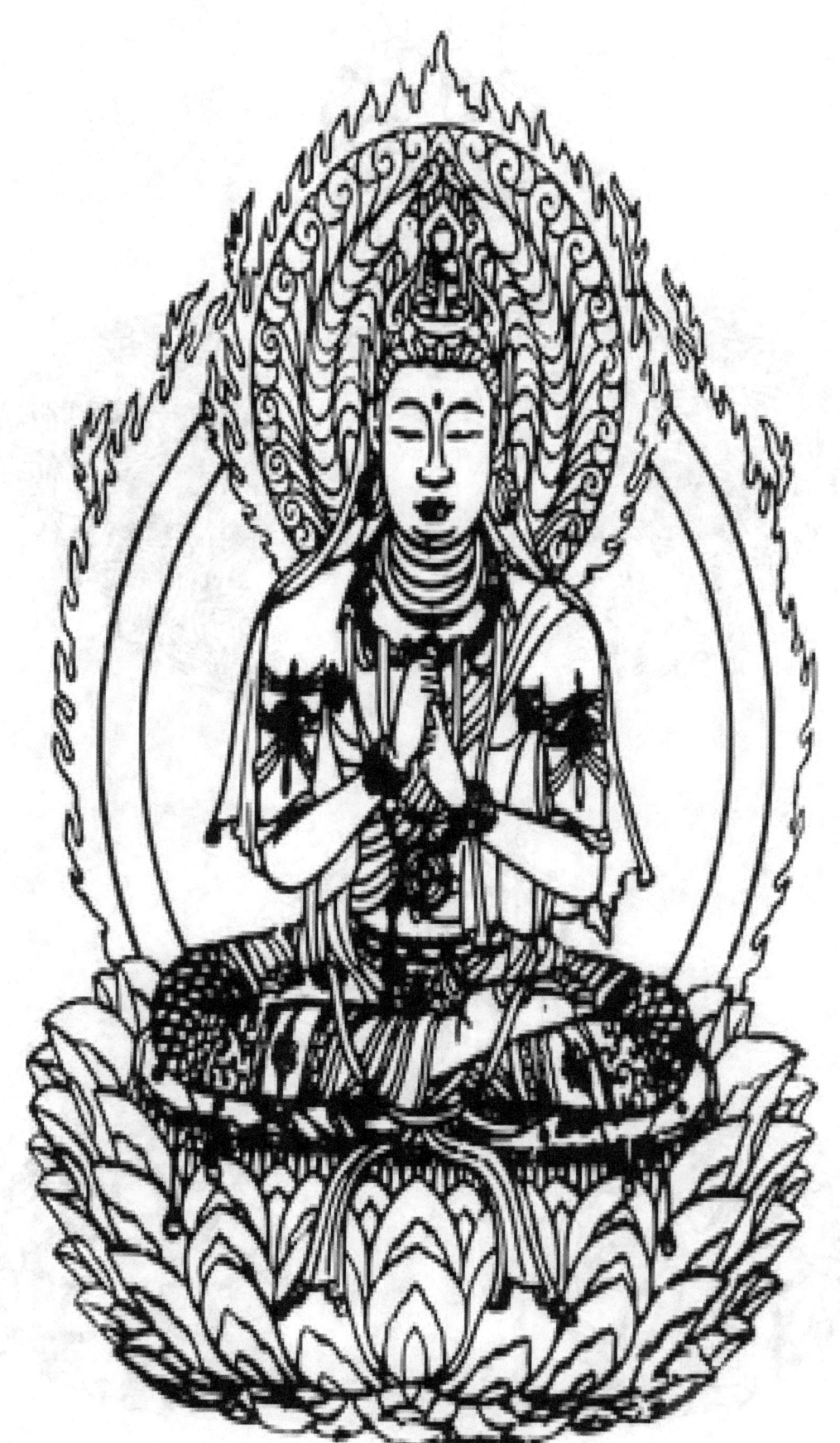

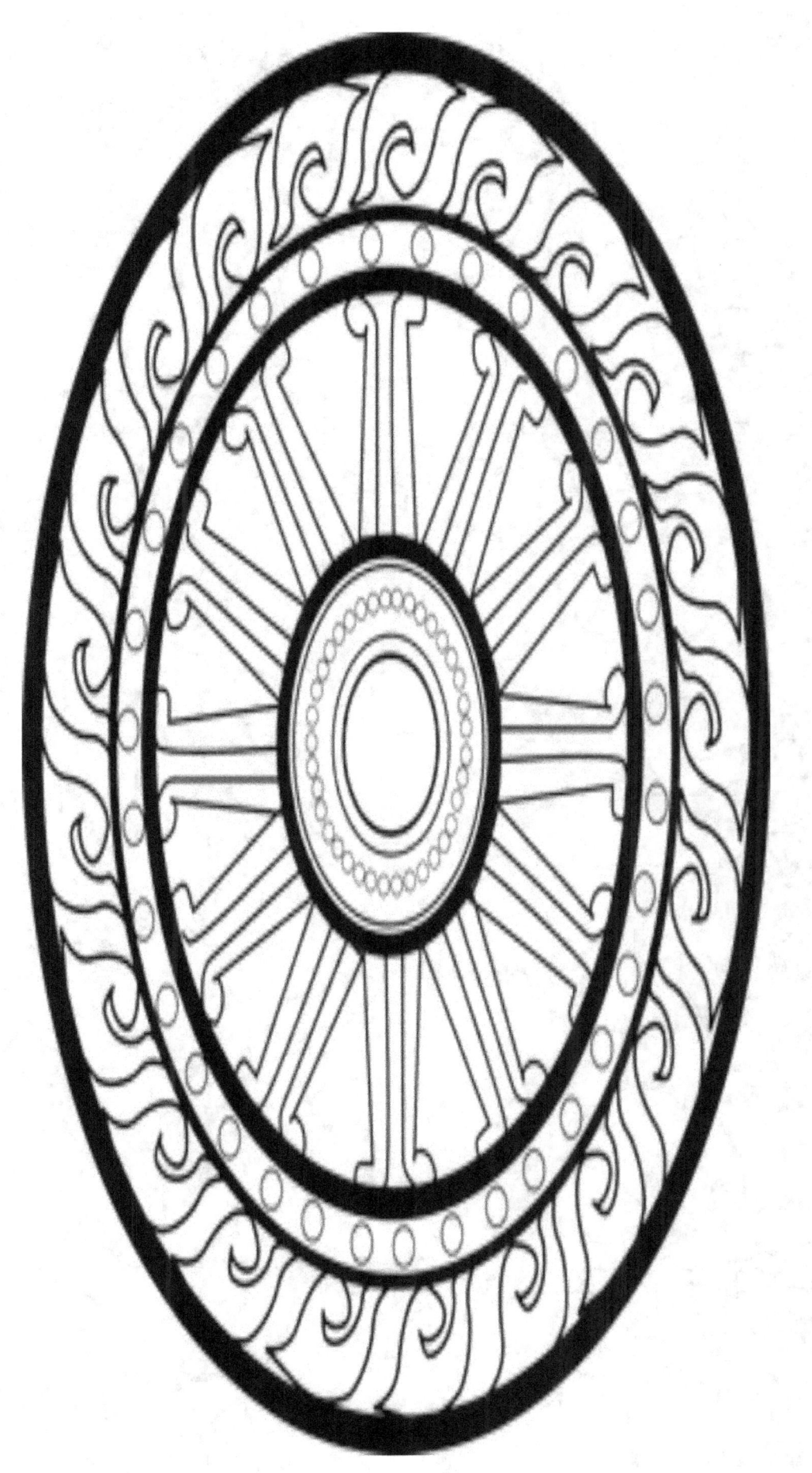

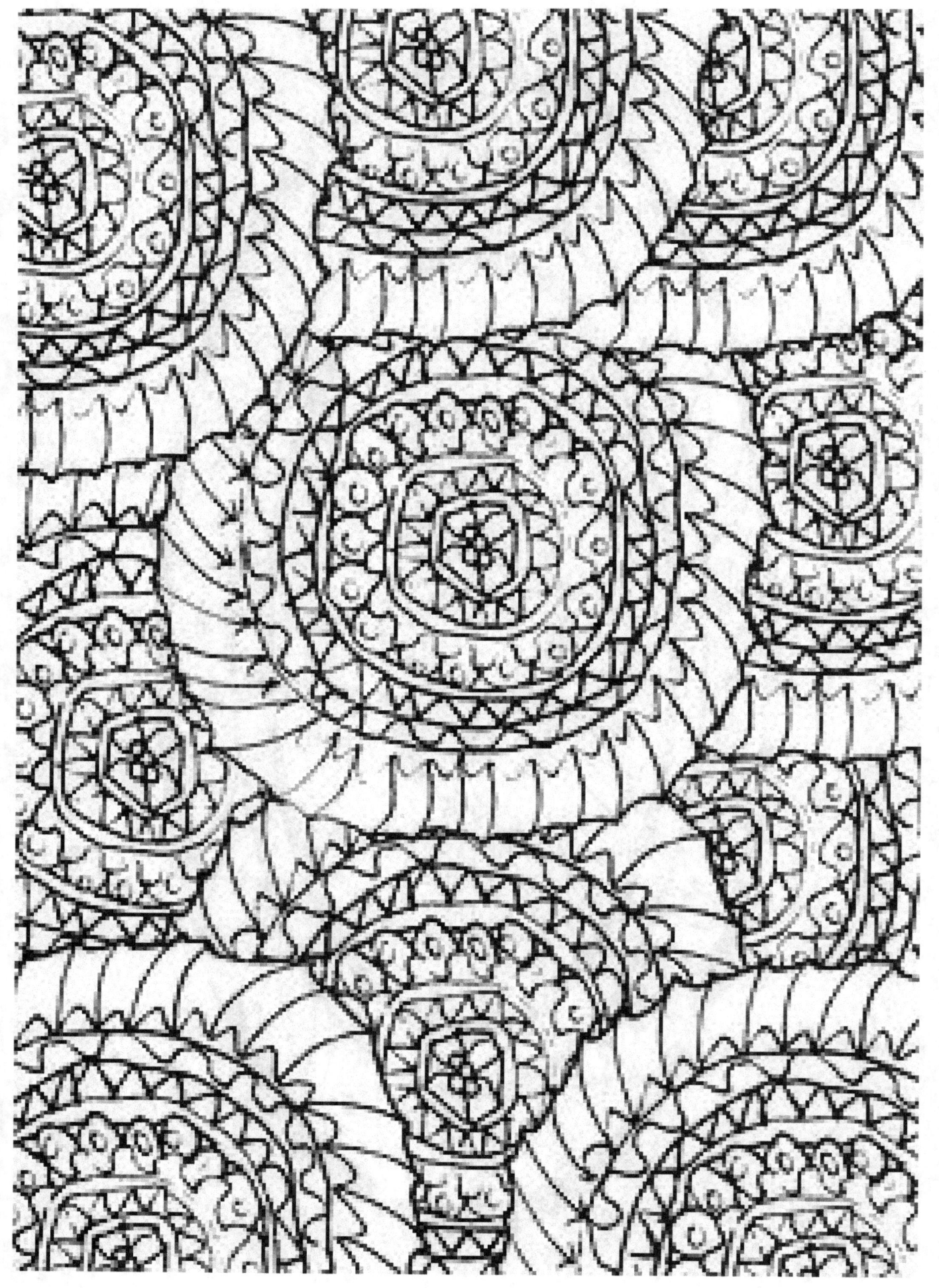

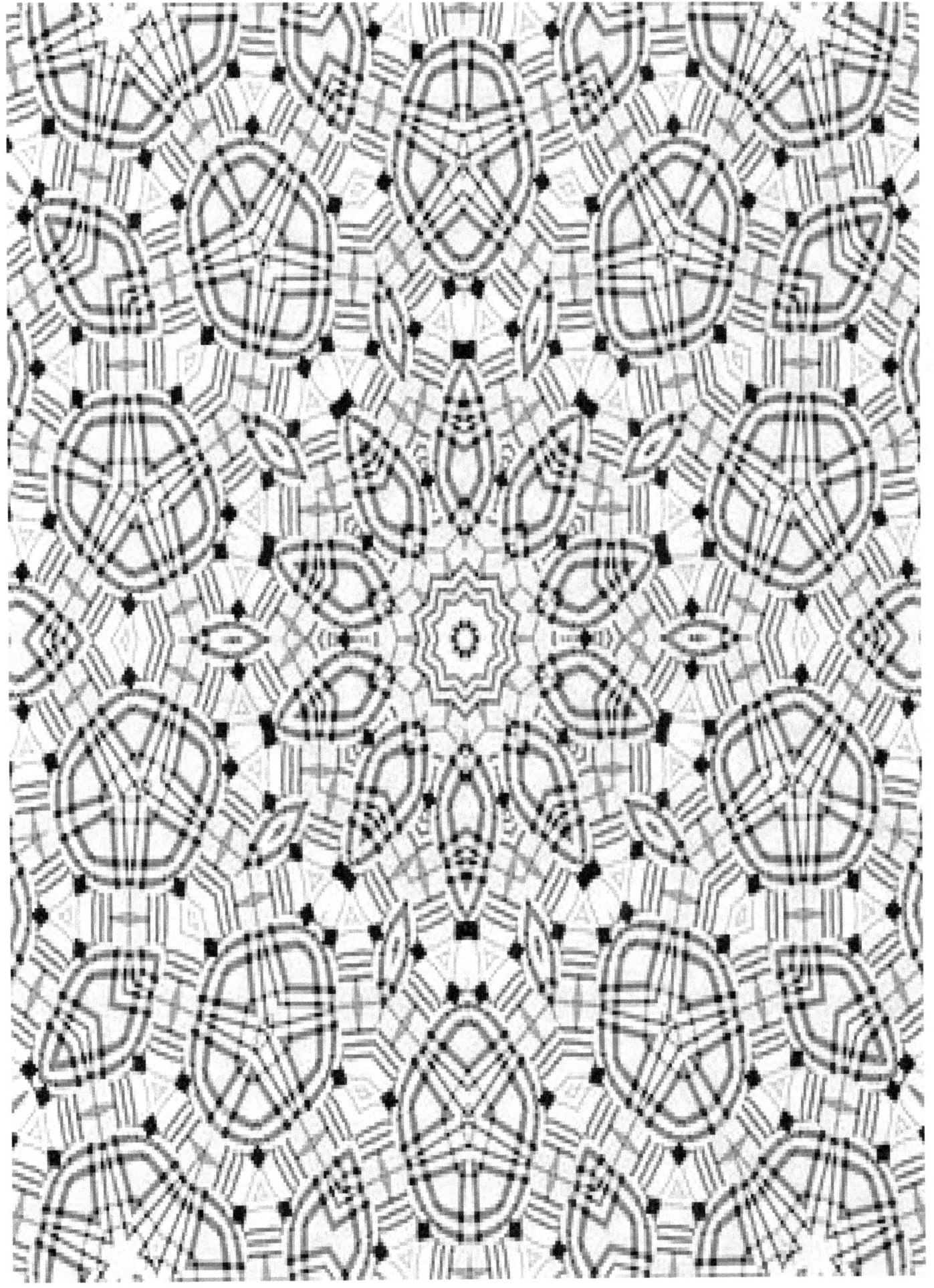

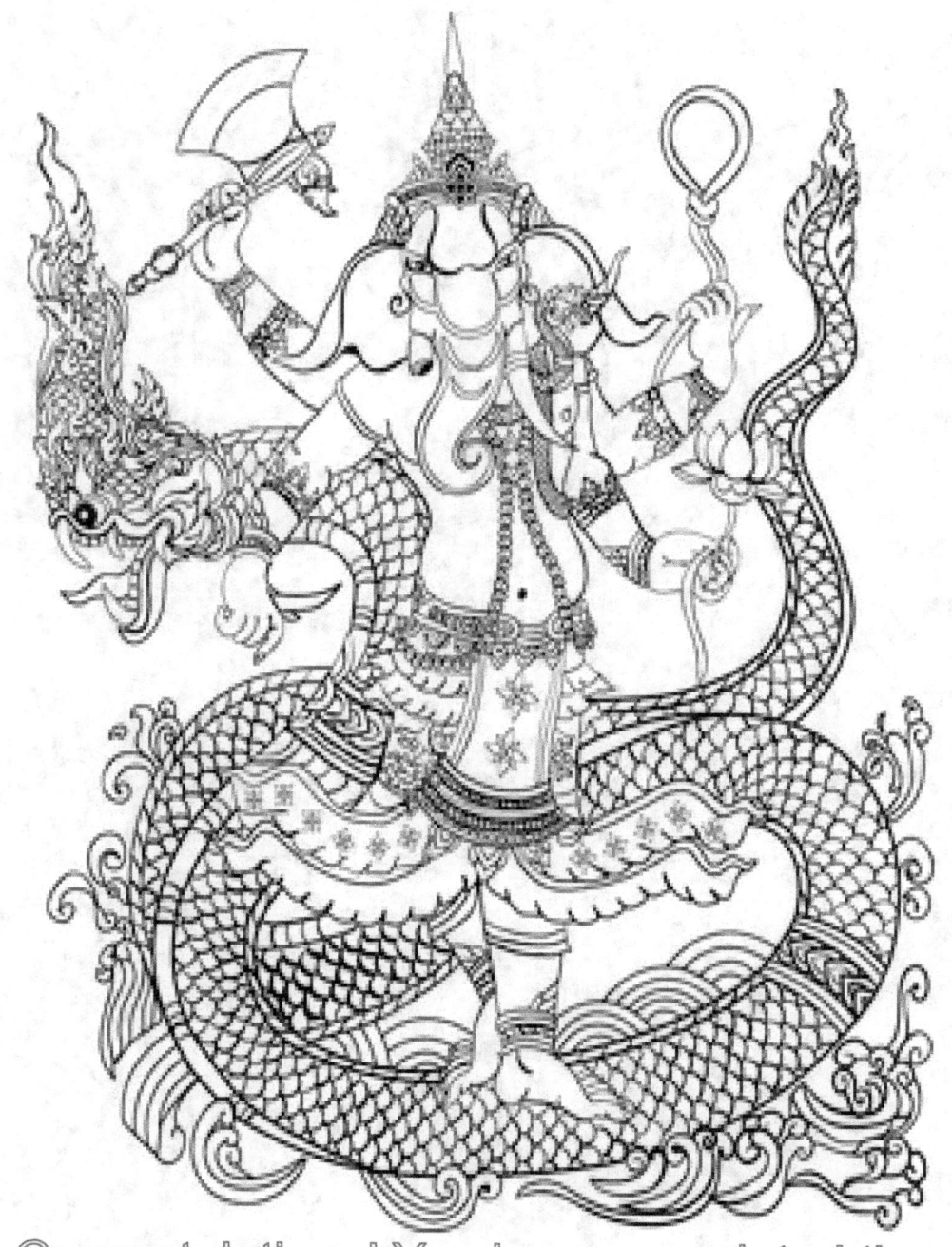

Congratulations! You have completed the psychedelic coloring book! Your prize is the freedom from all earthly desire. You are free to roam the Earth as an enlightened being. Love is all that matters now.